SCHOTTENSTEIN
JEWISH ■ YOUTH ■ COLLEGE

The Schottenstein Jewish Youth College is the umbrella of formal educational programs of the National Conference of Synagogue Youth (NCSY), which is under the auspices of the Union of Orthodox Jewish Congregations of America. Its programs are open to Jewish teens regardless of their affiliation or religious background.

The principle component of the Schottenstein Jewish Youth College is the Teen Torah Center Division, a tuition free after-school program of Jewish studies for public high school students aged 12-18. Though not yet ready for the rigors of a full day of Jewish studies — these youngsters are prepared to test the waters of traditional Jewish education by devoting a Sunday morning and a weekday to explore their heritage in depth. Their decision to enroll in a structured Teen Torah Center (TTC) environment provides the students with the opportunity to study classical texts within the framework of NCSY and under the guidance of trained educators attuned to the needs of beginner students.

The Teen Torah Center attracts youth in a journey that leads most of them to a full commitment to Jewish values — and that invariably enhances their Jewish identity. Without the Teen Torah Center, these Jewishly illiterate teenagers eager to learn the basics of Judaism have nowhere to go in order to satisfy their growing interest. The Teen Torah Center's atmosphere is noncontentious — no grades, no tests, and open to all Jewish teens regardless of their affiliation or religious background. The TTC combination of formal and informal educational techniques is deliberate and aimed at appealing to the youngsters heart and mind.

Other activities of the Schottenstein Jewish Youth College include Halachah Hotline; Yarchei Kallah; Halachah Yomis; Educational summer programs through Camp NCSY-East and Jolt II; 100 Schottenstein Young Leadership Scholars; and Chevrusa by phone.

ArtScroll Mesorah Series®

Rabbi Nosson Scherman / Rabbi Meir Zlotowitz

General Editors

tishah B'av

TISHAH B'AV — TEXTS, READINGS AND INSIGHTS / A PRE-SENTATION BASED ON TALMUDIC AND TRADITIONAL SOURCES.

Published by

Mesorah Publications, ltd

Compiled by Rabbi Avrohom Chaim Feuer
and Rabbi Shimon Finkelman

Laws by Rabbi Hersh Goldwurm

Eichah Commentary by Rabbi Meir Zlotowitz

Talmud Selection by
Rabbi Mordechai Kuber and Rabbi Yosef Davis

Overview by Rabbi Avrohom Chaim Feuer

FIRST EDITION
First Impression . . . June 1992

Published and Distributed by
MESORAH PUBLICATIONS, Ltd.
Brooklyn, New York 11232

Distributed in Israel by
MESORAH MAFITZIM / J. GROSSMAN
Rechov Harav Uziel 117
Jerusalem, Israel

Distributed in Europe by
J. LEHMANN HEBREW BOOKSELLERS
20 Cambridge Terrace
Gateshead, Tyne and Wear
England NE8 1RP

Distributed in Australia & New Zealand by
GOLD'S BOOK & GIFT CO.
36 William Street
Balaclava 3183, Vic., Australia

Distributed in South Africa by
KOLLEL BOOKSHOP
22 Muller Street
Yeoville 2198
Johannesburg, South Africa

ARTSCROLL MESORAH SERIES ®
"TISHAH B'AV" / Texts, Readings and Insights
© Copyright 1992, by MESORAH PUBLICATIONS, Ltd.
4401 Second Avenue / Brooklyn, N.Y. 11232 / (718) 921-9000

ISBN
0-89906-609-7 (hard cover)
0-89906-610-0 (paperback)

Typography by Compuscribe at ArtScroll Studios, Ltd.
4401 Second Avenue / Brooklyn, N.Y. 11232 / (718) 921-9000

Printed in the United States of America by Noble Book Press Corp.
Bound by Sefercraft, Quality Bookbinders, Ltd. Brooklyn, N.Y.

This volume is dedicated
to the memory of

ר' מנשה בן ר' שלמה יצחק ע"ה

נפטר בשם טוב ד' שבט תשנ"ב

עלקא בת ר' בנציון ע"ה

נפטרה בשם טוב ח"י מנחם אב תשנ"א

Menasche and Ella Krupka ע"ה

They were the most noble of people —
   beloved and respected by all.
The needs of others were placed before their own
as they were kind and sensitive to everyone,
whatever their station.
No obstacle could stand in the way
of their dedication to Yiddishkeit
as their love and loyalty to the Torah
survived every horror and dislocation.

They were truly honorable —
for most of all they succeeded in raising
two generations that honor their memory
by following the legacy of their example.

תנצב"ה

The Krupka Family

Table of Contents

◆§ Publishers' Preface

The publication of this volume fills a vacuum that many people have felt for a long time. Tishah B'Av, the day of tears and tragedy throughout Jewish history, is also a day when the opportunity for refreshing Torah study is sharply limited. Consequently, large numbers of conscientious Jews have requested for what might be called a "Tishah B'Av Companion," a reader with material suitable for the day, one that will enable them to understand its message and increase their Torah knowledge and sensitivity to its message.

Tishah B'Av is not only a day of destruction, it is the day when Messiah will be born, a day of rebirth and a day that will become a festival of renewal. But this can happen only if we hear and understand the cry of lament; only thereby can we learn to wipe away the tears and replace them with the smile of redemption. To help us do so is the purpose of this book.

We are proud to publish it in conjunction with THE SCHOTTENSTEIN JEWISH YOUTH COLLEGE, the formal educational division of the National Conference of Synagogue Youth / NCSY. Through its Schottenstein College and other dimensions of its multi-faceted program, NCSY reaches out to tens of thousands of young people, bringing them the timeless message of Torah in a timely manner. The ranks of Torah Judaism over the last generation have been filled with NCSYers, imbued with verve, knowledge and loyalty to their heritage. They are a priceless national resource.

We are equally proud of our personal and professional association with RABBI RAPHAEL BUTLER, National Director, Orthodox Union/NCSY. His infectious enthusiasm and wise leadership have already made a significant mark on the Jewish community in the United States and the former Soviet Union. We look forward to many more years of his fruitful work for our people and our collaboration with him. We acknowledge also the dedication and effectiveness of RABBI MOSHE KRUPKA, Director, National Programs, NCSY.

The primary authors of this volume are familiar to ArtScroll readers. RABBI AVROHOM CHAIM FEUER and RABBI SHIMON FINKELMAN are eminently skilled at bringing their considerable knowledge and insight to a

broad spectrum of readers. This book establishes them even further in the constellation of the written word. The section of Laws was compiled by RABBI HERSH GOLDWURM, General Editor of the Schottenstein Edition of the Talmud, whose encyclopedic knowledge is a mainstay of the ArtScroll Series. RABBIS MORDECHAI KUBER and YOSEF DAVIS prepared the Talmud elucidation from the forthcoming tractate *Gittin*.

The contents of this book are broad ranging, but they are united by their fidelity to the ideal that, as Rav Saadiah Gaon said, the Jewish people is a nation only by virtue of the Torah — and its corollary, that Jewry will again become the nation it once was and is destined to become only by virtue of the Torah. May this Tishah B'Av be the last one of weeping and the forerunner of the day that will be a celebration of the coming of Messiah and the erection of the Third and eternal Temple.

Rabbi Meir Zlotowitz / Rabbi Nosson Scherman
General Editors

Sivan 5752
June 1992

⮿ An Overview /
The Kingdom In Ashes

I. Galus: Homeless, Helpless, Heartbroken

II. For Whom the Lion Roars

III. The Source of Senseless Hatred

For perspectives on the inner meaning of Tishah B'Av and its historical sweep through the centuries, from the first day of tragedy in the Wilderness to our century; for an analysis of the flaws of character that gave birth to and perpetuated this day of tears and tragedy; and an exposition on impending Redemption, see the Overviews to the ArtScroll *Eichah* and the ArtScroll *Kinnos* / Complete Tishah B'Av Service by Rabbi Nosson Scherman.

The following Overviews, by Rabbi Avroham Chaim Feuer, deal with the Destruction from the perspective of Israel's drift from its legacy of Torah study.

An Overview —
The Kingdom in Ashes

I: Galus: Homeless, Helpless, Heartbroken

Rabbi Yose said: I was once traveling on the road and I entered one of the desolate houses in the ruins of Jerusalem to pray. Elijah the Prophet, may he be remembered for good, came and waited for me at the entrance until I concluded my prayers ... He asked me, "My son, what sounds did you hear from inside these ruins?" And I replied, "I heard a Heavenly voice [a bas kol], moaning like a dove, saying, 'Woe unto the children who, because of their sins, I destroyed My Temple, burned My Sanctuary and exiled them among the nations!' "

[Elijah] said to me, "[I swear] by your life and by the life of your head that not only at this time does it say thus, rather every single day it says thus; and not only that, but whenever Jews enter the synagogues and study halls and call out, 'May God's great Name be blessed'; the Holy One, Blessed is He, shakes His head and says, 'How fortunate is the King who is praised thus in His palace. What is left to the Father who has exiled His children? Woe to the children who have been exiled from their Father's table!' " (Berachos 3a).

Elijah Explains the Exile **W**ithout a penetrating understanding of the essential meaning of גָּלוּת, *exile*, a Jew cannot properly await the גְּאוּלָה, *Redemption*. This is what Elijah the Prophet, the Divinely designated herald of the future Redemption, revealed to Rabbi Yose.

Elijah explained, "Exile is not merely captivity and enslavement because, you, Yose, are free to travel as you please, yet you are in exile. Nor is exile religious persecution, because you, Yose, are free to pray where you wish. We cannot even say that exile means that we are not in our Holy Land, because, you, Yose, are right here in Jerusalem. Yet even here, God's Heavenly voice continuously moans and aches over the exile!"

What then is the nature of the exile? Why do Jews cry over it? What are we lacking? The answer is that we have everything — except the Beis HaMikdash!

What then is the nature of the exile? Why do Jews cry over it? What are we lacking? The answer is that we have *everything* — except the *Beis HaMikdash!* We have been driven from our ancestral home, banished from the "family residence." In spiritual terms, we are homeless!

"Homelessness" is a terrible thing. It stands out in the lexicon of suffering and woe as a tragic term describing a pitiful person, lost and restless, rejected and neglected, insecure and unprotected, abandoned to the mercy of the wild elements.

"Homelessness," taught Elijah, "sums up the heartache of the exiled Jew." Wandering to the four corners of the earth, the clever and capable Jew may settle down and prosper. He may strike new roots by erecting magnificent palaces and impressive houses — but the Jew in exile remains homeless, because he has no Temple.

Even when the Jew returns to the Land of his fathers, the Land of our history, the territory covenanted to our Patriarchs, the Jew is not yet *truly* home. For the Land of Israel is our estate and Jerusalem is our courtyard, but we are not truly home until we have the Holy Temple, the earthly abode of our Father.

The Land of Israel is our estate and Jerusalem is our courtyard, but we are not truly home until we have the Holy Temple.

מַה יְּדִידוֹת מִשְׁכְּנוֹתֶיךָ ה׳ צְבָאוֹת. נִכְסְפָה וְגַם כָּלְתָה נַפְשִׁי לְחַצְרוֹת ה׳ . . . גַּם צִפּוֹר מָצְאָה בַיִת וּדְרוֹר קֵן לָהּ . . . אַשְׁרֵי יוֹשְׁבֵי בֵיתֶךָ עוֹד יְהַלְלוּךָ סֶּלָה

How beloved are Your dwelling places, HASHEM of Legions! My soul yearns, indeed it pines, for the courtyards of HASHEM . . . Even the bird found a home, and the swallow, a nest for herself . . . Fortunate are those who dwell in Your home, continually they will praise You, Selah (Psalms 84:2-5).

An Overview / The Kingdom in Ashes [14]

In every generation of exile, pious Jews mourned the tragic irony that while the most insignificant bird can build its nest and establish its home, the nation of Israel wanders aimlessly with no place to call home. The Land of Israel is always ours and Jerusalem is forever our capital, but without the Temple we are homeless.

The Land of Israel is always ours and Jerusalem is forever our capital, but without the Temple we are homeless.

God mourns this exile and His children cry with Him.

The chassidic master Reb Izakel Safrin, the patriarch of the dynasty of Ziditchov, had five great sons. According to the family tradition, their pious mother, Hinda, awakened her babies at midnight, removed them from their cradles and put them on the floor, and let them cry for a little while. Then she would kiss away their tears and lovingly tuck them back into bed. Why did she do this? Because at midnight God cries, as it were, over the destruction of His Home and the exile of His children. Rebbetzin Hinda wanted her tiny infants to join God in His tears! From earliest childhood, let the Jewish soul feel the anguish of exile and hear the grief of our Father in Heaven!

At midnight God cries, as it were, over the destruction of His Home and the exile of His children.

Favorite Sons of the Heavenly Father

וְאָנֹכִי אָמַרְתִּי . . . וְאֶתֶּן לָךְ אֶרֶץ חֶמְדָּה נַחֲלַת צְבִי צִבְאוֹת גּוֹיִם וָאֹמַר אָבִי תִּקְרְאִי לִי וּמֵאַחֲרַי לֹא תָשׁוּבִי

And I [God] said to Myself . . . "I gave you a most desirable land, the heritage that is glorious to the hosts of nations." And I said, "You shall call Me, 'My Father,' and you shall never stray away from Me!" (Jeremiah 3:19).

The believing Jew is deeply attached to his Creator, he clings to his Maker with a passion and loves him with heart and soul. As King David sang, כִּי אָבִי וְאִמִּי עֲזָבוּנִי וַה׳ יַאַסְפֵנִי, *Though my father and mother have abandoned me, HASHEM will gather me in (Psalms 27:10).*

David felt as completely secure with God as, *a suckling child at his mother's side, like a suckling child is my soul (Psalms 131:2).*

This is the essence of the Jew's feelings for God. When he dwelled in the Holy Land, and periodically

visited his Father's home, the Holy Temple, he enjoyed security, dignity and a profound sense of worthiness. This explains the unique tragedy and trauma of the Jewish exile.

Can one imagine the shock and unbearable hurt of a beloved child, who is utterly rejected by his parents?

What excruciating pain sears the heart of a child whose father first expels him from his childhood home, then burns it down and sternly warns him not to return until further notice? This is how the Jew feels in exile.

What excruciating pain sears the heart of a child whose father first expels him from his childhood home, then burns it down and sternly warns him not to return until further notice? How utterly devastated this child would be, how stripped of self-esteem.

This is how the Jew feels in exile. His suffering is so unbearable not because of the hatred, not because of the persecution — other nations have suffered them too. It is the emotional anguish that makes us suffer so. For no other nation was God's firstborn, and no other son was ever so rejected by his father.

The painful month of exile is called אָב, *Av*, which means *father*, to teach that the primary anguish of exile is not the physical suffering, but the psychological pain of a wayward child rejected by his beloved father.

Three-Tiered Descent Into Darkness

Rabbi Eliezer taught: The night is divided into three watches and at every watch God sits and roars like a lion, as it is written: *HASHEM will roar from on high and from His Holy Residence His voice will cry out; He will roar and continue to roar over His [destroyed] dwelling (Jeremiah 25:30)*. The signal [for the commencement of each watch is as follows]: At the first watch, a donkey brays; at the second watch, dogs bark; at the third watch [near dawn], an infant suckles from its mother and a wife chats with her husband (*Berachos* 3a).

The allegory of night describes the bleak, gloomy exile, in which Israel is sinking in darkness and despair.

Maharal (*Netzach Yisrael*, ch. 18) explains that the allegory of night describes the bleak, gloomy exile, in which Israel is sinking in darkness and despair. Just as the actual night is divided into three parts, each with its own characteristic, so too, can we identify three progressively worsening phases of the exile.

The initial phase of exile is symbolized by a donkey braying in the night, because *galus* persecution begins when our oppressors treat us like a beast of burden, as they burden us with discriminatory taxes, penalties and forced labor. They confine us in ghettos and pales of settlement. But that is only the start; the exile get worse.

In the second stage, anti-Semitism increases violently and our enemies desire to eradicate us. This stage is symbolized by "barking dogs," because the Talmud (*Bava Kamma* 60b) teaches that when the Angel of Death is in the city, dogs suddenly begin to bark madly. Thus, the dogs barking at the second night watch symbolize that in the second phase of exile, our enemies seek to kill us through pogroms, blood libels, inquisitions, genocide and holocaust.

The most terrible threat of the exile appears in the third stage, as we approach the dawn of redemption.

But the most terrible threat of the exile appears in the third stage, as we approach the dawn of redemption. Those enemies who failed to destroy us with their hatred will adopt a new approach; they will try to kill us with love! Whereas in earlier times the Jew was despised, vilified and ostracized, as the end of days draws nearer, the Jew will be warmly welcomed and embraced. Whereas in earlier times intermarriage was unthinkable and unspeakable, the Jew will now be encouraged to assimilate. Thus, at the third watch of the night, "a wife chats with her husband," i.e. the enemies of the Torah will speak to us as intimately and lovingly as marriage partners. This insidious "Holocaust of Love" will be far more successful than the "Holocaust of Hate," and assimilation and intermarriage will decimate the ranks of the Jewish nation like no other scourge.

Yet, even as all hope for the Jewish future seems to fade, a faint glimmer of light will appear.

Yet, even as all hope for the Jewish future seems to fade, a faint glimmer of light will appear, when "... an infant awakens and suckles from its mother....," for even though most Jews will be assimilated and alienated from Torah values, there will be a handful who will be instinctively drawn back to the authentic wellsprings of Torah, just as an infant instinctively seeks nourishment at its mother's breast. This pure "return movement" will bring an end to the darkness of exile and herald the dawn of redemption.

This pure "return movement" will bring an end to the darkness of exile and herald the dawn of redemption.

This is the *Maharal's* prophetic interpretation of the

three levels of the long, black night of exile. Yet one point remains to be explained; what is the significance of the metaphor which describes God as roaring over every watch like a lion? *HASHEM will roar... (Jeremiah 25:30).*

How does the roar of a lion relate to the destruction of the Holy Temple?

II: For Whom the Lion Roars

עַל שְׂדֵה אִישׁ עָצֵל עָבַרְתִּי וְעַל כֶּרֶם אָדָם חֲסַר לֵב. וְהִנֵּה עָלָה כֻלּוֹ קִמְּשֹׂנִים כָּסּוּ פָנָיו חֲרֻלִּים וְגֶדֶר אֲבָנָיו נֶהֱרָסָה.

I passed by the field of a lazy man, and by the vineyard of a man lacking an [enthusiastic] heart. And behold, it was all overgrown with thorns, its surface was covered with thistles, and its stone fence crumbled into ruin (Proverbs 24:30-31).

I passed by the field of a lazy man — this refers to King Achaz [who closed the Torah academies and stopped the Temple service (Rashi)]. ...*and by the vineyard of a man lacking an [enthusiastic] heart* — this describes King Menashe [who went further and ripped God's Name from the Torah and destroyed the Temple Altar (Rashi)]. *and behold, it was all overgrown with thorns* — this refers to King Ammon [who continued the depravity]. *Its surface was covered with thistles* — this refers to King Yehoyakim. *And its stone fence crumbled into ruin* — this refers to King Tzidkiyahu (Zedekiah) in whose time the First Temple was destroyed (Sanhedrin 103a).

Three Insights Into Destruction No vision is as penetrating as that of our prophets and sages, who, with Divine inspiration and insight, studied Jewish history from a Torah perspective and revealed the true causes and meaning of everything that befell God's nation. Three Talmudic passages address

the crucial question: What brought about the destruction of the First Temple and the exile of the Jewish nation? Let us analyze and compare them.

Passage I:

מִקְדָּשׁ רִאשׁוֹן מִפְּנֵי מַה חָרַב? מִפְּנֵי שֶׁהָיוּ בָה שְׁלֹשָׁה
דְּבָרִים: עֲבוֹדָה זָרָה, גִּלּוּי עֲרָיוֹת, וּשְׁפִיכוּת דָּמִים
Why was the First Temple destroyed? Because during its period there were three [cardinal] sins: idolatry, immorality and bloodshed (Yoma 9b).

A nation that tramples upon the cardinal sins of the Torah forfeits its right to God's protection.

This passage speaks for itself: a nation that tramples upon the cardinal sins of the Torah forfeits its right to God's protection.

Passage II:

דָּבָר זֶה נִשְׁאַל לַחֲכָמִים וְלַנְּבִיאִים וְלַמַּלְאֲכֵי הַשָּׁרֵת
וְלֹא פְּרָשׁוּהוּ עַד שֶׁפֵּרְשׁוֹ הקב״ה בְּעַצְמוֹ . . . שֶׁאֵין
מְבָרְכִים בַּתּוֹרָה תְּחִלָּה
This question [why the First Temple was destroyed] was asked of the sages, the prophets and the ministering angels and they could not explain it, until The Holy One, Blessed is He, Himself explained it...because they did not make a blessing before studying the Torah (*Nedarim* 81a).

Let us carefully consider the implications of the above passage. The people of Israel *did* study and practice the Torah, so it was difficult to comprehend why they were punished. Therefore, only God Himself could explain. He had delved into the depths of their hearts and saw that the basis of their downfall was that even though they studied the Torah, it was not important to them and they studied with improper motives. The clear proof of this was their failure to recite the blessing for the Torah before they began their daily studies (*Ran* ibid. citing *Rabbeinu Yonah*).

Why were the sages, prophets and angels so bewildered by the First Destruction? Did they not know that people were guilty of idolatry, immorality and bloodshed? They did, but they were confused by contradic-

tory behavior. On the one hand, people were studying Torah, but on the other hand they were depraved enough to violate the three cardinal sins. How could anyone behave in such a contradictory manner? Only God Himself could give the answer. Appearances are deceiving. People can be shallow and insincere. Their study of Torah may not have penetrated into their character. If they do not realize it is a blessing, they recite no blessing over it. Therefore, their studies failed to elevate, sanctify and discipline them, and they succumbed easily to the temptation of the three cardinal sins.

People can be shallow and insincere. Their study of Torah, may not have penetrated into their character. If they do not realize it is a blessing, they recite no blessing over it.

Passage III:

The third passage is the one quoted above:

> *"I passed by the field of a lazy man,"* this refers to Achav [who closed the Torah academies and stopped the Temple service]... *"And its stone fence crumbled into ruin."* This refers to King Tzidkiyahu in whose time the First Temple was destroyed (*Sanhedrin* 103a).

Here the Sages of the Talmud delved even deeper. They wondered: How could it be that Israel failed to appreciate and bless God for giving them the Torah? How could the powerful message of Torah fail to penetrate their hearts? Why did Torah study fail to improve the character of the nation during the First Temple?

Why did Torah study fail to improve the character of the nation during the First Temple?

To explain why the Torah sometimes fails to make an impression on its students, the Sages formulated what might be called an axiom of "Torah physics": "The power of Torah to impact on its student is equal to the amount of energy and enthusiasm which the student invests in his studies." Studied with passive indifference, Torah remains lifeless — facts and figures, laws and lessons. For the lackadaisical student the Torah remains limp, lifeless and mute. But when he pores over and ponders it with wonder, awe and love — it comes alive. As the inspired student pours his life into the Torah, he breathes life into the words and letters, and

The power of Torah to impact on its student is equal to the amount of energy and enthusiasm which the student invests in his studies.

they dance and sing before his eyes. As he opens his heart to the Torah, the Torah reveals her secrets.

When the motivated student does that, it becomes the most powerful life force in the universe. Nothing stands in its path. All of nature bows before the Torah.

Torah: The Life Force of the Universe

We can appreciate the power of Torah by comparing it with the power of the mighty sun. The sun is a "life force." Although it is 93 million miles away, its prodigious nuclear heat and light travel that distance in moments and blanket the earth with the warmth and energy that make every living thing grow, and its light and energy travel to the most remote corners of the solar system. Moreover, the sun's gravitational pull locks all of the planets and moons and satellites of the solar system into obedient, undeviating orbits. An infinitesimal change in the sun's temperature or position would have an enormous effect on every part of the solar system and could spell life or death for organisms and heavenly bodies many millions of miles away.

Just as the sun is the life force of our "tiny" solar system, the Torah is the life force of the entire universe.

Just as the sun is the life force of our "tiny" solar system, the Torah is the life force of the entire universe. Indeed, it is through the Torah that God invested the sun with its gifts of light, heat and gravity.

God gave the Torah this mastery and dominion over the entire cosmos only for the sake of Israel. He desired that there be spiritual light and heat, energy and power in the world, so that Israel could harness it and elevate the mundane earth to the level of the highest heavens.

This concept introduces us to the great difference between all life forces of nature and the life force of Torah. At Creation, the Almighty decreed that all life forces should perform their tasks constantly, without deviation. No one has to press a button or flip a switch to turn the sun on and off; it functions continuously because such was God's will.

Not so the Torah. It *has* a "button," and God appointed Israel as its custodians. When *all* the Jews study the Torah with *all* their hearts and *all* their minds, they press the button so hard that the Torah springs to life with an awesome life force radiating energy,

abundance and blessing throughout the universe. But when Israel's enthusiasm wanes and dwindles, and only *some* Jews study Torah *sometimes*, with *some* fraction of their mental capacity — then the Torah gives forth only a fraction of its light and blessing, and a chilly darkness blankets the universe. A "dark age" of desolation and decay sets in. All progress and growth slow. The world regresses into confusion, conflict and chaos. And those who suffer the most are the Jews, for they are the guardians of the Torah. When they press the Torah buttons vigorously, they are the first to feel its blessings; but when they fail to press the button, they are the first to suffer the effects of failure.

If, Heaven forfend, there would be even one moment when no one anywhere was studying the Torah, then all the worlds would cease to exist.

If, Heaven forfend, there would be even one moment when no one anywhere was studying the Torah, then all the worlds would cease to exist. Thus, even one lonely Jew has abundant power, for he has the ability to sustain all the worlds and all of creation through his study of the holy Torah for its own sake [*lishmah*]. Moreover, it was worthwhile for the entire world to have been created for his sake.

Regarding such matters, the Sages stated (*Mishnah Sanhedrin* 4:5), "A person is obligated to say, 'Because of me was the world created' "(*Nefesh HaChaim* 4:13).

Laziness Leads to Lamentation

This is what the Sages taught in the third Talmudic passage, which identifies Israel's laziness in Torah study as the root cause of the Destruction. All other sins committed were but symptoms of a lethal malady. Isaiah denounced their dishonesty and harlotry. Jeremiah lashed out at their cruelty and arrogance. But terrible as they were, these transgressions were merely symptoms. Because if the Jews pour their prodigious energies into the study and support of intensive toil in Torah, they have no energy or desire for sin. But when they grow lazy in Torah, they need new outlets for their energy, and they channel their vigor into vanity and vice.

Jeremiah tried to direct the people back to intensive Torah study, but they rebuffed him. The Midrash (*Yalkut Shimoni; Shemos* 261) relates:

Jeremiah challenged the people: "Why don't you engage in deep Torah study?" They responded, "If we

engage in Torah study exclusively, how will we provide a livelihood for our families?"

Jeremiah went to the Holy Temple and brought out the jar of manna, which Aaron the *Kohen Gadol* had deposited there as a lesson for all future generations. Jeremiah said: "In the barren Wilderness, your ancestors did nothing but toil in the study of Torah! See how God provided them with a livelihood! You, too — immerse yourselves in Torah, and God will care for you!"

"In the barren Wilderness, your ancestors did nothing but toil in the study of Torah! See how God provided them with a livelihood! You, too — immerse yourselves in Torah, and God will care for you!"

But the people were smug and complacent. They ignored him and his exhortations. And the Sages teach us of the tragic results:

בַּעֲצַלְתַּיִם יִמַּךְ הַמְּקָרֶה וּבְשִׁפְלוּת יָדַיִם יִדְלֹף הַבָּיִת
Through slothfulness the ceiling sags, and through idleness of hands the house leaks (Koheles 10:18).

Because Israel was lazy in the days of Jeremiah and failed to repent, the roof [of the Temple] caved in (*Vayikra Rabbah* 19:4).

הִתְרַפִּיתָ בְּיוֹם צָרָה צַר כֹּחֶכָה
If you slackened then on the day of adversity, your strength will be feeble (Proverbs 24:10).

Whoever slackens his efforts in the study of Torah will find that he has no strength when he is confronted by adversity (*Yalkut Shimoni, Mishlei* §960).

וַיֵּלְכוּ בְלֹא כֹחַ לִפְנֵי רוֹדֵף
... they fled without strength from the pursuer (Lamentations 1:6).

The Rabbis taught: A man would approach his friend in Jerusalem and request, "Would you please read a page of the Written Law for me? Would you please study with me a chapter of the Oral Law?" The response would be, אֵין בִּי כֹחַ, *"I have no strength."* Said the Master of the Universe, "I promise that the day will come when you will really be drained of all strength," as it says: *they fled without strength from the pursuer* (*Midrash Eichah Rabbasi* 1:35).

With this in mind, our Sages (*Sifri* cited in *Yalkut Shimoni, Mishlei* §961) offered yet a deeper insight into the critique of the lazy man described in the words of King Solomon cited above in the third passage:

> *I passed by the field of a lazy man* — this describes the Torah scholar who does not review and discuss what he has learnt. *And by the vineyard of a man lacking in heart* — this Torah scholar will discover a vacuum in his heart and mind because he will start to forget important sections of his Torah. *And behold, it was all overgrown with thorns;* eventually, he will attempt to understand a portion of the Torah and it will be incomprehensible to him. *Its surface was covered with thistles;* afterwards his mind will be filled with distortions and misconceptions and he will issue erroneous Torah decisions. He will permit that which is forbidden and he will prohibit the permissible. *And its stone fence crumbled.* Finally, this lazy student will be corrupted and he will breach the fences and safeguards set up by the Rabbis. How will he be punished? Solomon stated, *He who breaches the fence will be bitten by a snake* (*Koheles* 10:8).

This lesson emerges also from the history of the world's greatest empires; nations that once seemed invincible eventually crumbled into dust and ashes. The underlying cause of decline and disintegration is always the same. Power, privilege and prosperity breed lethargy and indifference that sap the vitality and vigor of the national purpose. The industry and integrity that elevate the nation to imperial ascendancy give way to indolence and immorality, and the moral fiber of the nation withers.

The underlying cause of decline and disintegration is always the same.

The fortunes of Israel followed a similar pattern, but with us, the crucial factor was not the strength of our commitment to maintaining a robust military force or commercial strength. Rather, our fortunes depend on

our dedication to the wholehearted pursuit of Torah knowledge, and obedience to its commands and values.

When Israel slackened its grip on the Torah and its spiritual values, they plunged onto a slippery slope of decline, which ultimately led to the Temple's destruction.

Rabbi Eliezer taught: The night is divided into three watches and at every watch God sits and roars like a lion, as it is written (Jeremiah 25:30): HASHEM will roar from on high and from His Holy Residence His voice will cry out; He will roar and continue to roar over His [destroyed] dwelling (Berachos 3a).

יְהוּדָה בֶּן תֵּימָא אוֹמֵר: הֱוֵי עַז כַּנָּמֵר, וְקַל כַּנֶּשֶׁר, רָץ כַּצְּבִי, וְגִבּוֹר כָּאֲרִי לַעֲשׂוֹת רְצוֹן אָבִיךְ שֶׁבַּשָּׁמָיִם ... יְהִי רָצוֹן מִלְּפָנֶיךָ ה' אֱלֹקֵינוּ וֵאלֹקֵי אֲבוֹתֵינוּ שֶׁיִּבָּנֶה בֵּית הַמִּקְדָּשׁ בִּמְהֵרָה בְיָמֵינוּ וְתֵן חֶלְקֵנוּ בְּתוֹרָתֶךְ

Yehudah ben Tema said: Be bold as a leopard, light as an eagle, swift as a deer, and powerful as a lion, to carry out the will of your Father in Heaven ... May it be Your will, HASHEM, our God and the God of our forefathers, that the Holy Temple be rebuilt, speedily in our days, and grant us our share in Your Torah (Avos 5:23, 24).

Why does God mourn over the Temple with the roar of a lion? Because He wishes to remind us that if we had heard the powerful roar of the lion and emulated its energetic ways, the Temple would not have been destroyed!

Therefore, in the Mishnah in *Avos*, Yehudah ben Tema graphically described how vigorously we must pursue the study and practice of Torah learning by comparing it to the creatures of the world, especially the powerful lion.

Yehudah ben Tema concludes his statement in *Avos* in a fashion found nowhere else in this tractate or any other. He adds a prayer for the return of the Temple and for the acquisition of our portion in Torah. This combination of Temple and Torah highlights the connection between the two. Israel's lethargy in the

pursuit of its Torah portion led to the Destruction of the Temple. When we begin to pursue our portion in Torah with the energy of the lion, we will be worthy of the Temple's return. Until then, God will roar every night like a lion, to awaken us from our exile slumber!

When we begin to pursue our portion in Torah with the energy of the lion, we will be worthy of the Temple's return.

The lion is the ruler of the animal kingdom, and the essence of monarchy can be summed up in one word: control. A true king is master of every individual and every event. The sovereign imposes his will and his vision over everything and everyone in his domain. The king *acts* on his own initiative, he does not merely *react* to events initiated by others; he maps his agenda based on his own priorities and goals.

The Talmud (*Bava Basra* 3b) gives a simile to describe how nothing stands in the way of a king's will: even if a towering mountain were to stand in the king's path, he would level it so that it will not impede his progress.

The Jew must not allow any obstacle to intimidate or impede him in God's service.

In his service of the Almighty, the Jew should adopt the nature of the king of beasts. He must not allow any obstacle to intimidate or impede him in God's service. But when Israel grew lethargic, God punished Israel through a powerful king, whose desire for mastery knew no bounds and who resembled the royal lion in every way. If Israel could not be a lion in the spiritual sense, it fell prey to a human lion, who embodied the worst traits of a conquering beast.

The Lion of Babylon

אֲרִי נֹהֵם וְדֹב שׁוֹקֵק מֹשֵׁל רָשָׁע עַל עַם דָּל

A roaring lion and a bloodthirsty bear; such is a wicked ruler over an impoverished people (Proverbs 28:15)

A roaring lion — this refers to Nebuchadnezzar of whom Jeremiah says (4:7): *The lion is rising up from his dense jungle (Megillah 11a).*

רָכַב עַל אֲרִי זָכָר וְקָשַׁר תַּנִּין בְּרֹאשׁוֹ

He [Nebuchadnezzar] rode on a male lion [as his steed] and he tied a serpent to its head [as a bridle] (Shabbos 150a).

The Talmud continues that Nebuchadnezzar's power was so awesome that even after he died and descended

to *Gehinnom,* the inhabitants of that netherworld trembled in fear that he would exert his power to rule despotically over them!

Jeremiah desperately warned the people of Israel to examine their ways lest they be devoured by this ferocious Babylonian lion.

Jeremiah desperately warned the people of Israel to examine their ways lest they be devoured by this ferocious Babylonian lion.

כִּי כֹה אָמַר ה' לְאִישׁ יְהוּדָה וְלִירוּשָׁלַם נִירוּ לָכֶם נִיר
וְאַל תִּזְרְעוּ אֶל קוֹצִים

For HASHEM speaks thus to the men of Judea and Jerusalem, "Plow over your fallow fields and don't plant your seeds among the thorns" (Jeremiah 4:3).

The prophet was exhorting his people to learn a lesson from the farmers who prepare their fields in the summer by digging deep into the earth to rip out the roots and weeds that might ruin their crops in the winter. Similarly, the people of Israel must delve deep into their hearts to uproot the flawed character traits that are the cause of their evil (*Rashi*).

The people of Israel must delve deep into their hearts to uproot the flawed character traits that are the cause of their evil.

הַגִּידוּ בִיהוּדָה וּבִירוּשָׁלַם הַשְׁמִיעוּ וְאִמְרוּ תִּקְעוּ
שׁוֹפָר בָּאָרֶץ ... כִּי רָעָה אָנֹכִי מֵבִיא מִצָּפוֹן וְשֶׁבֶר
גָּדוֹל. עָלָה אַרְיֵה מִסֻּבְּכוֹ

Declare in Judea and proclaim in Jerusalem, and say, "Blow the shofar in the Land ... for I am about to bring evil from the north [Babylon], and a great devastation ... the lion [i.e. Nebuchadnezzar (Rashi)] is rising up from his dense jungle (Jeremiah 4:5-7).

Nebuchadnezzar was born of common stock and humble origins — how did he become a lion? The Talmud (*Sanhedrin* 96a) states that he was catapulted to great power by virtue of his zeal in protecting the glory of Hashem.

After King Chizkiyahu of Judah was miraculously cured of a mortal illness, King Merodach Baladin of Assyria sent him a congratulatory letter that began. "Peace unto King Chizkiyahu; peace unto the city of Jerusalem; peace unto the great God!" Nebuchadnezzar was the king's personal scribe, but he was not present at the writing of this particular letter. When Nebuchad-

nezzar returned and heard about these salutations he was shocked. "You refer to the Lord as the 'great God,' yet you place His Name last? You must always salute God first!" He jumped up and began to run after the messenger who was galloping away with the letter. After Nebuchadnezzar took four strides, the angel Gabriel came and stopped him. In the merit of those four steps, Nebuchadnezzar was given the power to destroy the Temple. God sent Gabriel to stop him because if he had taken any additional steps, he would have earned the power to eradicate the entire Jewish nation.

"You refer to the Lord as the 'great God,' yet you place His Name last? You must always salute God first!"

God's ways are measure for measure. As a young man, Nebuchadnezzar respected God and was steadfast in giving Him honor. It took an angel to stop him, because no earthly power could deter Nebuchadnezzar when he ran in God's honor. Measure for measure, he was rewarded with invincible power, and became a lion.

God's ways are measure for measure. As a young man, Nebuchadnezzar respected God and was steadfast in giving Him honor.

Tragically, this absolute power eventually corrupted him. He forgot that his powers were God given and he declared himself to be a god. When the Jewish people became fat and complacent, and allowed even slight obstacles to deter them from God's service, God used Nebuchadnezzar as His agent to punish Israel. Measure for measure, the lion of Babylon, who strove to honor God, arose to punish the Jews who failed to serve God like lions.

Measure for measure, the lion of Babylon, who strove to honor God, arose to punish the Jews who failed to serve God like lions.

The month of tragedy for Israel is אָב, *Av*, which literally means *Father*. The מַזָל, *zodiac sign*, of Av is Leo, the Lion. When Israel fails to serve its Father in Heaven with the power of the lion, the lion of Babylon pounces from his cruel jungle and devours its people. For this reason God cries every night like a roaring lion over the Temple's destruction — a lion, because that is the symbol of Israel's fall and Nebuchadnezzar's ascendancy.

III: The Source of Senseless Hatred

אֲבָל מִקְדָּשׁ שֵׁנִי שֶׁאָנוּ בְּקִיאִים בָּהֶם שֶׁהָיוּ עוֹסְקִים
בַּתּוֹרָה וּבְמִצְווֹת וּבִגְמִילוּת חֲסָדִים אַמַאי חָרֵב? מִפְּנֵי
שִׂנְאַת חִנָּם שֶׁהָיְתָה בֵּינֵיהֶם

. . . But in the Second Temple era — we know that they involved themselves with the Torah commandments and kind deeds — why was it destroyed? Because there was causeless hatred among them (Yoma 9b).

בְּלֵיל תִּשְׁעָה בְּאָב נִכְנַס אַבְרָהָם אָבִינוּ לְבֵית קוֹדֶשׁ
הַקֳּדָשִׁים אֲחָזוֹ הקב״ה בְּיָדוֹ וְהִנֵּה מְטַיֵּיל בּוֹ אֲרוּכוֹת
וּקְצָרוֹת. אָמַר לֵיהּ הקב״ה: מֶה לִידִידִי בְּבֵיתִי. אָמַר:
רִבּוֹנִי בָּנַי הֵיכָן הֵם? אָמַר לֵיהּ: חָטְאוּ וְהִגְלֵיתִים בֵּין
הָאוּמוֹת. אָמַר לֵיהּ: לֹא הָיוּ בָּהֶם צַדִּיקִים? אָמַר לֵיהּ
. . . הָיוּ שְׂמֵחִים בְּמַפַּלְתָם אֵלוּ עַל אֵלוּ [נ״א: הָיוּ
שׂוֹנְאִים זֶה אֶת זֶה]

On the night of Tishah B'Av, our Father Abraham entered the Holy of Holies. The Holy One, Blessed is He, grasped his hand and walked back and forth with him. God asked, "What brings My beloved one to My House?" (Jeremiah 11:15). Abraham responded: "My Lord, where are my children?" God said, "They sinned, so I have exiled them among the nations." Abraham argued, "But were there no righteous people among them?" God explained, ". . . Each one rejoiced over the downfall of the other [Alternate version: They hated one another]" (Midrash Eichah Rabbasi 1:21).

*When the
Ignorant
Despise
the Wise*

The Talmud (*Yoma* 9b) ascribes the ruination of the Second Temple to the sin of *causeless hatred*, but what does that actually mean? If there was no reason for animosity, why did they hate?

Rabbi Yonasan Eibeschutz (1690-1764) discussed this question. He explained that the breakdown of Jewish society began with a rift between the Torah scholars

and the ignorant masses. No bitterness can compare to that of an ignoramus who instinctively feels that the Torah is the most precious heritage of all Jews, yet fails to muster the initiative to take possession of it for himself. Dark feelings of intense frustration and resentment smolder in his soul, and he becomes jealous of Torah scholars who joyously master the myriad mysteries and intricacies of the rich Torah legacy (*Yaaros Dvash*, Part I; *Drash* 10).

Indeed, the Talmud (*Pesachim* 49b) describes the love of scholars for the Torah in terms of the relationship of a bride and groom. Therefore, when an ignoramus sees the scholars engaged in Torah study he is as angry as a groom watching his bride being torn from him before his very own eyes. The Talmud observed that the hatred of the ignorant for Torah scholars surpasses the hatred which the gentile idolaters have for the Jews!

The hatred of the ignorant for Torah scholars surpasses the hatred which the gentile idolaters have for the Jews!

The Talmud (ibid.) also cites the great Rabbi Akiva, who did not begin his Torah studies until he was forty years old. He told his students, "When I was still an ignorant person I used to say, 'If only I could get my hands on a Torah scholar, I would bite him as a donkey bites.'" Hearing this, his students asked, "Why don't you say that you would have bitten him as a dog bites?" Rabbi Akiva explained that a donkey's bite is worse: "A donkey bites and he breaks bones, while a dog's bite breaks no bones!" (*Pesachim* 49b).

This was the reason for the hatred that divided Jews, a very powerful reason: the envy of the ignorant for the Torah scholars.

The vicious nature of hatred is that once it is incited, it spreads (see *Tosafos* to *Pesachim* 113b) until, eventually, the rivals hate everything about one another even for no reason!

When Disciples Disregard Their Masters

תַּנְיָא אָמַר רַבִּי יוֹסֵי: מִתְּחִלָּה לֹא הָיוּ מַרְבִּים מַחְלוֹקֶת בְּיִשְׂרָאֵל ... מִשֶּׁרַבּוּ תַלְמִידֵי שַׁמַּאי וְהִלֵּל שֶׁלֹּא שִׁמְּשׁוּ כָּל צָרְכָּן רָבוּ מַחְלוֹקֶת בְּיִשְׂרָאֵל וְנַעֲשָׂה תוֹרָה כִּשְׁתֵּי תוֹרוֹת

Rabbi Yose taught: In early times, they avoided an increase of disputation in Israel... But when there was an increase of

students of Shammai and Hillel who did not serve [i.e. study from] their teachers as much as necessary, disputes proliferated in Israel and the Torah became tantamount to two Torahs (Sanhedrin 88b).

The hatred of the ignorant for the scholars was symptomatic of the times, but they were *not* the only source of hostility. Tragically, Israel's ruination began within the sacred Torah academies.

Tragically, Israel's ruination began within the sacred Torah academies.

From the time God gave the Torah at Sinai, it was faithfully transmitted from generation to generation, from teacher to student. The ultimate guarantee of the fidelity of this system was the total devotion of the disciples to the masters under whom they studied. The role of "disciple" was a calling, a lifelong career, and he committed himself to studying and comprehending the *entire* Torah.

This required tremendous physical and mental exertion and stamina, a discipline the Sages called עֲמֵלוּת בַּתּוֹרָה, *toiling over Torah*. In the Second Temple era, a significant group of disciples weakened in their commitment to this toil. They failed to devote themselves sufficiently to their teachers, so they ultimately failed to comprehend the tradition properly, resulting in misconceptions and disputes.

In the Second Temple era, a significant group of disciples weakened in their commitment, resulting in misconceptions and disputes.

Avos d'Rabbi Nosson (Chapter 1) describes Tzaddok and Beothos, disciples of Antigonos of Socho, who did not apply themselves properly to his teachings, and failed to clarify their doubts and errors. Eventually, these students twisted the teachings of their holy master into heretical beliefs. Ultimately, they rejected not only the teachings of their own teacher but also the lessons of *all* the Sages, and finally, they denied the validity of the entire Oral Law. From these heretics evolved the powerful sect of the Sadducees who hated the Sages and their teachings with causeless enmity.

The Rabbis taught that even someone who has studied the Scriptures and the Oral Law, but never "toiled in Torah" under genuine Torah scholars, is considered an ignoramus (*Berachos* 47b).

The key is שִׁמּוּשׁ תַּלְמִידֵי חֲכָמִים, *service of Torah*

scholars, i.e. to surrender one's heart and mind to a master teacher who molds and fashions raw human intellect into an organized, analytical, holy intellect capable and worthy of comprehending and applying the word of God. Only the fiercely loyal, not the lazy, will attain this level.

Self-Hatred Leads to Exile

אִם בְּחֻקֹּתַי תֵּלֵכוּ וְאֶת מִצְוֹתַי תִּשְׁמְרוּ וַעֲשִׂיתֶם אֹתָם וְנָתַתִּי גִשְׁמֵיכֶם בְּעִתָּם וְנָתְנָה הָאָרֶץ יְבוּלָהּ וְעֵץ הַשָּׂדֶה יִתֵּן פִּרְיוֹ

If you will follow My decrees [i.e. if you labor over Torah study (Rashi)] *and observe My ordinances and perform them; then I will provide your rains in their season, so that the land will give its produce and the tree of the field will give its fruit (Leviticus 26:3,4).*

Idyllic blessings await the Jewish people if they prove worthy of God's esteem by virtue of their devotion to Him.

That chapter of the Torah begins with a list of the idyllic blessings that await the Jewish people if they prove worthy of God's esteem by virtue of their devotion to Him, and the primary demonstration of Israel's devotion to God is summed up in *Rashi's* three pithy words that have become the motto of the Torah World:

שֶׁתִּהְיוּ עֲמֵלִים בַּתּוֹרָה, *that you labor over Torah study.*

Only one who has seen it can fully comprehend what this means. The following testimony of two great scholars provides a glimpse into this world:

> With truth and wholesomeness, I expended effort upon effort and toil upon toil. I did not become involved with any other matter; I did not grant sleep to my eyes or slumber to my eyelids for many years until I had made my goal a reality. I sifted and weighed [every point] upon a scale and reviewed every angle and every point of every angle — not once or twice, but one hundred and one times. I did this with distinguished and beloved colleagues, who gave their attention to my words. Anyone who was not with me would not believe it were he told of my exhaustive

efforts to search through the sea of Talmud and the codes until I had clarified everything (*R' Shabsi Cohen*, preface to his commentary on *Shulchan Aruch*).

Rav Chaim of Volozhin writes about the Vilna Gaon:

How much toil did this greatest of giants toil — it could not be believed were it to be described — until he had brought each topic into the clearest light, in accordance with absolute truth. Though he was endowed with a breadth of intellect and depth of understanding, a mind filled with wisdom the likes of which had not been seen for many generations, nevertheless his pure heart did not rely on this. He weighed each matter on the scales of his holy intellect many hundreds of times, with awesome effort. For many days and nights, he neither ate nor drank, shaking slumber from his eyes.

He dedicated his whole being to it, until Hashem illuminated his vision, bringing him to the peak of his understanding. In an instant, his pure countenance shone with the light and joy of Torah (Preface to the *Vilna Gaon's* commentary to *Sifra D'Tzniusa*).

The Torah paints a terrible word picture of the evils which will engulf the Jews if they abandon God's Torah. Further on, the tone of this chapter (*Leviticus* 26) turns dark and somber as the Torah paints a terrible word picture of the evils which will engulf the Jews if they abandon God's Torah. In this menacing section known as the תּוֹכָחָה, *Admonition*, Scripture makes it very clear that sloth and failure to toil in Torah will breed dissension and devastation.

But if you do not listen to Me [i.e. if you fail to labor over the Torah (*Rashi*)] *and do not perform all of these commandments; if you consider My decrees revolting, and if your being rejects My ordinances, in order not to perform My commandments, to annul My covenant* (*Leviticus* 26:14,15).

Rashi goes on to graphically illustrate how unenthusiastic, lethargic Torah study triggers a chain reaction of astounding spiritual decline:

1) If you will not dedicate yourself to intensive Torah study . . .
2) you will eventually stop performing the commandments . . .
3) and then you will be revolted by the others who remain steadfastly loyal to Torah . . .
4) and then you will despise all the sages who expound and teach Torah . . .
5) then you will attempt to prevent other Jews from being observant . . .
6) this will cause you to deny that God gave the Jews the Torah . . .
7) and finally you will deny the very existence of God, Who gave us the Torah and its commandments.

In short, the Jew cannot enjoy a "love bond" with Torah unless he is prepared to toil over it energetically and enthusiastically and make this love his highest priority.

In short, the Jew cannot enjoy a "love bond" with Torah unless he is prepared to toil over it energetically and enthusiastically and make this love his highest priority. If the Jew fails to forge this love bond, there can be no middle way; instead of love there will be hatred! The Torah makes it very clear: in relationships where intense emotion is not required, one can maintain a mood of neutrality. But where a relationship demands intense love and devotion — it is one or the other, either love or hate — there is no middle of the road!

יִשְׂרָאֵל וְאוֹרַיְיתָא וקוב"ה חַד הוּא

Israel, the Torah, and the Holy One, Blessed is He, are one . . . (*Rav Saadiah Gaon*).

Because Israel and the Torah are one, the Jew can love himself only as much as he loves the Torah; as he weakens his grip on the Torah, he becomes ever more alienated from himself. And because the Torah and God are one, the Jew who grows distant from himself and the Torah grows distant and removed from God — and God grows distant from him. God does not mince words; He tells the Jew exactly where he stands. When the Jew distances himself from God spiritually, God distances the Jew from his homeland physically and geographically. This is what we call *galus* — exile.

Torah Love
Breeds
Brotherly
Love

The *Beis HaLevi* emphasizes a point that is vital because the destiny of our nation depends on it: Causeless hatred is alien to the genuine Torah Jew. Such hatred can exist only in the heart of an ignorant, alienated Jew, who despises himself and transfers his bitterness to those who love the Torah. Where there is Torah, there is unity and brotherhood. The Talmud makes this clear over and over again in the following passage which serves as the concluding statement of many tractates (*Berachos* 64a; *Yevamos* 122b; *Nazir* 66b, *Tamid* 32b; *Kereisos* 28b):

אָמַר רַבִּי אֶלְעָזָר אָמַר רַבִּי חֲנִינָא: תַּלְמִידֵי חֲכָמִים
מַרְבִּים שָׁלוֹם בָּעוֹלָם. שֶׁנֶּאֱמַר: וְכָל בָּנַיִךְ לִמּוּדֵי ה׳,
וְרַב שְׁלוֹם בָּנָיִךְ. אַל תִּקְרֵי בָּנָיִךְ אֶלָּא בּוֹנַיִךְ שָׁלוֹם רָב
לְאֹהֲבֵי תוֹרָתֶךָ, וְאֵין לָמוֹ מִכְשׁוֹל.

Rabbi Elazar said in the name of Rabbi Chanina: Torah scholars increase peace in the world as it says: And all of your children will be students of HASHEM and your children will have abundant peace (Isaiah 54:13) — do not read [בָּנָיִךְ] *your children, but* [בּוֹנַיִךְ] *your builders. There is abundant peace for the lovers of Your Torah and there is no stumbling block for them (Psalms 119:165). . .*

The Almighty ordained that there must be tension and dissension in the world — but it must be channeled into a positive dynamic force.

The *Chasam Sofer* makes an observation about the nature of the world and the Jewish people. Conflict and controversy are not necessarily all bad. Not at all! In his Divine wisdom the Almighty ordained that there must be tension and dissension in the world — but it must be channeled into a positive dynamic force. The Talmud (*Kiddushin* 30b) teaches that in order to properly clarify a Torah concept, two study partners must become passionately involved in its elucidation. To paraphrase the Talmud:

"Even a father and his son may challenge each other in furious debate in Torah subjects, to the point where they appear to be אוֹיְבִים, *enemies*, as they vigorously argue their points. However, since they both seek truth rather than glory, they will not

leave the house of study until they arrive at the truth — and resume their genuine affection."

The abrasive, positive friction created by arduous toil in Torah purges the Jewish heart of base feelings and polishes it into a paragon of sterling qualities.

The abrasive, positive friction created by arduous toil in Torah purges the Jewish heart of base feelings and polishes it into a paragon of sterling qualities.

However, warns *Chasam Sofer*, when Jews grow lazy and fail to toil in Torah, new passions and desires fill their hearts — a passion for luxury and comfort, wealth and honor. Then they compete against one another and rivalry turns to rancor and animosity, and finally to hatred (*Drashos Chasam Sofer* vol. I, Sermon for 7 Adar 5554/1794).

In short, a heart brimming with genuine love for Torah is simultaneously overflowing with sincere love for the fellow Jew who is a partner in the incessant struggle to discover the truth. If only the Jews would return to the study hall in sincerity we would never again hear of "causeless hatred."

שִׁיר הַמַּעֲלוֹת לְדָוִד שָׂמַחְתִּי בְּאֹמְרִים לִי בֵּית ה' נֵלֵךְ. עֹמְדוֹת הָיוּ רַגְלֵינוּ בִּשְׁעָרַיִךְ יְרוּשָׁלָם. יְרוּשָׁלַם הַבְּנוּיָה כְּעִיר שֶׁחֻבְּרָה לָהּ יַחְדָּו.

A song of ascents, by David, I rejoiced when they said to me, "Let us go to the House of HASHEM." Immobile stood our feet within your gates, O Jerusalem. The built-up Jerusalem is like a city that is united together (Psalms 122:1-3).

The Sages (*Yerushalmi, Chagigah* 3:6) explain the phrase, *like a city that is united together,* to mean that Jerusalem is עִיר שֶׁנַּעֲשׂוּ בּוֹ הַכֹּל חֲבֵרִים, *the city wherein all Jews become comrades;* Jerusalem serves as a unifying social force. A wide variety of people converged upon this city for the festivals, young and old, rich and poor, learned and ignorant, from all stations and from all walks of life. Usually, these divergent peoples were divided by powerful social barriers, but when they made their pilgrimage to the Holy Temple, the abode of their Heavenly Father, they all recognized that they were the children of the same

An Overview / The Kingdom in Ashes [36]

We all study the
same Torah, we all
cherish the same
parchment and
letters, and we all
would gladly
sacrifice ourselves
for its glory. How
can we not all be
united as one?
Divine Parent and that they all shared one sacred home. They realized that in the heart of the Temple, the Holy of Holies, stood the Holy Ark housing the Torah. We all study the same Torah, we all cherish the same parchment and letters, and we all would gladly sacrifice ourselves for its glory. How can we not all be united as one?

The Light at the End of the Galus

In what merit will the Messianic king reign? In the merit of the Torah in which Israel toils (*Midrash Tanchuma, Parashas Terumah* §7).

The coming of Eliyahu HaNavi ... to herald the Redemption is dependent on intense Torah study (*Chida* in *P'nei Yosef, Parashas Pikudei*).

...The current exile is symbolized by Moses; therefore, they shall be redeemed in the merit of Torah. In this last exile, all the wonders [of Redemption] will be through the Torah... (*Vilna Gaon*).

The Second Temple was destroyed because of causeless hatred among Jews. *Yaaros Dvash* explains that this hatred resulted from the rise of the Sadducees, who splintered the Jewish people when they shattered the cornerstone of our faith by denying the Divinity of the Oral Law and the authority of the rabbis who transmit it. Because they hated the sages — the transmitters of the Oral Law — the Sadducees denied the truth of the Torah itself. This long exile cannot end until the nation of Israel atones for the primary sin that caused it: rejection of the Oral Torah. Therefore, as the exile draws close to its conclusion, the heretical urge to deny the Oral Law and the authentic rabbis will become more powerful than ever. Only those who remain steadfast in their belief in the Torah will be worthy of the final redemption (*Beis HaLevi, Parashas Bo*).

The Jewish people has sailed the storm-tossed sea of exile for almost two thousand years. We have been battered by wave after wave of suffering and persecution. After our tormentors plundered and stripped us of our possessions and drove us from their land, we discovered that only one acquisition is irrevocably ours forever — the Torah. Exile's primary lesson is that when we tighten our grip on the Torah, our bond with God grows stronger. Only the Torah confers on us the title "Children of God," and only children can demand re-entry into their Father's home, the Holy Land and the Temple. Torah study will illuminate the darkness of exile and turn night into day, as the prophet says: הָעָם הַהֹלְכִים בַּחֹשֶׁךְ רָאוּ אוֹר גָּדוֹל יֹשְׁבֵי בְּאֶרֶץ צַלְמָוֶת אוֹר נָגַהּ עֲלֵיהֶם, *The nation walking in darkness saw a great light; those living in the land of the shadow of death — suddenly a light shone over them (Isaiah 9:1).*

Exile's primary lesson is that when we tighten our grip on the Torah, our bond with God grows stronger.

יְהִי רָצוֹן מִלְּפָנֶיךָ ה' אֱלֹקֵינוּ וֵאלֹקֵי אֲבוֹתֵינוּ שֶׁיִּבָּנֶה בֵּית הַמִּקְדָּשׁ בִּמְהֵרָה בְיָמֵינוּ וְתֵן חֶלְקֵנוּ בְּתוֹרָתֶךָ וְשָׁם נַעֲבָדְךָ בְּיִרְאָה כִּימֵי עוֹלָם וּכְשָׁנִים קַדְמוֹנִיּוֹת
May it be Your will, HASHEM our God, and the God of our forefathers, that the Holy Temple be rebuilt, speedily in our days. Grant us our share in Your Torah, and may we serve You there with reverence, as in days of old and in former years.
(Final Meditation From *Shemoneh Esrei*)

Rabbi Avrohom Chaim Feuer

Miami Beach, Florida
20 Sivan, 5752

� Insights

A Place for Hashem

Times of Mourning

The Three Weeks

"He Proclaimed a Meeting Against Me"

Causes of Exile

Eternal Covenant

A Miniature Sanctuary

The Western Wall

Remembrance of the Destruction

A Place for Hashem

> ...*If I allow sleep to my eyes, slumber to my eyelids, until I find a place for HASHEM, resting places for the Strong One of Jacob (Psalms* 132:4-5).

"Make For Me a Sanctuary"

&sa Shortly after the Exodus from Egypt, God commanded the Jews to construct a Tabernacle *(Mishkan)* in the Wilderness. *They shall make for Me a Sanctuary so that I will dwell among them (Exodus* 25:8). The fact that almost half the Book of *Exodus* deals with the construction of the Tabernacle, its vessels and the Priestly garments worn by those who performed its service underscores the Tabernacle's central place among those in whose midst it stood. In his introduction to the Book of *Exodus, Ramban* writes:

> ...The exile in Egypt was not completed until the day they [Israel] returned to their place and returned to the eminence of their forefathers...When they arrived at Mount Sinai and made the Tabernacle, and the Holy One, Blessed is He, returned and rested His *Shechinah* (Divine Presence) among them — then they returned to the eminence of their forefathers who had God's mystery upon their tents, and who were themselves the "chariot" [i.e. the bearers] of His *Shechinah*. Then, they were considered finally redeemed...

The Tabernacle accompanied the Israelites throughout their wanderings in the Wilderness. When, after forty years, they crossed the Jordan and entered the Land of Canaan, they erected the Tabernacle at Gilgal, near Jericho. It remained there throughout the fourteen years of conquest and apportionment of the Land by Joshua, and was then re-established at Shiloh. There it was erected as a stone structure, replacing the portable structure that had served until that time.[1]

---

1. However, its roof was still made of tapestry material; according to *Rambam (Hilchos Beis HaBechirah* 1:2), these were the same cloth canopies which covered the Tabernacle in the Wilderness. The Tabernacle at Shiloh stood for 369 years; that the canopies lasted so long was a miracle.

The Tabernacle at Shiloh was destroyed in a war with the Philistines. It was then that the portable Tabernacle that had been used in the Wilderness was re-established, first at Nov and later at Giveon where it stood for a combined total of fifty-seven years.[1]

In the fourth year of King Solomon's reign, the First Temple was built. Upon its completion, Solomon uttered a paraphrase of the words of his father David: קוּמָה ה' לִמְנוּחָתֶךָ, אַתָּה וַאֲרוֹן עֻזֶּךָ, *Arise, HASHEM, to Your resting place, You and the Ark of Your strength (Psalms 132:8)*. With these words, God was invited to change His dwelling place, so to speak, from His temporary abode in the Tabernacle to His permanent resting place in the Temple. A glorious cloud which embodied the essence of God's Presence appeared and accompanied the Ark as it entered the Holy of Holies (*II Chronicles* 5:14).

Eye of the Universe

◆§ The Sages teach, "Jerusalem is holier than the rest of the Land of Israel" (*Mishnah Keilim* 1:8). For almost one thousand years, from the time it was dedicated by King David until it was destroyed by the Romans, Jerusalem was the focal point of the Jewish people. The Kingdom of David, Divinely ordained to govern the Jewish nation, ruled from Jerusalem. Aside from the Temple service, many observances, such as the consumption of the second tithe (*ma'aser sheni*) could be performed only in Jersualem. The Great *Sanhedrin*, the Jewish nation's supreme judicial court, convened regularly in the Temple Courtyard.

If Jerusalem was the focal point of the Land of Israel, the Temple (*Beis HaMikdash*) was the focal point of Jerusalem. There the daily service was performed by the *Kohanim* (Priests). There and only there could sacrifices be offered unto God. There did the *Levi'im* (Levites) sing the song of the day in conjunction with the daily offerings. There was the Temple outer chamber (the *Heichal*) in which sat the Menorah, Altar of Incense Burning and Table of Gold, upon which the miraculous Show-Bread[2] was placed each week. There was the Holy of Holies (*Kodesh HaKodashim*) in which sat the Ark containing the Tablets which Moses brought down from Heaven, upon which were

---

1. This is the opinion of *Rambam* (commentary to *Mishnah Zevachim* 14:7). *Rashi* (*Pesachim* 38b s.v. זאת), however, differs.

2. The Show-Bread was as warm and fresh when it was removed from the Table as when it had been placed on it a week earlier.

were inscribed the Ten Commandments.[1] It was in the Holy of Holies that God's Presence was most manifest, so much so that no man was permitted to enter there, save for the *Kohen Gadol* (High Priest) on Yom Kippur.

Three times a year, before Pesach, Shavuos and Succos, Jews the world over streamed into the Holy City where they offered sacrifices unto God in the Temple Courtyard and received spiritual nourishment that sustained them throughout the year.

God's Chosen Place

◂§ The significance of the Temple Mount began with Creation itself. In the Holy of Holies was the אֶבֶן שְׁתִיָּה, *foundation stone*. Creation of the world began from this point and this rock was the first of the earth to be created *(Yoma* 54b). Adam was formed from the dust of what would be the site of the Courtyard Altar, to symbolize "that it would be on atonement for him that he might be able to endure" *(Rashi* to *Genesis* 2:7). After partaking of the Tree of Knowledge, Adam built an altar on the Temple Mount and offered a sacrifice to God. This altar was used by successive generations until the Deluge and was subsequently rebuilt by Noah *(Bereishis Rabbah* 34:9).

It was there that Abraham prepared to offer his beloved son Isaac as a sacrifice, until God instructed Abraham to let his son live, for the command to sacrifice Isaac had been intended only as a test of faith. It was upon the Temple Mount that Jacob had slept and had his prophetic dream in which he perceived that *this is the abode of God and this is the gate to the heavens (Genesis* 28:17). Jacob had perceived that the site of the future Temple was the conduit through which prayers from all corners of the earth ascend Heavenward. Indeed, to this day, wherever a Jew prays, he faces toward the site of the Holy of Holies *(Mishnah Berachos* 4:5).

David's Search

◂§ It is noteworthy that nowhere in the Pentateuch is the site of the Temple identified. Always, it is referred to as הַמָּקוֹם אֲשֶׁר יִבְחַר ה׳, *the place that HASHEM shall choose*. According to *Talmud Yerushalmi*

---

1. The Ark was not in the Holy of Holies in the Second Temple. According to *Mishnah Shekalim* (6:2), it was hidden by King Yoshiyahu toward the end of the First Temple era out of concern that it not fall into enemy hands (see *Yoma* 53a).

(Sanhedrin 10:2), the tradition of where the Temple would be built was recorded on a secret scroll which was transmitted through the ages and which the prophet Samuel gave to David. However, since this scroll was not part of Scripture, Samuel and David did not rest until they discovered a Scriptural reference to the specific place where the Temple was to be built (see *Rashi* to *Zevachim* 54b). Toward the end of his life, David purchased this site from Aravna the Jebusite. He found the location of the altar upon which Adam, Noah and Abraham had sacrificed. Using that spot as a starting point, he then surveyed and measured exactly where the Holy of Holies would be built, the position of the Temple Courtyard, etc.[1]

Why was all this necessary? Why did God not reveal in the Torah precisely where the Temple would stand? *Malbim* explains this in light of the command to erect a permanent dwelling for God's Presence: *For only to the place that HASHEM will choose from among all your tribes to place His Name there — [a place for] the manifestation of His Presence you shall seek and there you shall come (Deuteronomy* 12:5).[2] David understood the term לְשִׁכְנוֹ תִדְרְשׁוּ, *the manifestation of His Presence you shall seek,* to mean that to be worthy of God's Presence, one must actively *seek* it. The Torah specifically concealed the Temple's site so that it would be discovered only through intense, relentless spiritual yearning, the kind which David expresses in *Psalm* 132:

> O HASHEM, remember unto David all his suffering, how he swore to HASHEM, and vowed to the Strong One of Jacob: "If I enter the tent of my home, if I go upon the bed that is spread for me; if I allow sleep to my eyes, slumber to my eyelids, until I find a place for HASHEM, resting places[3] for the Strong One of Jacob (v. 1-5).

For God to continue to manifest His Presence among His people, it was necessary that they live their lives in a manner that reflected a yearning for His closeness. When the Jews' yearning waned and they became overtaken by sinful desires, the Divine Presence ceased to dwell among them. The Temple was then transformed into a hollow structure and their fate was sealed.

---

1. Though it was Solomon who built the First Temple, it was David who made the preliminary preparations.

2. See *Rambam, Hilchos Melachim* 1:1.

3. The plural *resting places* alludes to the three Temples (including the future one) that would be built upon that site *(Radak)*.

The First Temple stood for four hundred and ten years. In the year 3338 (from Creation; 422 B.C.E.), the armies of Nebuchadnezzar, king of Babylon, swept across the Jewish kingdom and on the Ninth of Av, destroyed the Temple.

The prophet Jeremiah foretold, *For thus said God, "When seventy years are completed for Babylon, I shall remember you, to return you to this place" (Jeremiah* 29:10). Exactly seventy years after the Destruction, the building of the Second Temple began (see *Megillah* 11b).

Four hundred and twenty years later on the Ninth of Av, the Roman armies, led by Titus, destroyed the Second Temple. When this exile will end remains hidden, until the moment when redemption will arrive.

Times of Mourning

The Four Fasts

◆§ *Rambam (Hilchos Taaniyos* 5:1-4, based on *Mishnah Taanis* 4:6) writes:

> There are days when all Israel fasts because of the misfortunes that occurred then, in order to awaken the hearts and to open the ways of repentance. Let this be a reminder of our evil deeds and our forefathers' deeds that were like our present deeds until they caused those misfortunes for them and for us. For through the recollection of these matters, we will repent to improve, as Scripture states *(Leviticus 26:40): And they shall confess their transgression and the transgression of their fathers.*
>
> These days are:
>
> The third of Tishrei, on which Gedaliah ben Achikam was killed and [therefore] the remaining ember of Israel [in their Land] was extinguished, thus bringing about the completion of their exile.
>
> The Tenth of Teves, when the wicked King Nebuchadnezzar laid siege to Jerusalem, bringing it to dire straits and distress.
>
> Five [tragic] events occurred on the Seventeenth of Tammuz: The [First] Tablets were broken; the *Tamid* offering

was discontinued in the days of the First Temple; the walls of Jerusalem were breached in the days of the Second Temple; the wicked Apostumos burned the Torah, and placed an idolatrous image in the Temple.

Five [tragic] events occurred on Tishah B'Av: It was decreed upon Israel in the Wilderness that it [i.e. that generation] should not enter the Land [of Israel]; the First and Second Temples were destroyed; and the great city of Betar was conquered. In that city were tens of thousands of Jews led by a great king whom all of Israel and its Sages thought was the Messiah. The city fell to the Romans and all its inhabitants were killed; it was a catastrophe akin to the Temple's destruction.

And on this day that was designated for punishment, the wicked Turnus Rufus plowed up the area of the Temple and its surroundings, in fulfillment of the verse, *Zion will be plowed like a field* (Jeremiah 26:18).[1]

The Seventeenth of Tammuz

◆§ The following is a brief explanation of the events which occurred on the Seventeenth of Tammuz:

On the seventeenth of Tammuz after the Torah was given at Sinai, Moses descended the mountain bearing the first Tablets upon which the Ten Commandments were written. As Moses descended, he saw the people worshiping the Golden Calf. He then smashed the Tablets at the foot of the mountain (*Exodus* ch. 32).

Rambam, as cited above, asserts that the cessation of the *Tamid* offering to which the Mishnah refers occurred during the First Temple. However, *Talmud Yerushalmi* cites two Tannaic opinions, both of which place this event in the Second Temple era. According to Rabbi Shimon, it took place during a siege of the Temple by the Greeks. Rabbi Levi maintains that it took place during the siege of Jerusalem by the Romans. Support for *Rambam*'s opinion is found in a Talmudic passage *(Arachin* 11b) which associates the cessation of the *Tamid* with a Scriptural verse related to the First Destruction.

Jerusalem's walls were breached on this day prior to the destruction of the Second Temple. Prior to the destruction of the First

---

1. The last two tragedies mentioned here are elaborated upon in "The Destruction of the Second Temple" found later in this volume.

Temple, the city's walls were breached on the ninth of Tammuz, as it says, *In the fourth month on the ninth of the month, and the famine became severe in the city . . . And the city was breached* (Jeremiah 52:6-7). The Sages did not want to burden the nation with two fasts in such close proximity; therefore, they selected the seventeenth of Tammuz as a fast since it was a prelude to the present exile and it also commemorates the other tragic events which occurred on it *(Tur, Orach Chaim 549).*

The above is the opinion of *Talmud Bavli (Taanis 28:b). Talmud Yerushalmi* (cited by *Tosafos* to *Rosh Hashanah* 18b s.v. זה ט' בתמוז), however, is of the opinion that at the time of the First Destruction, the walls were, in fact, breached on the seventeenth of Tammuz. However, the people were so thoroughly consumed by fear and dread of the enemy that they mixed up all their calendar dates. In their confusion, they thought that the seventeenth of Tammuz was actually the ninth, and that is the date which the prophet Jeremiah recorded in Scripture for all time, to teach us how utterly distraught and terrified the people of Jerusalem were when the Destruction occured.

Apostumos, a Greek general, burned the Torah that was kept in the Temple Courtyard. This scroll was written by Ezra the Scribe; it was the most authoritative copy of the Torah extant at that time and was used to check the accuracy of other scrolls. Therefore, its burning was deemed a great tragedy.

An alternative explanation is that Apostumos burned any Torah scroll that he could find, with the intent of causing Torah to become forgotten from the Jewish nation *(Tiferes Yisrael* to *Mishnah Taanis* 4:6).

According to *Rambam,* Apostumos was also responsible for the next tragedy cited in the Mishnah, the placing of an idolatrous image in the Second Temple during the Greek occupation of the Land. However, *Rashi's* version of the Mishnah's text, וְהוּעֲמַד צֶלֶם בַּהֵיכָל, *and an image was placed in the Temple,* indicates that this event is unrelated to the previous one. According to *Rashi,* this refers to the placing of an idolatrous image in the First Temple by Menashe, king of Judah, as recorded in *Targum Yerushalmi* to *Isaiah* ch. 66.

Tishah B'Av

◆§ In the second year of the Jews' sojourn in the Wilderness, Moses sent twelve great men, one from each tribe, to scout out the Land of Canaan in advance of Israel's conquest of it. When they returned from

their mission, ten of the spies delivered a slanderous, demoralizing report about the Land and the Jews' ability to conquer it. The people accepted this report as fact and wept throughout the night.

> R' Yochanan said: That day [when the spies returned] was Tishah B'Av eve. The Holy One, Blessed is He, said, "You wept in vain. I will establish it for you as a time of weeping for all generations" (Taanis 28b).

God decreed that, because of this sin, the Jews would wander in the Wilderness for forty years and all adult males of that generation would not enter the Land (Numbers ch. 13-14).

The Talmud (Taanis 29a) deduces from Scriptural sources that the First Temple was set on fire on the ninth of Av (Tishah B'Av). With regard to the date of the Second Temple's destruction, the Talmud states, מְגַלְגְּלִין זְכוּת לְיוֹם זַכַּאי וְחוֹבָה לְיוֹם חַיָּיב, Good things are brought to pass on an auspicious day and bad things on an ominous day. Meiri comments that certainly the Sages of the Mishnah clearly knew the date of the Second Temple's Destruction, which occurred during the Mishnaic period. In making the above statement, the Talmud is merely observing that the fact that both Destructions occurred on the same calendar date coincides with the principle that misfortune is brought about in an ominous time.

בֵּין הַמְּצָרִים / The Three Weeks

A Nation of Mourners

> כָּל רֹדְפֶיהָ הִשִּׂיגוּהָ בֵּין הַמְּצָרִים
> All her pursuers overtook her in narrow straits (Lamentations 1:3).
> "Bein HaMetzarim" [can be interpreted as "within the days of distress" and] refers to the days of distress from the Seventeenth of Tammuz until Tishah B'Av, for it is during these days that spiritual forces of destruction are most potent (Eichah Rabbah 1:29).

๛ The twenty-two-day period of mourning which commences with the Seventeenth of Tammuz and ends with Tishah B'Av[1] is refered to in halachic literature and common Hebrew usage as בֵּין הַמְּצָרִים, *Bein HaMetzarim*. It is known colloquially as "The Three Weeks." The mourning of this period intensifies with the advent of the month of Av, intensifies still further during the week in which Tishah B'Av falls and reaches its peak on the day of Tishah B'Av itself.

The halachic details of this period are not within the scope of this work. The best-known restrictions of the days from the Seventeenth of Tammuz until Rosh Chodesh Av are the prohibitions of weddings, playing music and cutting one's hair. From Rosh Chodesh Av and on, the eating of meat, drinking of wine and wearing of freshly laundered clothing are among those restrictions added to those already in force.[2]

A Time for Vigilance

๛ As is apparent from the Midrash cited above, as well as the words of R' Yosef Karo in *Shulchan Aruch (Orach Chaim* 551:18), the national tragedies which occurred to the Jewish nation during this period have transformed it until the Final Redemption into days of misfortune and require more than the usual vigilance with regard to matters of personal health and safety.

As mentioned above, the tragedy of the Spies' failed mission brought forth a Heavenly decree that Tishah B'Av become a day of weeping for generations. R' Moshe Wolfson *(Emunas Itecha)* comments that it is not coincidental that during this time of year, Jews the world over go on journeys of their own, as they leave their city dwellings for summer resorts and other destinations. Relaxation from the strains of daily life is important, but it brings with it many a spiritual test — particularly in the summer, when the outdoors is inviting and the streets abound with sights that a Jew's eyes must not behold. How does one react to these challenges? Will his relaxed pace prevent him from arising in time to attend the *minyan?* Will his daily Torah sessions fall to the wayside in favor of extracurricular activities? Will he be careless in not avoiding places where the laws of *tznius* (modesty in dress) are ignored?

---

1. Actually, the *Halachah* requires that some forms of mourning continue until noon of the tenth of Av. See Laws section of this volume.

2. Sefardic customs may differ from those cited here. The laws of the Three Weeks are detailed in *Shulchan Aruch, Orach Chaim* ch. 549-559.

When Moses instructed the Spies prior to their mission, he exhorted them, וְהִתְחַזַּקְתֶּם, *and take courage (Numbers* 13:20). Realizing that personal interest and desire might impede their mission, Moses urged the Spies to muster the spiritual strength needed to overcome their inclinations and see the Land with a clear vision. They failed and brought disaster upon themselves and their people. During the Three Weeks, we can rectify their sin by garnering the strength to scrupulously observe God's commandments no matter where our travels may take us.

A Time to Pray

◆§ Only two of the Spies returned from their mission with a positive report which reflected their deep faith in God and His promise that the nation would indeed conquer and settle the Land which "flows with milk and honey." The power of prayer figured significantly in both Joshua and Caleb remaining wholly untainted by the wicked designs of their companions. Moses prayed that Joshua (his closest disciple) be saved "from the plans of the [other] Spies," while Caleb prostrated himself in prayer before God at the graves of the Patriarchs and Matriarchs — and their prayers were answered.

As we mourn the suffering and destruction that has its roots in the Spies' sin, we should take a lesson from Moses and Caleb. The power of prayer is awesome; even when the sword is upon one's neck, he should not give up hope, for prayer can still save him *(Berachos* 10a). The mourning of the Three Weeks demands that we not divert our minds from the Temple's destruction and that we pray with renewed fervor for its re-establishment.

When the Jewish people are exiled, the *Shechinah,* Divine Presence, goes into exile as well, as it were *(Megillah* 29a). The Chassidic masters teach that during the Three Weeks, this exile is of a different, more pronounced nature. The *Maggid* of Mezritch drew an analogy to a king who takes leave of his palace and goes out to the streets and markets to be among his subjects. When the king is in his palace, he is not easily accessible, but when he walks among the people, anyone can approach him and put forth his requests. During the Three Weeks, God is likened to a king who has taken leave of his palace. He is easily accessible and He awaits the sincere requests of His subjects that they be restored to their former glory.

The *Maggid* interpreted כָּל רֹדְפֶיהָ הִשִּׂיגוּהָ בֵּין הַמְּצָרִים homiletically:

All those who sincerely pursue a closeness with God can reach Him within the "days of distress" — the Three Weeks.

The Nine Days

When Av begins, we curtail joy (Mishnah Taanis 4:6).

§ As mentioned above, the period from Rosh Chodesh Av through Tishah B'Av, known as "The Nine Days," is one whose mourning is of an even greater degree than that which begins with the Seventeenth of Tammuz. It was in Av that the Destructions actually occurred and this is sufficient reason to mandate further reflection, introspection and sadness. *Magen Avraham* (*Orach Chaim* 552:1) writes that in stating מְמַעֲטִין בְּשִׂמְחָה, *[When Av begins,] we curtail joy,* the Sages' intent was to prohibit *all* forms of rejoicing.

The Talmud contrasts the month of Av with that of Adar, the Jewish people's most auspicious month, in which the Purim miracle occurred. *Just as when Av begins we curtail joy, so, too, when Adar begins we increase joy (Taanis 29a).* It would seem that in drawing this contrast, the Sages were alluding to a relationship between the sadness of Av and the joy of Adar.

Tishah B'Av's tragedies are rooted in the sin of the Spies, which was triggered by a serious lapse of faith. God had promised His people that they would inherit the Land of Canaan. Yet, the spies returned from their mission with a negative assessment. *The people that dwell in the land are strong. . .we are not able to go up against the people for they are stronger than us (Bamidbar 13:28,31).* These words implied a denial of God's ability to fulfill His promise, and it was for this that they were punished so severely (see *Ramban* to *Numbers* 13:27).

A primary cause of the First Destruction was a laxity in the observance of *Shemittah*, the seventh year, when the Land must lie fallow. *Then the Land will be appeased for its sabbaticals during all the years of its desolation, while you are in the land of your foes (Leviticus 26:34).* *Shemittah* observance is a demonstration of faith that it is God's blessing and not man's efforts that is the ultimate source of one's livelihood. Laxity in this regard is predicated on a lack of faith.

The primary cause of the Second Destruction was *sinas chinam*, senseless hatred among Jews. People become resentful of one

another when they lose faith in God and see their neighbor as a threat to their success.[1]

The Sabbath preceding Tishah B'Av is known as *Shabbos Chazon*, after the *Haftarah* which opens with the words חֲזוֹן יְשַׁעְיָהוּ בֶן אָמוֹץ, *The vision of Isaiah son of Amotz (Isaiah 1:1)*.[2] In that vision, the prophet declares in the name of God: *An ox knows his owner and a donkey his master's crib; Israel does not know, My people does not consider* (ibid. v. 3). Faith in God is as natural as the ox's recognition of who his owner is or the donkey's recognition of the crib from which it eats. It is sin that creates the barriers that result in a lack of faith *(R' Eliyahu Lopian)*.

At the time of the Purim miracle, the Jews saw clearly how even in times of exile, God is with them, orchestrating events in a hidden manner in accordance with His will. As recounted in the Book of *Esther,* a series of seemingly unrelated events, which occurred over a period of nine years, came together to bring about the salvation of the entire Jewish nation from the hands of their enemies. As the story reached its climax, the Jews rose to a heightened level of faith and renewed their commitment to God and His Torah.

Moreover, it was their demonstration of faith through fasting and repentance which merited their salvation.

Faith in God brings with it tranquility and happiness. Lack of faith breeds tension and distress. During the Nine Days, a Jew should ponder the contrast between the distress and sadness borne of lack of faith and the joy for all generations which was inspired by the faith shown at the time of the Purim miracle.

❧ ❧ ❧

אֶסְתֵּר מִן הַתּוֹרָה מִנַּיִן? ,,וְאָנֹכִי הַסְתֵּר אַסְתִּיר פָּנַי.''
Where is there an allusion to Esther in the Torah? "And I will conceal My countenance" (Deuteronomy 31:18).

(Chullin 139b)

The verse in *Deuteronomy* speaks of a time when Israel will sin grievously and as a result will be subject to Divine wrath. *My wrath will rage on that day; I will forsake them and I will conceal My countenance from them* (ibid. v. 17). The double form הַסְתֵּר אַסְתִּיר

---

1. See p. 65.

2. The Sabbath following Tishah B'Av is known as *Shabbos Nachamu*, for the *Haftarah* of that week opens: נַחֲמוּ נַחֲמוּ עַמִּי יֹאמַר אֱלֹהֵיכֶם, *Comfort, comfort My people, says your God* (Isaiah 40:1).

represents utter concealment, when the punishments and sufferings are acute and only those pure of faith can perceive the Divine hand at work. It is they who know that "in reality, wherever they may be, I [the Divine Presence] am to be found there, as our Sages said, *Wherever Israel was exiled, the Divine Presence was with them (Megillah* 29a). Rather, I shall but *hide My face* from saving them" (*Sforno* ibid.).

The miracle of Purim happened during the period between the two Temples when the Jews were in exile. It serves as an eternal reminder that God never abandons His people. Even in the darkness of exile, when the swords of our oppressors are at the necks of our people, He is there.

We are incapable of gaining a true understanding of events from our present limited perspective. Clarity will not be ours until the End of Days, when the meaning inherent in every event will become evident. One thing, however, we do know: *Behold! He was standing behind our wall, observing through the window, peering through the cracks (Song of Songs* 2:9). Just as God was with us at the time of the Purim miracle, so, too, He is with us in the most trying moments of this exile.

R' Elchonon's Parable

◄§ R' Elchonon Wasserman, the great European *Rosh Yeshivah* and Torah leader, was martyred in the Kovno ghetto in 1941, after returning to Poland in the summer of 1939 from a trip to the United States. R' Elchonon was fully cognizant that to return home was to risk death, yet he did so because he knew that his students needed him during those perilous times.

Among the first American troops to enter the death camps in the United States Army's sweep across Europe was First Lieutenant Meyer Birnbaum, an Orthodox Jew who served in the United States Signal Corps. Birnbaum performed heroically to help save lives and bring comfort to the starving, stricken survivors. One day in Buchenwald, a gaunt Jewish survivor approached him and asked whether he had ever heard of R' Elchonon. Lt. Birnbaum told the man that he remembered R' Elchonon well from his stay in the United States in 1938-39. The Jew was happy that he had found a listener. He proceeded to tell his new friend that he had been with R' Elchonon during those frightful, final days in Kovno. The fugitives had asked R' Elchonon to explain why these horrors were befalling

them. R' Elchonon spoke, and this is what he said:

Once a man who knew nothing at all about agriculture came to a farmer and asked to be taught about farming. The farmer took him to his field and asked him what he saw. "I see a beautiful piece of land, lush with grass, and pleasing to the eye." Then the visitor stood aghast while the farmer plowed under the grass and turned the beautiful green field into a mass of shallow brown ditches.

"Why did you ruin the field!" he demanded.

"Be patient. You will see," said the farmer.

The farmer then showed his guest a sackful of plump kernels of wheat and said, "Tell me what you see." The visitor described the nutritious, inviting grain — and then, once more watched in shock as the farmer ruined something beautiful. This time, he walked up and down the furrows and dropped kernels into the open ground wherever he went. Then he covered the kernels with clods of soil.

"Are you insane?" the man demanded. "First you destroyed the field and then you ruined the grain!"

"Be patient. You will see."

Time went by, and once more the farmer took his guest out to the field. Now they saw endless, straight rows of green stalks sprouting up from all the furrows. The visitor smiled broadly.

"I apologize. Now I understand what you were doing. You made the field more beautiful than ever. The art of farming is truly marvelous."

"No," said the farmer. "We are not done. You must still be patient."

More time went by and the stalks were fully grown. The farmer came with a sickle and chopped them all down as his visitor watched open-mouthed, seeing how the orderly field became an ugly scene of destruction. The farmer bound the fallen stalks into bundles and decorated the field with them. Later, he took the bundles to another area where he beat and crushed them until they became a mass of straw and loose kernels. Then he separated the kernels from the chaff and piled them up in a huge hill. Always he told his protesting visitor, "We are not done, you must be more patient."

The farmer came with his wagon and piled it high with grain, which he took to a mill. There, the beautiful grain was ground into formless, choking dust. The visitor complained again. "You have taken grain and transformed it into dirt!" Again, he was told to be patient.

The farmer put the dust into sacks and took it back home. He took some dust and mixed it with water while his guest marveled at the foolishness of making "whitish mud." Then the farmer fashioned the "mud" into the shape of a loaf. The visitor saw the perfectly formed loaf and smiled broadly, but his happiness did not last. The farmer kindled a fire in an oven and put the loaf into it.

"Now I know you are insane. After all that work, you burn what you have made."

The farmer looked at him and laughed. "Have I not told you to be patient?"

Finally, the farmer opened the oven and took out a freshly baked bread — crisp and brown, with an aroma that made the visitor's mouth water.

"Come," the farmer said. He led his guest to the kitchen table where he cut the bread and offered his now-pleased visitor a liberally buttered slice.

"Now," the farmer said, *"now* you understand."

God is the Farmer and we are the ignorant visitors who do not begin to understand His ways or the outcome of His plan. Only when the process is complete and Redemption is a reality will the Jewish people know why all that transpired during this long and bitter exile had to happen. Until then, we must be patient and have faith that everything — even when it seems destructive and painful — is a part of the process that will produce goodness and beauty.

Tishah B'Av and Pesach

◆§ Our Sages note an inner connection between Tishah B'Av and Pesach. In *Lamentations* we read, הִשְׂבִּיעַנִי בַמְּרוֹרִים הִרְוַנִי לַעֲנָה, *He filled me with bitterness; sated me with wormwood* (3:15). The Midrash links בַמְּרוֹרִים, *bitterness*, with מָרוֹר, the *bitter herbs* eaten at the Pesach *seder*, and comments that the first day of Pesach always falls on the same day of the week as Tishah B'Av. Common custom is to begin the *seder* meal with the eating of a hard-boiled egg, a food that traditionally is eaten by mourners. This is to evoke a sense of mourning over the absence of the Temple and its Altar, upon which the Pesach lamb was offered.

The fact that so many national tragedies occurred on Tishah B'Av is in itself testimony to the fact that these events were not accidents of

history,[1] but powerful proclamations of God's special relationship with the Jewish people and that He instructs them *as a father instructs his son (Deuteronomy* 8:5).

On the night of the Exodus, when God inflicted punishment upon the Jews' oppressors and freed His people from bondage amid great miracles, the nation achieved a heightened awareness of and closeness to Him. In the verdicts of Tishah B'Av, too, one can recognize the eternal providence of God and thereby, achieve a renewed awareness of and closeness to Him *(Moreinu R' Yaakov Rosenheim).*

"He Proclaimed a Meeting Against Me"

Source of Comfort

קָרָא עָלַי מוֹעֵד לִשְׁבּׂר בַּחוּרָי

He proclaimed a meeting against me to crush my young men (Lamentations 1:15).

◆§ In its plain meaning, the word מוֹעֵד, *meeting,* refers to the meeting of invading armies which converged on the Land of Israel at the time of the Destruction *(Rashi).* On another level of interpretaion, our Sages understand the term מוֹעֵד to mean *festival* as it is so often used in Scripture. This has halachic implications: The *Tachanun* prayer is not recited on Tishah B'Av, just as it is not recited on Festivals and certain other days of celebration *(Shulchan Aruch* 559:4).

In what sense can Tishah B'Av be viewed as a festival?

Chasam Sofer explains that our mourning over the Temple's destruction is in itself a cause for wonder. Through the course of history, many nations have suffered destruction and loss of nationhood at the hands of their conquerors, yet all this becomes forgotten with the passage of time. Surely, there are none who mourn their losses collectively as do the Jewish people each year on Tishah B'Av. Almost two thousand years have passed since the Second Destruction, yet we continue to weep. Why?

---

1. In addition to the five tragedies listed above, the expulsion of the Jews from Spain occurred on Tishah B'Av of 1492 and World War I erupted on Tishah B'Av of 1914 (see pp. 157-158).

Our Sages state that the fact, that with the passage of time, the memory of the deceased becomes forgotten from his loved ones to the point that they can be consoled and overcome their grief, is a Divine decree. Because this is a decree, one who mourns a loved one — whom he *believes* to be dead but is actually alive — will never be consoled (see *Rashi* to *Genesis* 37:35). Similarly, says *Chasam Sofer*, other nations can overcome their loss of country and nationhood, because when this occurs, it is final. They have no hope of ever regaining their lost empires, of being restored to their former glory. Their once glorious status is "dead" and therefore, becomes forgotten as time goes on.

Israel, however, can never be consoled, for its collective soul knows that its former glory will yet return. *The city that was great with people has become like a widow (Lamentations* 1:1): She is *like* a widow but she is not *really* a widow; rather, she is like a woman whose husband went to a foreign country, but with the intention of returning to her *(Sanhedrin* 104b).

The fact that we still mourn, that we still yearn for the Jerusalem of old with its Temple service and awesome spiritual aura, is of itself the greatest source of consolation.

It is this aspect of Tishah B'Av that confers a degree of מוֹעֵד upon this day of profound mourning, to the extent that a prayer which is not recited on Festivals is omitted on this day as well.

Strengthening of Faith[1]

⋖ In citing the *halachah* that one does not say *Tachanun* on Tishah B'Av, *Aruch HaShulchan* writes: "This serves as a sign that we trust in the Holy One, Blessed is He, that [He will redeem us from this exile, at which time] these days will be transformed into joyous festivals" *(Orach Chaim* 552:14).

The mourning that Tishah B'Av demands of us must not be confused with despair. Despair has no place where faith and trust are present. The Jew of faith knows that not only is redemption inevitable, but that its roots lie in the destruction itself.

The prophet exhorts Israel, *Return, Israel, unto HASHEM your God, for you have stumbled by your sins (Hosea* 14:2). The Talmud derives from this verse that *teshuvah*, repentance, reaches to the throne of

---

1. This piece is based, in part, on the thoughts of R' Chaim Shmulevitz, as recorded in *Sichos Mussar*.

the Almighty (עַד ה' אֱלֹהֶיךָ) (*Yoma* 86a). Whence does it draw such power? *For you have stumbled by your sins.* The depths of retribution and rejection which Tishah B'Av represents spur the Jewish people on to greater spiritual heights and a renewed closeness with their loving God.

In the Torah reading of Tishah B'Av morning, Moses speaks of Israel's downfall as the product of lethargy: *When you will beget children and grandchildren, and will have been long in the Land . . .* (Deuteronomy 4:25). *Ramban* relates the word וְנוֹשַׁנְתֶּם, *and you will be long*, to יָשָׁן, *old* and *well worn*. It was the force of habit, of becoming set in one's ways, that bred an atmosphere that made destruction a painful necessity. The mourning of Tishah B'Av should inspire us to ponder this fact and thus, has the potential to bring us *to the throne of the Almighty*.

This is why the prophet states that at the time of the Redemption, the days of fasting will themselves become days of rejoicing (Zechariah 8:14-15). At that time, we will clearly perceive how the Destruction and exile were for our good and we will rejoice in the salvation whose seeds they bore.

In the meantime, we omit *Tachanun* on Tishah B'Av, to strengthen our belief that the day which is called a מוֹעֵד, *festival*, will one day be celebrated as such.[1]

"Ani Ma'amin" / *"I Believe"*

◆§ The mourning of Tishah B'av is somewhat lessened in the afternoon, when, for example, it is permissible to sit on a bench or chair (see

---

1. *Tachanun* is also omitted on the Fifteenth of Av, which was a day of great celebration when the Temple stood (*Shulchan Aruch, Orach Chaim* 131:6; see *Mishnah Taanis* 4:8) One reason for this celebration is that on this date, the Jews in the Wilderness realized with certainty that all those who were to die because of the sin of the Spies had already died — and that those who were still alive would enter the Land (*Taanis* 30b; see *Rashi*). From the time that the decree of death had been issued as a result of the Spies' sin until the last person had died, God did not speak to Moses in the particular and affectionate manner that He employed before issuing the decree. However, when the dying ended, this intimate tenor of prophecy was restored to Moses — for the benefit of the entire nation (see *Gevuros Ari* ad loc.). Therefore, the Fifteenth of Av was established as a permanent day of festivity and celebration.

Perhaps our omission of *Tachanun* on this day can also be seen as an expression of faith: Just as God renewed His closeness with Moses when the decree in the Wilderness had been carried out, so, too, will He one day heed the plea with which the reading of *Lamentations* concludes: *Bring us back to You, HASHEM, and we shall return, renew our days as of old.*

Mishnah Berurah 555:3). It is in the afternoon that we recite נַחֵם, in which we beseech the Almighty to comfort the mourners of Jersualem. The Chofetz Chaim (ibid.) writes that the reason for this recitation is to make mention, even while we mourn, of our ultimate consolation. In discussing customs of certain communities on Tishah B'Av afternoon, *Birkei Yosef* (§554) cites the statement of the *Midrash* that the Messiah is born on Tishah B'Av. He stresses the importance of reinforcing on this day belief in the Final Redemption through the coming of the Messiah.

Belief in the coming of the Messiah is the twelfth of the Thirteen Principles of Faith as formulated by *Rambam*:

אֲנִי מַאֲמִין בֶּאֱמוּנָה שְׁלֵמָה בְּבִיאַת הַמָּשִׁיחַ, וְאַף עַל פִּי שֶׁיִּתְמַהְמֵהַ, עִם כָּל זֶה אֲחַכֶּה לוֹ בְּכָל יוֹם שֶׁיָּבוֹא.

I believe with complete faith in the coming of the Messiah, and even though he may delay, nevertheless I anticipate every day that he will come.

Scripture is replete with references to the Final Redemption through the coming of the Messiah, a scion of King David. The Messiah will restore the kingdom of David, gather in the exiles of Israel and rebuild the Temple *(Rambam, Hilchos Melachim* 11:1).

As is apparent from *Rambam's* wording of this principle of faith, a Jew is required to not only believe in the Messiah's ultimate coming, but also to forever anticipate his arrival. The Talmud *(Shabbos 31a)* states that when a person is brought before the Heavenly Tribunal, one of the questions he is asked is, "צִפִּיתָ לִישׁוּעָה?", *Did you anticipate the Redemption?"* This means that we are required to believe that the Messiah's arrival can occur at any time and to hope for his possible coming at any moment. As the prophet Malachi foretold, *And suddenly, the master whom you are seeking will come (Malachi* 3:1); he can arrive *suddenly*, at a moment's notice, if such be the will of God.

The Chofetz Chaim wrote an essay entitled צִפִּיתָ לִישׁוּעָה?, in which he exhorted the Jewish people to truly yearn for the Redemption. He notes an apparent contradiction in the words of the prophet *(Habakuk* 2:3), where one verse begins, *If he [the Messiah] delays, wait for him,* and concludes, *He [the Messiah] shall surely come without delay.* The Chofetz Chaim resolved this with a parable:

A king became incensed with his wayward son and banished him to exile for five years. The son was sent to a distant land, so far away that it took years for him to reach it. Eventually, the king regretted his

decree, but knowing that it could not be nullified, he sought to at least find a way to bring his son home swiftly as soon as the sentence would end. He ordered that roadways be carved through the mountains and paved, and the fastest train be built to speed his beloved son back home to the palace.

Similarly, God has banished us into exile until that moment when He will deem it time for our redemption. As we wait for that moment, we should not be given to despair, for when it comes, God will have everything prepared in advance so that the Messiah can redeem us instantly.

Rabban Yochanan ben Zakkai

∞§ A classic illustration of grief for the Destruction combined with hope for the future and practicality for the present is the legislation enacted by Rabban Yochanan ben Zakkai soon after the Second Temple's Destruction. At the time of the Destruction, Rabban Yochanan, his colleagues and disciples were in the port city of Yavneh.[1] As our Sages relate:

> Rabban Yochanan was hoping and dreading. . .When the news arrived that Jerusalem was destroyed and the Holy Temple burnt, he rent his garments, as did his disciples; they wept and lamented *(Avos D'R' Nassan* ch.4).

Soon after the Destruction, Rabban Yochanan, as the leading sage of his generation, prepared three important Rabbinic ordinances in advent of the approaching High Holidays. The Talmud *(Rosh Hashanah* 29a-30b) enumerates these ordinances:

1) The Torah mandates that the *mitzvah* of *arbah minim*, four species, on Succos be performed for seven days in the Temple Courtyard, but only on the first day of the holiday elsewhere. Rabban Yochanan ben Zakkai decreed that the four species be taken for seven days everywhere as a זֵכֶר לְמִקְדָּשׁ, *remembrance of the Temple.* The concept of such remembrance was first expressed by the prophet Jeremiah: צִיּוֹן הִיא דֹּרֵשׁ אֵין לָהּ, *She is Zion; she has no one inquiring about her (Jeremiah* 30:17). The way to show concern for Zion, the Sages determined, was to perform *mitzvos* that recall the Temple service.

---

1. See p. 136.

2) Before the Destruction, when Rosh Hashanah fell on the Sabbath the *shofar* was sounded only in the Temple. After the Destruction, Rabban Yochanan decreed that it be sounded on the Sabbath in every place where there is a *beis din*, Rabbinic court *(Mishnah Rosh HaShanah* 4:1). This ordinance emphasized that the observance of Torah was not dependent on the physical presence of the Temple. The study hall, as represented by the Rabbinic court, had now taken the place of the Temple as the focal point of Judaism.

3) When the Temple stood, the new grain crop was forbidden until after the *Omer* offering was brought on the sixteenth of Nissan of that year. According to Scriptural law, when the Temple is not standing the new grain becomes permissible at sunrise of the sixteenth. After the Destruction, however, Rabban Yochanan decreed that the new grain be forbidden the entire sixteenth day. His reason? מְהֵרָה יִבָּנֶה בֵּית הַמִּקְדָּשׁ, *The Temple might speedily be rebuilt*; i.e. the Messiah might arrive on the eve of the sixteenth of Nissan and rebuild the Temple, thus necessitating the bringing of the *Omer* offering. Preparation of the offering might stretch into the next afternoon, and the new grain would be Scripturally prohibited all that time — but many, in the habit of partaking of the new grain at sunrise, might not realize that this year is different. To preclude such a mistake from occurring, Rabban Yochanan decreed that until the Temple is rebuilt, the new grain should not be eaten until the sixteenth of Nissan has passed.[1]

Active Anticipation

◆§ How does one demonstrate that, indeed, he does anticipate and yearn for the Redemption? One way is by striving for self-improvement. *Tana D'vei Eliyahu* (ch. 16) relates that a disciple once asked Elijah the prophet when all of Isaiah's prophecies concerning the Messiah will be fulfilled. Elijah replied, "If the Jewish people would repent sincerely, out of love of God, He would immediately rebuild the Temple and shower them with eternal love."

---

1. Note that one reason for the ritual washing of one's hands before eating bread is so that when the Temple will be rebuilt and the eating of sacred produce will require such washing, we will already be accustomed to it *(Mishnah Berurah* 158:1). Thus, every time a Jew washes his hands before eating bread, he is demonstrating belief in the Redemption.

It has been said on behalf of the Chassidic masters that we, on earth, have the capacity to rebuild the Temple through the performance of *mitzvos*. Each good deed creates a vessel in the Heavenly Temple, but each sin destroys a portion of the structure. If only the performance of good deeds could continue uninterrupted, the heavenly Temple would be completed and it would descend to earth.

Another means of anticipation is to maintain an ever-present awareness that Israel is a nation apart, and even in exile must remain distinct from those in whose land it dwells. *"And he sojourned there (Deuteronomy* 26:5) — this teaches that Jacob did not go to Egypt to settle there permanently, but merely to stay there for a time. *And he became there a nation* (ibid.) — this teaches that the Jews were distinctive there" *(Passover Haggadah)*.

The *Netziv (She'eiris Yisrael)* notes that Scripture uses fire as a metaphor for Israel *(Ovadiah* 1:18) and water to describe the gentile nations *(Song of Songs* 8:7). When water is placed upon fire with a barrier (i.e. a pot) separating them, the fire will warm the water, which in turn can cook food or serve some other beneficial purpose. However, when the two come in direct contact with one another, co-existence is impossible; the water will douse the fire. So, too, says the *Netziv*, is it with Israel and the nations. The Jewish people have much to offer the world as a light unto the nations, but to fulfill this role, they must remain distinct. It is absolutely essential that the Jewish people maintain their pure faith, fidelity to Torah and distinct way of life. If, however, they lose their distinctiveness, then their fire becomes nothing more than useless, suffocating smoke.

Service of the Heart

◆§ *Yaaros Devash* exhorts every Jew to shed an endless stream of tears in the daily *Shemoneh Esrei (Amidah)* while reciting the prayers for the rebuilding of Jerusalem and the re-establishment of the Davidic dynasty. He writes that their absence fills the Almighty with pain, as it were, and causes the ministering angels to weep day and night. How, then, can *we* remain calm and serene? Every Jew's heart should be filled with sorrow and misery over the Destruction and this should be manifest each day in the manner in which he recites the above-mentioned prayers.

The Talmud states, "The son of David [the Messiah] will not come until the Jewish people give up all hope for redemption and there will

be no help or support for Israel" (Sanhedrin 97a). This seems to cont-
radict the many Scriptural and Rabbinic sources which emphasize
that a Jew should never give up hope or yearning for the Messiah.

Rabbi Yaakov Kamenetzky explained the above statement as
follows: Jews are misguided when they place their hopes for
salvation in gentile powers that dominate the world or in their own
political and financial influence. Kings and their governments are
nothing but pawns in the hand of the King of kings and Jewish
influence does not guarantee gentile favors. The Messiah will come
when we place our full faith in God and realize that it is He and only
He Who can rescue us from our bitter plight and bring about our
Redemption.

Causes of Exile

The Power of Our Deeds

◌§ In discussing the sins that brought about the Destruction, it is fitting
to quote the following from Nefesh HaChaim by R' Chaim
Volozhiner:

> Let not any Jew say, "What am I and what power do my
> lowly deeds have to accomplish anything in this world?"
> Rather, he should know... that not a single detail of his
> deeds, words and thoughts at any moment are ever for
> waste, Heaven forfend. How great are his deeds, how
> exalted are they! — for each one of them accomplishes in its
> own way in the loftiest heights, in the Upper Worlds...
>
> In truth, a man of wisdom...will be gripped by awe and
> dread, when his heart perceives the damage and destruction
> that is caused [in the Upper Worlds] by even a minor sin —
> a damage far greater than the destruction wreaked by
> Nebuchadnezzar and Titus. The wicked deeds of Nebuchad-
> nezzar and Titus did not effect any blemish or ruination in
> the Upper Worlds, for they [Nebuchadnezzar and Titus] had
> no lot or root in those worlds which would enable their
> deeds to reach anywhere. Rather, it is our sins which
> weakened and diminished, as it were, the might of Heaven;

they defiled the Temple of God, that is, the Heavenly Temple. It was through this that Nebuchadnezzar and Titus [respectively] acquired the strength to destroy the Temple below which corresponds to the Temple above. It is as the Sages have stated, "[Jersualem said to the daughter of Babylon:] Ground meal have you ground [a burnt city did you set ablaze]!" *(Eichah Rabbah 1:43).*

Thus did our sins destroy the Sanctuary in the Holy Spheres above, while they [Nebuchadnezzar and Titus] destroyed only the Sanctuary below.[1]

(Nefesh HaChaim 1:4)

The Palace Is Proof

Why was the First Temple destroyed? Because during its period there were three sins: idolatry, immorality and bloodshed ... But [regarding the period of] the Second Temple, we know that they studied Torah, performed the mitzvos and did kind deeds; why was it destroyed? Because there was senseless hatred among them. This teaches us that senseless hatred is equivalent to the three sins of idolatry, immorality and bloodshed.

Said Rabbi Yochanan: Better the claws of the earlier generations than the bowels of the later generations. [And if you contend that this is not so, then] the palace [i.e. the Temple] is proof, for it was returned to the former but has not yet been returned to the latter (Yoma 9b).

◆§ The Torah identifies kosher animals as ruminants (i.e. cud-chewing animals) whose hooves are cloven. Nearly all non-kosher animals lack both of these signs. The Torah lists but four animals which have one sign and not the other: the camel, rabbit, hare and pig. The first three chew their cud, while the pig is cloven hooved. The Sages *(Vayikra Rabbah 13)* state that these four animals are symbolic of the four kingdoms which subjugated Israel since the time of the First Destruction: Babylon, Greece, Persia and Rome. Of these kingdoms,

---

1. In this vein, *Nefesh HaChaim* offers a novel interpretation of דַּע מַה לְמַעְלָה מִמְּךָ, whose plain meaning is, *Know that which is above you: [A watchful Eye. . .] (Avos 2:1).* Nefesh HaChaim interprets: דַּע מַה לְמַעְלָה — *Know that that which occurs above,* מִמְּךָ — *is because of you;* i.e. the result of your deeds.

the first three were characterized by negative desires which were easily identified as they and their subjects pursued wealth, lust and other forms of earthly gratification. In this, these kingdoms are likened to those animals whose unkosher status is the external sign of uncloven hooves. The Roman Empire, however, was different. Outwardly, it appeared civilized, concerned with human welfare and pursuit of justice. Inwardly, however, the Romans were concerned with nothing but self-worship and glory. Rome, therefore, is likened to the pig which thrusts its feet in the air displaying its cloven hooves, while its inner inability to ruminate identifies it as non-kosher.

During the First Temple era, the Jews were guilty of serious external offenses. They were overtaken by lust, so they turned to idolatry to justify their behavior and murder as a means of attaining their corrupt goals. They were punished measure for measure by being subjugated under the rule of kingdoms which sought these very same pursuits. During the Second Temple, however, the Jewish people served God faithfully — externally. Inwardly, however, their hearts were tainted with selfishness. They lost faith in God, believed success and failure to be in their own hands and consequently, saw their fellow man as a threat to their own pursuits. The result was *sinas chinam*, senseless hatred. Therefore, they were conquered by Rome, a nation which feigns civility but inwardly, is rotten with corruption.

Said R' Yochanan: Better the claws of the earlier generations than the bowels of the later generations. "Claws" (i.e. uncloven hooves) alludes to the impure external nature of the earlier generations, while "bowels" (i.e. non-ruminant) alludes to the corrupt inner nature of the later generations. It is far easier to harness one's desires when one's inner nature is basically sound than to eradicate deep-rooted feelings of self-aggrandizement, self-interest and jealousy.

Our task in this long and bitter exile is to overcome the test of self-worship while living among nations where such is the norm. When the Jewish people will finally overcome this test, and strive to faithfully serve its Creator like one man with one heart, the purpose of this exile will have been accomplished and the Messiah will arrive (based on the teachings of the *Vilna Gaon* as elucidated in *The Juggler and the King* by Rabbi Aharon Feldman).

The Gift of Torah

Who is the wise man who will understand this, to whom the mouth of HASHEM speaks — let him relate it: "For what reason did the Land perish?. . .Because they forsook My Torah that I put before them. . ."(Jeremiah 9:11-12).

The Holy One, Blessed is He, was yielding regarding the three cardinal sins [i.e. idolatry, immorality and murder] but He was unyielding regarding the rejection of Torah (Yerushalmi Chagigah 1:7).

ֵ§ In citing the above verse, the Talmud (*Nedarim* 81a) states that the generation at the time of the First Destruction was guilty of "not reciting the [required] blessing on the Torah prior to learning." Rabbi Aharon Kotler (*Mishnas R' Aharon* I, p. 26)[1] explains: "They believed in Torah and *mitzvos* and fulfilled their religious obligations, including involvement and toil in Torah study, but they failed to appreciate the inestimable value of Torah, that without it there is no purpose whatsoever to creation and that the whole eternal purpose of life can be fulfilled only through Torah. Therefore, they failed to recognize the magnitude of the obligation to offer praise [to God] for the Torah [by reciting the blessing on the Torah]. Because of this, they lacked the benefit of the full spiritual light that radiates from Torah.

". . .Though the First Temple was destroyed because of the three cardinal sins which were found among a portion of the people, nevertheless, had their appreciation for Torah been adequate, God would have been yielding — because they would have been in a position to repent and better their ways. However, once they lacked a proper appreciation of Torah, it was impossible to ignore their sins."

Our Task

With regard to the current exile, the Chofetz Chaim writes:

Well known is the statement of our Sages that the generation at the time of the Second Destruction performed *mitzvos* and studied Torah sufficiently, but caused the Temple to be

---

1. Based on *Rabbeinu Yonah* as cited by *Ran* to *Nedarim* 81a. *Rabbeinu Yonah's* comment is further elaborated upon in the Overview.

destroyed through *sinas chinam* (senseless hatred) and *lashon hara* (forbidden speech). The early commentators have written that if these sins had the power to cause a standing edifice to be destroyed, then certainly their continued presence [among the Jewish people] will prevent a new Temple from being built. This fact is alluded to in our Sages' statement that any generation in which the Temple is not rebuilt is considered as if it had destroyed it *(Yerushalmi Yoma* 1:1). We, therefore, have no choice but to strengthen our efforts to correct this sin...for how long are we to remain in exile?

...To our misfortune, even those who have an understanding of Torah law do not accord these sins the severity of other sins. Proof of this is the fact that if a person discovers that he somehow mistakenly ate non-kosher food, his heart is pained and the matter reaches to the depths of his soul, literally. He might even fast over this, and all his life he will never forget the time that he ate non-kosher food. Such is not the case with this sin [of *lashon hara*]. Even if his words will cause hurt to another Jew, or if he will embarrass someone, or speak words of *lashon hara* and *rechilus* [which causes animosity between Jews]...his heart will remain unmoved...After a few days, he will forget the matter entirely, as if he had never experienced such sins at all. It is clear that the *yetzer hara* (evil inclination) successfully prevents even inspired individuals from paying heed to these matters.

It is therefore imperative that every serious-minded Jew strengthen himself to be zealous in these matters, so that the word of God not be treated as something unimportant.

...It is written that a single congregation which is meticulous in maintaining peace amongst itself can merit bringing the Messiah. Thus, the coming of the Messiah is in our hands. It is well known that true peace is impossible without zealousness in avoiding *sinas chinam* and *lashon hara*. Every person who will strive to correct these sins will have a share in the building of the Third Temple, for without such people, the Temple would remain destroyed forever, Heaven forfend.

(Shemiras HaLashon 2:7)

A Time to Forgive

~§ A well-known principle regarding Divine judgment is that God exacts retribution *midah k'neged midah*, measure for measure; the punishment fits the crime. This principle applies not only to the judgment of an individual act, but also to the general attitude with which one's behavior is viewed. If a person judges others harshly, is critical and speaks badly of them, then Heaven will be quick to scrutinize that person's deeds and find any existing faults. Conversely, one who refrains from speaking badly of others and instead judges them favorably will be judged accordingly Above.

Still greater is the person who has been clearly wronged, yet chooses to be forgiving, even without being asked for forgiveness.

> Rava said: For anyone who refrains from exacting his measure [of retribution — מַעֲבִיר עַל מִדּוֹתָיו], the Heavenly Court removes from him all his sins, as it is written, "[God] forgives transgression and passes over sin" (Michah 7:18) — Whose transgression does He forgive? One who passes over sins committed against himself (Yoma 23a).

The Mirrer Yeshivah in Jerusalem is situated not far from the pre-1967 border between Israel and Jordan. During the Six Day War, the yeshivah's basement dining room served as a bomb shelter for the neighborhood. Hundreds huddled together in that room as shells whistled above, striking dangerously close. Once, there was a direct hit. The ensuing explosion shook the building. Many thought the end was near and began to recite שְׁמַע יִשְׂרָאֵל, *Hear O Israel. . .*, as is done when death seems imminent.

Among the group was a woman who lived next door to the yeshivah. She was an *agunah,* a woman whose husband had abandoned her twenty years earlier. Her life was one of endless misery and torment. Now, as everyone feared the worst, her voice could be heard above the others. "Master of the Universe! My husband left me abandoned for twenty years. I have suffered so much — but I forgive him! Please, God, forgive the Jewish people for all we have done wrong." Rabbi Chaim Shmulevitz, legendary Mirrer *Rosh Yeshivah*, was in the shelter at that time. He later expressed the conviction that it was this woman's prayer that had saved them all.

R' Moshe Chaim Luzzato wrote, "God loves the Jewish people, and the more a person loves his fellow Jew, the greater is the love

that God showers upon him" *(Mesilas Yesharim* ch. 19). The current exile is the result of *sinas chinam. Ahavas Yisrael,* love of one's fellow Jew — even when such love seems unwarranted — can bring this exile to an end.

Eternal Covenant

Chosen Forever

◆§ In two sections of the Torah, God warns His people of the punishments that will befall them if they fail to live up to their obligations as the Chosen People. Known as the *Tochachah* [Admonition], these punishments are meant not as revenge, but to awaken the people to repent.

Ramban is of the opinion that the *Tochachah* of *Leviticus* 26 foretells the sins of the First Temple era and its aftermath, while that of *Deuteronomy* 28 speaks of the Second Temple era. At the conclusion of the first *Tochachah*, God comforts the Jewish nation, lest they think that the ravages of exile indicate their having lost their status as God's Chosen People:

וְאַף גַּם זֹאת בִּהְיוֹתָם בְּאֶרֶץ אֹיְבֵיהֶם לֹא מְאַסְתִּים וְלֹא גְעַלְתִּים לְכַלֹּתָם לְהָפֵר בְּרִיתִי אִתָּם כִּי אֲנִי ה' אֱלֹהֵיהֶם.

But despite all this, while they will be in the land of their enemies, I will not have been revolted by them nor will I have rejected them to obliterate them, to annul My covenant with them — for I am HASHEM, their God (Leviticus 26:44).

Ramban (Deuteronomy 32:26) explains the nature of this covenant and why it will never be annulled:

God created man so that man perceive his Creator's existence and [serve Him and] praise His Divine Name. Man was given the option to do good or evil. Mankind willfully sinned and denied His existence. Only this nation [Israel] remained loyal to Him and through them, He demonstrated His omnipotence through signs and wonders and thus became recognized by the nations of the world [once more]. If it were conceivable that Israel ever be lost, the truth of God's omnipotence would be lost to mankind forever. . . .and

the purpose of creation would come to naught. Therefore, that same will of God with which He willed creation must guarantee the eternal existence of this people, for they are the ones close to Him and who perceive Him more than any other nation.

God's design and Israel's fate are intertwined. The Jewish people are the bearers of Divine Glory on earth and therefore, there is within them a core of holiness which can never be destroyed.

Miracle of Survival

   In the Torah, Moses proclaimed that God is הָאֵל הַגָּדֹל הַגִּבֹּר וְהַנּוֹרָא, *the great, mighty and awesome God (Deuteronomy* 10:17). The Talmud *(Yoma* 69b) relates that centuries later, after the First Temple's destruction, Jeremiah cried out, "The gentiles desecrate His Sanctuary without restraint — where is His awesomeness?" Thereafter, Jeremiah did not mention הַנּוֹרָא, *the awesome One,* in his prayers. When Daniel witnessed the Jews' oppression at the hands of the Babylonians, he exclaimed, "Where is His might?" He ceased to mention הַגִּבֹּר, *the mighty One,* in his prayers. Later, the אַנְשֵׁי כְּנֶסֶת הַגְּדוֹלָה, *Men of the Great Assembly,* took a different view of things. God displays His might when He controls His fury against the gentile oppressors and waits for what He determines as the correct moment to punish those who persecuted His flock. God displays His awesomeness when Israel is in exile, by ensuring their survival even while they are surrounded by a myriad of hostile enemies.

Tosafos Yeshanim (ibid. citing *Midrash Tanchuma*) relates that the Roman emperor Hadrian once told the Mishnaic sage Rabbi Yehoshua, "Great is the lamb [Israel] that remains standing while surrounded by seventy wolves [the gentile nations]." Rabbi Yehoshua responded, "Great is the Shepherd Who rescues her."

Rabbi Yitzchak Breuer *(Der Neue Kusari)* writes that the miracle of Israel's survival in exile is foretold in a number of verses of the *Tochachah* in Leviticus. Though they would be exiled, the Land from which they had been driven would still be called *their* Land — *And you I will scatter among the nations, I will unsheathe the sword after you;* **your** *Land will be desolate and* **your** *cities will be a ruin (Leviticus* 26:33). Until their return, the Land would reject any attempt by its conquerors to settle and cultivate it — *I will make the Land desolate; and your foes who dwell upon it will be desolate* (ibid. v. 32). The

Jews would remain distinct even among the nations and they would never lose their status as the Chosen People — *I, too, will behave toward you with casualness and I will bring them to the land of their enemies* — *perhaps then their unfeeling heart will be humbled and they will gain appeasement for their sin* (ibid. v. 41).

But despite all this, while they will be in the land of their enemies, I will not have been revolted by them nor will I have rejected them to obliterate them, to annul My covenant with them — for I am HASHEM, their God. (ibid. v. 44).

Survival of Torah

◆§ In *Lamentations* we read: בְּמַחֲשַׁכִּים הוֹשִׁיבַנִי כְּמֵתֵי עוֹלָם, *He has placed me in darkness like the eternally dead* (3:6). The Talmud *(Sanhedrin 24a)* comments that these words allude to the study of the Oral Law in Babylon.[1]

The Chassidic master Rabbi Simchah Bunim of P'shischa interpreted הוֹשִׁיבַנִי (lit. *He placed me*) homiletically as related to מְשִׁיבַת נֶפֶשׁ, *[The Torah of HASHEM is perfect,] it restores the soul (Psalms 19:8)*. As Jeremiah laments the Destruction, he tells us that in the darkness and bitterness of exile, God has granted the Jew one means by which to restore his soul: *Talmud Bavli*, the primary body of Oral Law. The study of Talmud has inspired, stimulated, revived and mended the souls of our brethren in all four corners of the earth, throughout these past two thousand years. In the words of Rabbi Chaim Ozer Grodzensky, leader of Lithuanian Jewry in the pre-Holocaust years:

> From the day that Israel was exiled from its Land, the everlasting and unbroken chain of Talmudic transmission and commentary was never broken. In the days of religious persecution, decrees, oppression and wanderings, they

---

1. *Ramban* (cited by *Ritva* to *Yoma* 57a and quoted by *Ein Yaakov* to *Chagigah* 10a) explains that this refers to periods when the Jewish community of Babylon suffered severe persecution. The academies of learning were closed, while the Torah leaders and their scholars were scattered as they sought a safe haven from their pursuers. Their incessant wanderings and suffering prevented them from studying a topic thoroughly as they normally would, and they were left with many a matter unresolved. Thus, they remained "in the dark" on many topics.

The phrase כְּמֵתֵי עוֹלָם, *like the eternally dead,* could thus be explained simply: In the morning prayers, we offer praise of God Who *gave us the Torah of truth and implanted eternal life within us*. To study Torah while robbed of inner peace, incapable of proper understanding, is, by comparison, to be *like the eternally dead.*

toiled with self-sacrifice to prepare a dwelling place for Torah...To those that merited it, the study of Torah was always a potion of life...

Rabbi Saadiah *Gaon* said, "Our nation is a nation only through Torah." Israel's survival since the First Destruction as a nation of Torah is one of the great miracles of history.

Until the end of the First Temple era, Babylon was never a factor in Jewish history. King Chizkiyahu referred to Babylon as a "far-off nation" (*II Kings* 20:14) because Israel had had no contact with Babylon until that time. In the fourth year of King Yehoyakim's reign, Nebuchadnezzar assumed the throne of Babylon. The world underwent dramatic change: Assyria was no longer a power, Egypt was defeated and Babylon became a mighty power. Nebuchadnezzar conquered Israel and destroyed its Temple — and Babylon ceased to be a world power shortly thereafter.

One factor above all shaped world history at that time: the destiny of the Jewish people. The inevitable Destruction and exile that Israel's sins demanded made it necessary that a nation appear on the stage of history who could conquer the Land, exile its inhabitants and yet, make it possible for the Jews to remain a nation of Torah while in exile. Assyria and Egypt did not meet this last requirement, but Babylon did. Thus, Babylon's rise to glory. Once it had served this purpose, it disappeared from history's center stage (*Netziv* in *She'eiris Yisrael*).

Eleven years before the First Destruction, Nebuchadnezzar took Israel's King Yehoyachin from his seat of royalty in Jerusalem and imprisoned him in Babylon. At that time, ten thousand of Israel's best people were taken away.

> And [Nebuchadnezzar] carried away into exile all Jerusalem, and all the leaders, and all the mighty warriors, ten thousand exiles, and all the craftsmen and locksmiths (הֶחָרָשׁ וְהַמַּסְגֵּר). . . And the king of Babylon took them into exile to Babylon (*II Kings* 24:14,16).

The *charash* and *masgeir*, craftsmen and locksmiths, were a group comprised of a thousand of Israel's most distinguished Torah scholars, including several prophets.[1] Nebuchadnezzar's plan was

---

1. The letters חרש (*charash*) can also mean *silence* (as in חֵרֵשׁ). "Craftsmen" hints that as soon as these men opened a learned discussion, all the others became as though speechless (*Sanhedrin* 38a). The root of מֵסְגֵּר, *masgeir*, is סגר, *closed*. Once they had closed a halachic discussion, it was never reopened (for none were able were to cast doubt on their ruling (ibid.).

simple. By removing Jersualem's leading scholars and *all the leaders and all the mighty warriors* (i.e. its civil and military leadership), he would ensure that it would never again flout his authority.

Unwittingly, Nebuchadnezzar brought about the failure of his own plans. The *charash* and *masgeir* and those that accompanied them built the foundations of a flourishing Torah community in exile and of the later generation that would return home and build the Second Temple.

There is more to the miracle.

> R' Chisda said in the name of Mar Ukba — others state that Mar Ukba quoted it from a lecture of Mari bar Mar — What is meant by the verse, "And so HASHEM has hastened the evil and brought it upon us; for HASHEM our God is righteous" (Daniel 9:14)? Can one call it "righteousness" [i.e. charity] that He hastened to bring the evil upon us?! Yes! The Holy One, Blessed is He, did a righteous [i.e. charitable] thing for Israel, in that He brought the exile of Tzidkiyahu [at the time of the Destruction] while the exiles of Yechanyah [Yeho-yachin, who had arrived eleven years earlier] were still alive (Sanhedrin 38).

In hastening the final exile of that period, God ensured the proper transmission of Torah from the *charash* and *masgeir* to the new generation of scholars who were then arriving. The survival of Torah, in all its richness, depth and clarity had been accomplished.

❧ ❧ ❧

It was clearly the workings of Providence that ensured the proper transmission of Torah at the time of the Second Destruction. Rabbi Yochanan ben Zakkai, the leading sage at that time, was spirited out of Jerusalem at the risk of his life in order to meet with Vespasian, general of the Roman army. Deeply impressed by Rabban Yochanan's words, the general allowed him to request anything he wished. Rabban Yochanan's first request was *Give me Yavneh and its Sages!* — so that the study of Torah be properly maintained.[1]

The Pattern of Galus

◦§ In a lengthy commentary to *Leviticus* 26:44, *Meshech Chachmah* explains that there is a distinct pattern to the long and bitter exile and

---

1. See p. 135.

that its nature is, in fact, a fulfillment of *But despite all this . . . I will not . . . obliterate them . . . for I am* HASHEM, *their God.*

> . . . Jews arrive in a new land. They and their children gradually prosper and become important citizens of their adopted country. They organize into communities to build and maintain their own institutions. With the passage of time, they become more deeply involved in the culture of their surroundings. Acclimation leads to assimilation, as the Jew abandons his Divine mission and his hope for spiritual salvation in favor of the seductive glitter of the non-Jewish world. After a time, the host country turns against its Jewish citizenry,[1] and several hundred years after its founding, the Jewish community is completely destroyed by the unleashed wrath of its erstwhile hosts. The survivors, impoverished and broken in spirit, return to God once again and with His help, escape into a more hospitable country to rebuild in an atmosphere of relative peace — until they are again subjected to harsh treatment.

Meshech Chachmah explains that whenever Jews fled from persecution to settle in a new land, they initially experienced a reawakening of spirit and felt impelled to strive for the Torah glory of old. Indeed, great achievements in Torah were always attained. Eventually, however, a later generation always came along which sought to make its mark in other areas and this attitude led to a denial of the worth of its heritage. This generation abandoned its traditions in favor of the culture of its adopted country.

> He thinks of Berlin as his Jerusalem and learns to behave in a manner typical of the lower elements of his host society. A storm of destruction follows which uproots him and deposits him in a distant land. . .This brings him to the realization that his adopted language and culture were, in fact, foreign to him. . .His true "culture" is Torah, his language is the Holy Tongue and his sources of comfort are the words of the prophets.

In our verse, God tells His people:

---

1. The hatred which the Egyptian people demonstrated towards the Jews after the death of Joseph (*Exodus* ch.1) was a portent of future exiles. Of that phenomenon, King David said, *He [God] turned their [the Egyptians'] hearts to hate His nation* (*Psalms* 105:25).

This revulsion and rejection is not final, to destroy them or annul My covenant, Heaven forfend. Rather, it is through this that My Name will be exalted and the nation of the seed of Abraham will survive. . .

A Miniature Sanctuary

לָכֵן אֱמֹר כֹּה אָמַר ה' אֱלֹהִים: כִּי הִרְחַקְתִּים בַּגּוֹיִם וְכִי הֲפִיצוֹתִים בָּאֲרָצוֹת, וָאֱהִי לָהֶם לְמִקְדָּשׁ מְעַט בָּאֲרָצוֹת אֲשֶׁר בָּאוּ שָׁם.

Therefore say: Thus says my Lord HASHEM / ELOHIM: "Though I have removed them far off among the nations, and though I have scattered them among the countries, yet I have been for them a small Sanctuary in the countries where they came" (Ezekiel 11:16).

"I have been for them a small Sanctuary" — R' Yitzchak said: These are the synagogues and study halls in Babylon (Megillah 29a).

◆§ Before citing the above verse, the Talmud (ibid.) teaches that whenever the Jewish people are exiled, the *Shechinah*, Divine Presence, accompanies them. "Come and see how beloved are the people of Israel before the Holy One, Blessed is He. When they were exiled to Egypt, the *Shechinah* was with them. . .when they were exiled to Babylon, the *Shechinah* was with them. . .and when they will be redeemed in the future, the *Shechinah* will return with them, as it is written, *And HASHEM will return with your returning exiles* (Deuteronomy 30:3).

The Talmudic Sages asked, "In Babylon where can the *Shechinah* be found?" Abaye answered, "In the synagogue of Hutzal and in the synagogue of שַׁף וְיָתִיב ('That Moved and Settled') of Nehardea" (Megillah 29a).

Of the latter, Rabbi Sherira *Gaon* writes in his *Iggeres* (Letter):

> You should know that at the beginning, when the Jewish people were exiled in the dispersion of Yehoyachin (i.e. some eleven years before the First Destruction), and with them went the "craftsmen" and the "locksmiths" including several prophets (see p. 72), they were first brought to Nehardea. There, King Yehoyachin and his followers built a synagogue,

putting into its foundation stones and earth that they had brought with them from the Temple in fulfillment of the verse: "For Your servants hold her stones dear and cherish her very dust" (Psalms 102:15). And they called it, "The synagogue that moved and settled" ["moved" from its place in Jerusalem and "settled" in Nehardea]. This means that the [holiness of the] Temple settled here [in Babylonia] and the Shechinah rested among them.

Alshich comments that the Divine Presence must accompany the Children of Israel into exile, for if not, they would become assimilated among the nations to the point that they would be lost forever as a distinct and holy people ל"ר. It follows, then, that for the individual Jew to survive in exile as a Jew faithful to God and His Torah, he must seek to find the *Shechinah* in his midst.

And where can the *Shechinah* be found?

In the synagogue; in the study hall; in the Jewish home; in the soul of every Jew.

The Synagogue

◆§ When Jews come together in a synagogue for communal prayer, they are, in a sense, transported to another world. In the words of *Maharal*:

> ... the *Shechinah* is with Israel in exile ... and when they gather together ... as for example, during communal prayer, that is considered a "gathering in" of the dispersion which is Israel's lot among the nations, and it can be viewed as a redemption from among the nations. Know then, that Israel among the nations, even when a thousand of them are in one place, are considered "scattered." But while they pray they are as one community, gathered in and drawn to God. And through this they leave [their exile] among the nations and rise up from among them *(Ohr Chadash 4:16).*

The Torah states, *Observe My Sabbaths and revere My Sanctuary — I am HASHEM (Leviticus 26:2).* The status of the synagogue and study hall as "miniature Sanctuaries" demands proper reverence. "Regarding synagogues, one may not conduct himself with levity in them, one may not eat in them, nor may one drink in them, nor may one adorn himself in them, nor may one stroll around in them, nor may

one enter them in the summer to escape the heat or in the rainy season to escape the rain..." (*Megillah* 28a). Included under "levity" is mundane conversation, such as matters pertaining to business. The Chofetz Chaim (*Mishnah Berurah* 151:1 citing *Semak*) writes that the sin of speaking mundane talk in the synagogue "transforms it into a place of idol worship." He further notes that the *Zohar* speaks of this sin in most severe terms. To gossip or engage in other forms of forbidden speech is a particularly grave sin when done in the synagogue or study hall. . .

> for in doing so, one shows lack of regard for the *Shechinah*; [furthermore,] there is no comparison between one who sins in private and one who does so in the palace of the King, in the King's presence. This evil is compounded when one causes others to join in his sin. . .so that from a few individuals come many groups which engage in strife with one another — until the synagogue becomes like one huge torch. . .And who is the cause of this, if not the one with whom it all started? Surely, that individual will be "rewarded" for all that he has caused.
>
> Therefore, one who is truly God fearing should be forever vigilant that he not engage in any mundane talk neither in the synagogue nor in the study hall. Rather, these places will be used by him strictly for Torah study and prayer (*Mishnah Berurah* 151:2).

[It should be noted that conversation while prayers are in progress is a particularly severe offense. *Shulchan Aruch* (*Orach Chaim* 124:7) states, "It is forbidden to engage in conversation while the *chazzan* repeats the *Shemoneh Esrei*. One who speaks is a sinner; his sin is too great to bear and one should rebuke him." *Mishnah Berurah* (§27) cites the testimony of *Kol Bo*: "Woe to those who converse during prayers, for we have seen many synagogues destroyed on account of this sin."]

The Study Hall

> *From the day that the Temple was destroyed, the Holy One, Blessed is He, has nothing in this world, save for the four amos (cubits) of Halachah (Berachos 8a).*

◈§ When the Temple stood, the Great Sanhedrin which met in the Temple Courtyard's Chamber of Hewn Stone was the supreme authority for deciding and interpreting Jewish law. Surely the *Shechinah*, Divine Presence, was there with them.[1] Since the Destruction, the place where any Torah scholar sits and delves into the profundities of Talmudic law is like the Chamber of Hewn Stone in earlier times and the *Shechinah* is there with him (*Maharsha* ibid.).

Nefesh HaChaim (4:34) writes:

> Since the Destruction of our Holy Temple when the children were banished from the table of their Father, the *Shechinah* moves about, as it were, for it can find no rest. *And there is nothing left but this Torah*.[2] When the holy nation of Israel discusses and delves into Torah properly, they become a miniature Sanctuary for the *Shechinah* . . . It dwells among them and spreads its wings over them, as it were. It [the *Shechinah*] is thus granted somewhat of a respite, as the Sages have taught, "From the day that the Temple was destroyed, the Holy One, Blessed is He, has nothing in this world, save for the four *amos* of *Halachah*." They have further taught (*Avos* 3:7) that even when one studies Torah alone, the *Shechinah* is with him, as it is written, *In every place where I cause My Name to be mentioned, I will come to you and bless you* (Exodus 20:21).[3]

The Jewish Home

◈§ The Sages relate that the tent of the matriarch Sarah had three extraordinary qualities: a cloud hung by the entrance of her tent;

---

1. Scripture states, *God stands in the Divine assembly, in the midst of judges shall He judge* (Psalms 82:1).

2. A passage from the Yom Kippur *Ne'ilah* service reads:
   The holy city and the suburbs have become a disgrace and been looted, all her treasures have been buried and hidden — and there is nothing left but this Torah. Restore the captivity of Jacob's tents and save us for Your Name's sake.

3. It should be noted that the sanctity of a *beis midrash*, study hall, is greater than that of a *beis haknesses*, synagogue. *Shulchan Aruch* (*Orach Chaim* 90:18) therefore rules that if one has a choice between praying in a *beis midrash* that is used by the public for Torah study or a *beis haknesses*, he should choose the former. Citing the Talmudic teaching that "God loves the select entranceways of Talmudic study more than synagogues and ordinary study halls" (*Berachos* 8a), *Mishnah Berurah* (§54) adds that this rule applies even when the *minyan* (quorum) in the synagogue is of greater size.

there was a blessing in her dough, meaning that her guests left her table with lingering feelings of satisfaction which lasted for a long time; and the lamp which she lit each Sabbath eve remained burning all week long (Bereishis Rabbah 60:16). These qualities paralleled three constant miracles of the Tabernacle (Mishkan) and Temple: the שְׁכִינָה, Divine Presence, was constantly manifest; the לֶחֶם הַפָּנִים, Loaves of Show-Bread, retained their initial warmth and freshness throughout the week that they lay on the Table of God; and the נֵר מַעֲרָבִי, Western Lamp, was the first to be lit each evening, yet was the only one to burn bright until the next evening's lighting.

The Heavenly cloud that hovered over Sarah's tent bore witness to what went on within her tent. Because she lived her life in a manner worthy of God's Presence, He therefore set His cloud atop her dwelling (Shem MiShmuel).

The Sages refer to the Jewish home as a *mikdash me'at*, a miniature sanctuary. According to *Ramban* (introduction to the Book of Exodus) (see p. 41), the *Mishkan* was meant to be a replica of Sarah's tent — the prototype Jewish home! A Jewish home can be imbued with God's holiness — if its inhabitants will allow it to enter.

The Jewish Soul

⤳ In commanding the Jews in the Wilderness to construct the Tabernacle, God declared:

וְעָשׂוּ לִי מִקְדָּשׁ וְשָׁכַנְתִּי בְּתוֹכָם.

Make for Me a Sanctuary so that I may dwell among them (Exodus 25:8).

Noting the Torah's use of בְּתוֹכָם, [so that I may dwell] among them, as opposed to בְּתוֹכוֹ, [so that I may dwell] in it (i.e. the Tabernacle), the Sages comment: "בְּתוֹכָם, among them — [so that I may dwell] within each and every one of them"(Seder Olam Rabbah 6).

Nefesh HaChaim (footnote to 1:4) elaborates upon this teaching, stating that "...Man's heart should be gripped by awe when pondering the "sanctuary" that his being encompasses." In defining the nature of this sanctuary, the author first expounds upon the essence of the Tabernacle and Temple:

> The Tabernacle and Temple encompassed within them all the spiritual forces and worlds and all the orders of sanctity

in their entirety. All its [the Temple's] sections, hidden recesses, upper and lower chambers and all its holy vessels were a replica of that which is in the Upper Worlds, an image of the Holy Spheres and the order of the components of the Divine Chariot. . .Thus it is stated in *Midrash (Tanchuma, Parashas Pekudei)* that the construction of the Tabernacle corresponded to the creation of the universe. There, the *Midrash* lists in order the various stages of Creation and how their concepts were found in the Tabernacle as well.

Thus did our Sages teach: "Bezalel [the Tabernacle's primary builder] knew how to arrange the holy letters through which heaven and earth were created."

How does all this relate to the individual Jew?

Man . . . is an image of the Tabernacle and Temple and all their vessels. All this is the [hidden] intent within the order of connection between man's various limbs, sinews and all his innate strengths. In this vein does the *Zohar* analyze the construction of the Tabernacle and its vessels, showing how they are alluded to in man, each item in its proper order.

It is thus certain that the primary purpose of the Temple, and of God manifesting His presence there, is man. If man will sanctify himself appropriately through the observance of all the *mitzvos,* each of which is connected to a specific Heavenly root among the "limbs" that form the "body" of the totality of spheres, as it were, then he is a Temple — literally — and the *Shechinah* rests within him; as it is written, "The Sanctuary of Hashem are they" *(Jeremiah 7:4).*

. . . In this vein, we can interpret the words וְעָשׂוּ לִי מִקְדָּשׁ וְשָׁכַנְתִּי בְּתוֹכָם. . .וְכֵן תַּעֲשׂוּ, *Make for Me a Sanctuary so that I may dwell among them. . .and so you shall do,* to which our Sages comment (*Sanhedrin* 16b): וְכֵן תַּעֲשׂוּ – לְדוֹרוֹת, *And so shall you do — for all generations.* We can explain this as follows: [God is saying,] "Do not think that My ultimate intention is the construction of the Temple edifice; rather . . . My desiring the Tabernacle and its vessels is merely so that you should infer from it how to make yourselves; namely, that through your deeds you should be as desirable as the Tabernacle and its vessels — all of you holy, fitting and prepared to be receptacles for My Presence in a literal sense."

Nefesh HaChaim concludes:

> ..And so did the Holy One, Blessed is His Name, tell Solomon after the completion of the [First] Temple: *"This House that you are building — If you will follow My statutes and carry out My laws, and safeguard all My commandments. . .then I shall dwell among the Children of Israel, and I will not forsake My nation Israel"* (I Kings 6:12-13). Therefore, when they ruined the inner Sanctuary that resided within their beings, then the external Sanctuary (i.e. the Temple) was of no use and its foundations were razed.

The Western Wall (Kosel Ma'aravi)

God's Oath

הִנֵּה זֶה עוֹמֵד אַחַר כָּתְלֵנוּ. . .

Behold! He stands behind our wall (Song of Songs 2:9).

"He [God's Presence] stands behind our wall" — behind the Western Wall of the Temple. Why? Because God has sworn that it will never be destroyed (Shir HaShirim Rabbah 2:9).

The Shechinah [Divine Presence] has never departed from the Temple's Western Wall (Zohar, Shemos 5b).

◄§ While the above Aggadic statements speak of the "Temple's" western wall, the commentators apply them to the Western Wall of the Temple Mount, the *Kosel Ma'aravi* or *Kosel (Kotel)*. Since the recapture of the Old City of Jerusalem during the Six Day War, hundreds of thousands of Jews the world over have poured out their hearts in prayer at the Western Wall.

One reason given for the Western Wall's uniqueness is its close proximity to the site of the Holy of Holies *(Kodesh HaKadoshim)*, the chamber which housed the Holy Ark and where the *Shechinah* was most strongly manifest.

There is a tradition that the foundation of this wall was laid by King David, who made many of the preparations for the First Temple which was built by his son King Solomon. The Talmud *(Sotah 9a)*

states that the works of Moses and David are invulnerable to the onslaughts of our enemies.[1]

The *Midrash* states: When Vespasian besieged Jerusalem at the time of the Second Destruction, he assigned four different generals to raze the four sections of the city. The western sector fell to the lot of a general named Pangar. While the other three generals destroyed their sectors, Pangar allowed the Western Wall to stand intact. Vespasian summoned him and demanded an explanation, to which Pangar responded, 'I swear that my intention is only to glorify your reputation, O royal master! Had I obliterated every last vestige of this metropolis of Jerusalem, later generations would have no idea of the scope of your victory, for they might think that Jerusalem was no more than a tiny town. But now that I have left over this massive Western Wall as a memorial, it will be known for all time that your majesty conquered a major city of colossal proportions!'''

Pangar lied. The true reason why he did not destroy the Western Wall was because he *could not* destroy it. For God had decreed that the place from which the *Shechinah* has never departed should remain standing forever (*Midrash Eichah* 1:32).

☙ ☙ ☙

The Talmud (*Rosh HaShanah* 31a) describes the ten-stage withdrawal of the *Shechinah* from the Temple at the time of the First Destruction. How is this reconciled with the Midrashic statement that the *Shechinah* has never departed from the Western Wall, or with the statement of *Rambam (Hilchos Beis HaBechirah* 6:16) that the eternal sanctity of the Temple Mount is due to the eternal presence of the *Shechinah* there? Rabbi Yechiel M. Tikuchinsky *(Ir HaKodesh V'HaMikdash)* explains that these passages refer to different manifestations of God's Presence. On one plane, the *Shechinah* has been present on the Temple Mount since the beginning of time. Thus did Jacob exclaim upon awakening from his prophetic dream, *Surely HASHEM is present in this place and I did not know! (Genesis* 28:16), which *Targum Yonasan* interprets as, *Surely the glory of God's Shechinah dwells in this place!* However, the *Shechinah* is manifest there to a greater degree when Israel dwells upon its Land and is worthy of serving God in the Temple. *Now as Solomon finished praying [at the inauguration of the First Temple], the fire came down from heaven and consumed the burnt offer-*

---

1. See *Lamentations* 2:9 with *Rashi*.

ings. . .and the glory of HASHEM filled the Temple (II Chronciles 7:1).

The Talmud *(Yoma* 21b) states that the *Shechinah* was one of five things which were present in the First Temple but not in the Second. This means that God's Presence was perceived more strongly in the First Temple than in the Second Temple.

Even after the Destruction, the *Shechinah* remained present to some degree — and it is present to this day at the Western Wall.

Gate of the Heavens

◄§ Upon awakening from his prophetic dream at the Temple Mount, Jacob called that place *the gate of the heavens,* meaning, the gate through which all prayers ascend *(Genesis* 28:17; see *Rashi)*. At the inauguration of the First Temple, Solomon spoke of the Temple as the center of all prayers on earth *(II Chronicles* ch. 6). Indeed, Jews everywhere are required to face in the direction of the Holy of Holies when they recite the *Shemoneh Esrei* (Amidah), for it is from that place that all prayers ascend Heavenward.

Siddur Minchas Yerushalayim states, "Prayer at this place [the Western Wall] is most efficacious, for the gate of the heavens is there and it stands open so that one's prayers may be heard. Prayers that are offered there flow from the depths of one's heart; anyone whose lot is bitter, whose soul is downcast, goes to the Western Wall where he prays and pours out his woes. There is a tradition that a prayer offered at the Wall is never returned unanswered. The author of *Chayei Adam*, in his work *Shaarei Tzedek,* composed a special prayer to be said at the Western Wall."[1]

Mourning at the Wall

◄§ Upon approaching the Western Wall for the first time in thirty days, one is required to perform an act of mourning over the Temple's destruction.[2]

---

1. A collection of prayers to be recited at the Wall can be found in *Sefer Shaarei Dimah*.

2. One should note that even after the Temple was destroyed, the Mount upon which it stood still retained its special sanctity. Therefore, today when we are all in a state of *tumah*, ritual defilement, it is strictly forbidden for a Jew to enter the Temple Mount *(Radbaz* 691, *Teshuvos Chasam Sofer, Yoreh Deah* 233,234; *Magen Avraham* 561:2; and *Mishnah Berurah* 561:5). The *Kosel* Plaza is on the outside of the Mount.

"When he sees the sight of the Temple, he says, בֵּית קָדְשֵׁינוּ
וְתִפְאַרְתֵּנוּ אֲשֶׁר הִלְלוּךְ בּוֹ אֲבוֹתֵינוּ הָיָה לִשְׂרֵפַת אֵשׁ וְכָל מַחֲמַדֵּנוּ הָיָה לְחָרְבָּה,
*The House of our sanctity and glory in which our forefathers praised
You has been consumed by fire and all that we cherished has become
a ruin. He then rends his garment"* (Shulchan Aruch, Orach Chaim
561:2). The Chofetz Chaim (citing *Bach*) adds:

> One should bow, rend his garment, cry out and mourn over
> the Temple's destruction. He should lament and recite Psalm
> 79 [*A song of Assaf: O God! The nations have. . .defiled the
> Sanctuary of Your holiness. . .*] in its entirety. When rending
> one's garment, one should say:
>
> בָּרוּךְ דַּיַּן אֱמֶת, כִּי כָל מִשְׁפָּטָיו צֶדֶק וֶאֱמֶת. הַצּוּר תָּמִים פָּעֳלוֹ כִּי כָל דְּרָכָיו
> מִשְׁפָּט, אֵל אֱמוּנָה וְאֵין עָוֶל, צַדִּיק וְיָשָׁר הוּא. וְאַתָּה צַדִּיק עַל כָּל הַבָּא
> עָלֵינוּ, כִּי אֱמֶת עָשִׂיתָ וַאֲנַחְנוּ הִרְשָׁעְנוּ.
>
> *Blessed is the true Judge. The Rock! — perfect is His work, for
> all His paths are justice; a God of faith without iniquity, right-
> eous and fair is He [Deuteronomy 32:4]. And You are right-
> eous in all that has come upon us, for You have acted truth-
> fully while we have caused wickedness [Nechemiah 9:33].*
>
> (Mishnah Berurah §6)[1]

Rabbi Avraham HaLevi

◄§ The seventeenth-century commentator Rabbi Zvi Hirsh Kaidanover
writes the following in his *Kav HaYashar* (ch. 93):

> I have received the following authentic tradition: Whoso-
> ever's heart is incessantly pained over the exile of the
> *Shechinah*, as it were, merits the crown of Torah. Know that
> which the *Arizal*[2] wrote regarding our master, Rabbi
> Avraham HaLevi, who lived in Safed and composed the
> *Tikkunei Shabbos*. Each night at midnight, he would walk the

---

1. *Shulchan Aruch* also speaks of a requirement to demonstrate mourning upon seeing
the cities of Judea and the Old City of Jersualem. For more on the subject, see *Mishnah
Berurah* to ch. 561; *Har HaKodesh* by Rabbi Nachum Moshe Shapiro; *Ir HaKodesh
V'HaMikdash* vol. III, by Rabbi Yechiel M. Tikuchinsky; *Igros Moshe, Orach Chaim* III and
IV; and a monograph on the subject by Rabbi Serayah Dovletsky.
2. R' Yitzchak Luria, sixteenth-century kabbalist and fountainhead of modern kabbalistic
thought.

streets of the Jews and in a mournful voice would say, "Our brethren, the House of Israel: You are well aware that the *Shechinah* is in exile, due to our many sins, and our Temple has gone up in flames. Let us arise and cry out to God, Who is a merciful and compassionate King. Perhaps our prayers will be heeded and He will take pity on His nation, the remnants of Israel."

This exceedingly pious Jew would continue to cry out, not allowing the city's inhabitants to rest. All of them would rise together and make their way to the synagogues and study halls where they would recite *Tikkun Chatzos*. [1] Then each man would study Torah according to his own level of scholarship; some would delve into Kabbalah and *Zohar*, some would study Talmud and Mishnah, while others would study Scripture. They would then recite additional prayers until morning, thereby awakening Divine compassion. The *Rav*, the *Arizal*, would extol R' Avraham's piety and would say that he was a *gilgul* (transmigrant) of the prophet Jeremiah.

Kav HaYashar continues that the *Arizal* once revealed to R' Avraham that his (R' Avraham's) time to leave this world had come. However, he would be granted an additional twenty-two years of life if he would journey to Jerusalem and pour his heart out in prayer at the Western Wall — he would merit to perceive the *Shechinah*. R' Avraham spent the next three days in seclusion, fasting and wearing sackcloth. He then journeyed to the Western Wall, where he shed a torrent of tears as he prayed fervently for the Redemption. He then perceived an image clothed in black upon the Wall; immediately, he fell to the ground in awe and cried out as he wept, "Woe is to me that I have perceived You in such a manner! Woe unto my soul!" He continued to cry out and weep until he fainted. It was then that R' Avraham had a dream in which he perceived an image clothed in finery. A voice called to him, "Be comforted, My son Avraham. *There is hope for you ultimately, for the children shall return to their border.* [2] *I will bring back their captives and show mercy to them.*"[3]

---

1. Special prayers recited at midnight over the Destruction. The order of these prayers is based on the writings of the *Arizal*. See *Shulchan Aruch, Orach Chaim* 1:3 with *Mishnah Berurah*. Also, see Overview to ArtScroll's *The Complete Tishah B'av Service*.

2. Cf. *Jeremiah* 31:16.

3. Cf. Ibid. 33:26.

זֵכֶר לְחוּרְבָּן
Remembrance of the Destruction

אִם אֶשְׁכָּחֵךְ יְרוּשָׁלָיִם תִּשְׁכַּח יְמִינִי.
If I forget you, O Jerusalem, let my right hand forget its skill (Psalms 137:5).

Year-Round Mourning

◄§ As the above verse makes obvious, remembering and feeling pain over the Temple's destruction is not a concept limited to the Three Weeks. In discussing man's daily routine, the opening chapter of *Shulchan Aruch* states: "It is proper for every God-fearing person to feel pain and anguish over the destruction of the Temple" (*Orach Chaim* 1:3).

The Talmud (*Bava Basra* 60b) relates that when the Temple was destroyed, many Jews began to deprive themselves of meat and wine as a token of mourning. Rabbi Yehoshua asked them why. They answered, "How can we eat meat which was once placed upon the Temple Altar, or drink wine which was once poured upon the Altar?" Rabbi Yehoshua told them, "In that case, do not eat figs or grapes, because they were brought to the Temple as first fruits. Do not eat bread, because bread was used in the Temple service." Rabbi Yehoshua concluded that while we *are* required to grieve, we should not grieve excessively.[1] While the Sages did enact legislation formulated under the heading of זֵכֶר לְחוּרְבָּן, *Remembrance of the Destruction,* they did not impose restrictions that are overly difficult.[2]

---

1. *Mishnah Berurah* comments that one's anguish over the Destruction must not interfere with the joyous spirit that is so integral to prayer and Torah study.

2. Nevertheless, there were individuals, even in recent times, who accepted personal stringencies which reflected their own heightened sensitivity toward the sufferings of their people. For example, Rebbetzin Chana Perl Kotler, wife of R' Aharon, did not permit herself to partake of sweets from the time of the Holocaust until her death in 1986. "So many *tzaros* (tribulations) for the Jewish people," she would say, "such a *Churban!* How can I enjoy sweets?"

Among the remembrances they enacted are:

1) If someone plasters his home, he should leave an *amah* (cubit) square of wall opposite the entrance unfinished (see *Orach Chaim* 560 and *Igros Moshe, Orach Chaim III* §86).

2) When a women adorns herself, she should omit some of her ornaments (ibid.).[1]

3) A bridegroom should place ashes upon his head before making his way to the *chupah*, marriage canopy *(Tosefta, Sotah* 15:4,5).

4) At the conclusion of the marriage ceremony, a glass should be broken *(Rama, Orach Chaim* 360).

Weddings Without Music

◦§ If you attend a wedding in the Old City of Jerusalem or in the neighborhoods adjacent to it, you may be surprised by the absence of one of a traditional wedding's most essential components — instrumental music. At best, you may hear a drummer beating out a dancing rhythm, or a talented vocalist whose humming sounds like a violin or a flute. But why is there no band of musicians?

The answer takes us back over a century to the year 1865, when a terrible cholera epidemic raged through the Jewish community in Jerusalem. The plague attacked young and old; scores upon scores of fresh graves dotted the cemetery on the Mount of Olives. Even the most pious Sages were not immune to the terrible plague, as three of Jerusalem's most venerable rabbis succumbed to the cholera within a short period.

The entire community was in a panic. Even before the epidemic, life in Old Jerusalem was filled with struggle and suffering. Now, death stared every family in the face and the epidemic showed no signs of abating. The populace increased their prayers, their fasting, their charity and their learning — but seemingly to no avail. Death stalked them at home and in the streets.

1.The Chofetz Chaim *(Mishnah Berurah* §8) finds another reason why Jewish women should never show themselves fully adorned; namely, because this arouses jealousy among the gentiles. In *Shaar HaTziyun* (§11), he cites *Genesis* 42:1, where Jacob advises his sons to join their neighbors in journeying to Egypt in search of food during a hunger — though his family still had food. Jacob told his sons, "Why show yourselves?" that is, "Why show that you are better off than your neighbors and thereby arouse their fire?"

Finally, in sheer desperation, one of Jerusalem's most outstanding Rabbinic leaders, Rabbi Meir Auerbach (formerly *Rav* of Kalish, Poland and author of the classic work, *Imrei Binah*), fasted and prayed fervently that the cause of this epidemic might be revealed to him in a "prophetic dream-vision." Because of his purity and unique personal merits, R' Meir was granted this vision and a cryptic message was relayed to him in his dream.

With the assistance of the holy mystics (the *mekuballim*) of Jerusalem, he understood that the Heavenly Tribunal was making the following demands of Jerusalem's pious and God-fearing citizens: From the time the Temple was destroyed almost two thousand years ago, the Jewish people have been plunged into dark mourning which is expressed in many ways throughout the year. However, the Jews who are privileged to reside near the Western Wall, near the site where the Temple once stood and where the *Shechinah* still resides, are expected to intensify their mourning more than anyone else in the world because they see the *Churban*, the Destruction, before their very eyes, all the time. Therefore, although wedding music is permissible and commendable for Jews the world over, it is inappropriate for the Jews of Old Jerusalem, lest the joyous music distract them from their constant level of heightened mourning over the Temple and its ruins.

Not long after this revelation, all of the Jews of Old Jerusalem — men, women and children — assembled at the Western Wall at midnight. At this awesome gathering, the Chief Rabbi of Jerusalem arose and publicly banned the playing of music at weddings in Jerusalem until the Redemption, when it shall *be heard in the cities of Judah and the streets of Jerusalem, the sound of joy and the sound of gladness, the voice of the groom and the voice of the bride* (cf. Jeremiah 33:10-11).[1]

The Jerusalem community accepted this strict ban and affirmed it. Only once did someone dare to defy this rabbinic decree. In 1873, a new family of settlers arrived from Europe and they prepared to make a wedding for their daughter in Jerusalem. The bride's mother adamantly refused to accept the ban and she insisted that there be live music at the wedding. When she could find no Jewish musicians who would defy the ban, she hired gentile musicians. Rabbi Meir

---

1. Music is not played at other forms of celebration as well. Music *is* played in Jerusalem during the *simchas beis hasho'eivah* festivities held during the Intermediate Days (*Chol HaMoed*) of Succos, as a remembrance of the joyous celebrations held in the Temple during those days.

Auerbach sent her a final warning not to defy the ban, but this warning was ignored.

The morning after the wedding, the city of Jerusalem was in an uproar. The bride's mother had disappeared! She simply vanished without a trace and was never seen again.

Taking Matters to Heart

⋙ It is customary to cover or remove the bread knife from the table before reciting *Birkas Hamazon* at a meal's conclusion. One source for this custom is an incident where a man, upon reciting the words וּבְנֵה יְרוּשָׁלַיִם עִיר הַקֹּדֶשׁ, *And rebuild Jerusalem, the holy city,* became so distressed over the Destruction that he picked up the knife and stabbed himself *(Beis Yosef, Orach Chaim* 180 citing *Rabbeinu Simchah)*. We seem far from such emotions; yet, some people are not.

When the legendary Torah pioneer R' Shraga Feivel Mendlowitz[1] taught *Al Naharos Bavel* (On the Rivers of Babylon — *Psalm* 137) to his students, he could rarely get out a word or two before being so overcome with emotion that he was incapable of continuing.

On a Friday night in the summer of 1948, word reached America of the fall of Jerusalem. That evening, while reciting the words וּבְנֵה יְרוּשָׁלַיִם עִיר הַקֹּדֶשׁ, R' Shraga Feivel suffered a heart attack. His disciple Rabbi Yitzchak Chinn attended to him during that illness and watched as he pounded his fist against his bed while in an oxygen tent and exclaimed, *"Vas vet zein mit Eretz Yisrael* (What will be with *Eretz Yisrael)?"*

A Home Like His Master's

⋙ After General Allenby took Palestine from the Turks in World War I, the British mandate was established over *Eretz Yisrael*. In the year 1920, the British government appointed a Jew, Sir Herbert Samuel, to be the High Commissioner of Palestine. When Sir Herbert arrived, he made it his first order of business to visit and pay his respects to the religious leaders of the Holy Land. He visited the heads of the various

---

1. 1886-1948. Among his many great accomplishments were the founding of Mesivta Torah Vodaath in New York and Torah Umesorah, the umbrella organization of *yeshivos* and day-schools in North America.

Christian churches and the Grand Mufti of the Moslems. He paid his respects to Rabbi Avraham Yitzchak Kook and finally made an appointment to visit the Chief Rabbi of Jerusalem, Rabbi Yosef Chaim Sonnenfeld, in his humble apartment in Batei Machse, inside the walls of the Old City of Jerusalem facing the Temple Mount.

R' Yosef Chaim was a humble and holy man. For sixty years, he had lived in his squalid apartment and he was perfectly satisfied with it. He ignored the fact that it was a basement apartment, situated mostly underground. This dwelling consisted of only one room — small, dark and damp — whose walls were always covered with moisture and mold. The rickety furniture was literally falling apart. To enter the apartment one had to descend a steep flight of stairs and then crouch to enter the low door.

The famous statesman of Jerusalem's Orthodox community, Rabbi Moshe Blau, who was R' Yosef Chaim's devoted disciple, and Dr. Wallach, the head of Shaarei Tzedek Hospital, both pleaded with the *Rav* of Jerusalem to change his residence so that he would make a favorable impression on the High Commissioner. R' Yosef Chaim refused, explaining that he had not invited the High Commissioner, rather the High Commissioner had invited himself and expressed a desire to visit R' Yosef Chaim in *his* house. R' Yosef Chaim also refused the offer his two admirers made to get him new furniture. "However," R' Yosef Chaim suggested, "you may place a new tablecloth on my table in honor of this important visitor."

The day of the visit arrived. Sir Herbert Samuel was escorted into the Old City by a cortege of soldiers and police. The fanfare drew huge crowds and all the media were there to report this special event. As the procession reached the *Rav's* residence, Rabbi Blau and Dr. Wallach came out to greet the visitors and to escort the High Commissioner down the steep steps leading to R' Yosef Chaim's cellar-like apartment. As Sir Herbert entered the cramped, dark dwelling he greeted the *Rav* with a jest, "The *Rav* couldn't find himself a home deeper in the earth?"

R' Yosef Chaim Sonnenfeld did not respond. His features were covered with a most serious and sorrowful look. Silently, he approached Sir Herbert, took him gently by the hand and led him across the room to a shuttered window. The *Rav* opened the shutters and before the two men was a panoramic view of the Temple Mount, the holiest spot in the world, now lying in ruins and covered with a gentile shrine. Two great teardrops welled up in the *Rav's* eyes and

rolled down his cheeks. R' Yosef Chaim turned to the High Commissioner and said, "As long as the dwelling place of my beloved God lies in ruins, my home need not be any better than His!"

Those simple and sincere words were expressed by the *Rav* with such reverence and awe that the High Commissioner was left thunderstruck. He simply could not utter another word. Such love of God, such yearning for the Temple — it was unheard of! Sir Herbert just turned around quietly and took his leave. Outside, the reporters flocked around the High Commissioner to interview him. But when the reporter for the *London Times* asked him, "Sir, please share with us your impressions from this short visit," Sir Herbert said nothing at all and maintained an awestruck silence.

(Heard from Rabbi Yosef Scheinberger of Jerusalem)

The Quality of Mourning

◆§ When the Old City of Jerusalem was captured during the Six Day War, Israeli soldiers from all walks of life caressed the holy stones of the Western Wall as their prayers and tears poured forth. Two soldiers, however, stood back, seemingly detached from this moment in history. They were secularists from birth and the significance of the capture of their people's most coveted shrine was somewhat lost to them.

Suddenly, one of these soldiers burst into tears. "לָמָה אַתָּה בּוֹכֶה, Why are you crying?" his friend asked. He replied, "אֲנִי בּוֹכֶה עַל מַה שֶׁאֲנִי לֹא בּוֹכֶה, I am crying for not feeling any need to cry."

The *S'fas Emes* was once asked: "And what should someone do if he feels no anguish over the *Churban* (Destruction)?" The *S'fas Emes* replied, "Let him mourn over his own personal *Churban*." If a Jew is not pained by the absence of God's dwelling place on earth and all that its existence represents, then his soul is surely in a sorry state.

> "Make glad Jerusalem and rejoice with her, all those who love her; be elated with her, all those who mourn for her" (Isaiah 66:10) — From here the Sages said: Whoever mourns for Jerusualem will merit to witness her joy; and whoever does not mourn for Jerusalem will not merit to witness her joy (Taanis 30b).

The above teaching is worded in the present tense: כָּל הַמִּתְאַבֵּל עַל יְרוּשָׁלַיִם זוֹכֶה וְרוֹאֶה בְּשִׂמְחָתָהּ, which, translated literally, means, *Whoever mourns for Jerusalem merits and witnesses its joy.* As *Chasam Sofer*[1] explains, a Jew's ability to mourn over Jerusalem is in itself a great source of consolation, for it is proof that this long and bitter exile will not, Heaven forfend, last forever. We cannot be consoled over the Destruction because we know with certainty that the glory and splendor of the Jerusalem of old will one day return — and our souls yearn for that day when our fondest dreams will become a reality.

As long as we mourn for Jerusalem, we are assured that, indeed, we shall someday witness its joy.

Rambam concludes the Laws of the Fasts with the following:

> All these [four] fasts will be abolished in the Messianic era. Moreover, they will each become a *yom tov,* a day of joy and gladness, as it is written, *So says HASHEM, Master of legions: The fast of the fourth,* [2] *the fast of the fifth, the fast of the seventh and the fast of the tenth will be to the house of Judah for joy and gladness and happy festivals — [if they will] but love truth and peace* (Zechariah 8:19).

May that time come speedily and in our day.

---

1. See p. 56.

2. The numbers in this verse refer to months of the Jewish calendar, in which Nissan is the first month. The fourth month is Tammuz, in which the fast of the Seventeenth of Tammuz falls (though the verse actually refers to the ninth of Tammuz — see p. 47); the fifth month is Av, in which Tishah B'Av falls; the seventh month is Tishrei in which the Fast of Gedaliah falls; and the tenth month is Teves in which the fast of the Tenth of Teves falls.

ເຈ Tishah B'Av Tragedies — A Concise History

First Temple

Second Temple

Megillas Eichah*

Targum Sheni**

Psalm 22***

* This section is reprinted from *The Book of Megillos,* translated and annotated by Rabbi Meir Zlotowitz, Mesorah Publications Ltd.

** This section is reprinted from *Tz'enah Ur'enah,* vol. II, translated by Miriam Stark Zakon, Mesorah Publications Ltd.

*** This section is abridged from *Tehillim,* by Rabbi Avrohom Chaim Feuer, Mesorah Publications Ltd.

More than a day of lamenting, Tishah B'Av is a day of learning — learning essential lessons from the terrible errors of our past so that we may never repeat them in the present or future. Evidently, we have not yet learned these lessons, for as the Sages teach, any generation in which the Temple is not rebuilt is considered as if it had destroyed it (Yerushalmi Yoma 1:1).

It is imperative that we peruse and analyze ourselves and our deeds through the pure eyes of Torah Sages whose vision has been carefully adjusted and clarified by many long years of studying the word of God.

Here we present a brief outline of the history of the major tragedies which befell the Jewish nation on Tishah B'Av beginning with the Destruction of the First Temple. The tragedies and events leading up to them are presented from the vantage point of the Sages of the Talmud and Midrash who were endowed with pure Torah vision.

For further sources and details about the Destruction of the First Temple, the reader is referred to Rabbi Shlomo Rottenberg's masterpiece, Toldos Am Olam. The Overview to ArtScroll's Ezekiel provides deep insight into this period.

Much of the information presented here pertaining to the Destruction of the Second Temple and its aftermath was culled from ArtScroll's History of the Jewish People, vol. I and II.

It is prohibited to study the pleasant portions of the Torah on the day of Tishah B'Av, but we are permitted, nay, encouraged to delve into the Torah lessons which exhort us to learn from our mistakes. Such intense introspection is painful — yet most profitable. We fervently hope that the reader will gain much from the historic insights presented forthwith.

THE DESTRUCTION
OF THE FIRST TEMPLE

I. The Sun Begins to Set

With the ascension of Menashe, the son of Chizkiyahu, to the throne of Jerusalem and Judea in the year 3228 (from Creation), the sun began to set upon the era of the First Temple. For one hundred and ten more years, until the destruction of the Temple by the Babylonians in the year 3338, the faith and fortunes of **Menashe** various Jewish kings would wax and wane, but the essential direction of the Jewish nation was downward, because the evil Menashe had thrust the nation towards its doom. Slowly but surely the soul of the Jewish people would crumble, eroded by the rot of idol worship which Menashe planted in their heart. In the end, the physical destruction of the Land and the Temple would be no more than the outward manifestation of the inner decay to which the nation had gradually succumbed.

Menashe's father, Chizkiyahu (3199-3228), had carried his people to a glorious zenith of spiritual attainment. He had been a "Prince of Peace" (*Isaiah* 9:5) and had come tantalizingly close to becoming the מָשִׁיחַ, *Messiah* (*Sanhedrin* 94a). In his Divinely inspired vision, however, he saw that he would give birth to a son whose destructive wickedness would go beyond anything that had been known before — and this knowledge was the sorrow of his life. In desperation, he decided not to marry so that the evil potential within his loins would not be realized. But the prophet Isaiah told him:

בַּהֲדֵי כַּבְשֵׁי דְרַחֲמָנָא לְמָה לָךְ? מַאי דְמִפַּקְדַתְּ אִיבָּעֵי לָךְ לְמֶעֱבַד, וּמַה דְּנִיחָא קַמֵּיה קוּדְשָׁא בְּרִיךְ הוּא לֶעֱבִיד.
Why do you meddle in God's mysteries? You must do what you are commanded to do, and the Holy One, Blessed is He, will do what pleases Him (Berachos 10a).

His worst fears were confirmed. Menashe imitated the abominations of the idolatrous nations. He even went so far as to place an idol inside the Holy Temple. He was also guilty of much bloodshed and even murdered his own grandfather, the prophet Isaiah! Although Menashe eventually repented (*II Chronicles* 33:12), the period of his wickedness

was so destructive and the moral fiber of the people so thoroughly weakened, that the fate of Jerusalem was sealed (*II Kings* 21:10-15). The Land would be laid waste and the Temple would be destroyed, because of the *anger which Menashe had angered Him* (ibid. 23:26).

The darkness which Menashe cast over Jerusalem would not lift for more than half a century. His own reign of fifty-five years was followed by that of his son Ammon (3283-3285) whose wickedness exceeded even that of his father (*Sanhedrin* 103b).

Ammon followed in Menashe's evil footsteps until he was assassinated by his own servants. His son, Yoshiyahu, became king.

J ust as a flame flickers most brightly just before it dies, hope shone once more in Jerusalem. Yoshiyahu, Ammon's son (3285-3316), rejected the heritage of evil which had come to him from his father and grandfather. With unprecedented energy (*II Kings* 23:25), Yoshiyahu set

Yoshiyahu   about to forge a renewed covenant between God and His people (ibid. v. 3), and to cleanse the land of the idolatrous filth by which it had been inundated (ibid. v. 4-20).

Only eight years old upon assuming the throne, Yoshiyahu was a righteous person who unswervingly followed the ways of his ancestor, David. His first major project was to appoint officials to supervise the repair of the Temple. Chilkiyahu, the High Priest, found a Torah scroll in the Temple and had it read to the king. Yoshiyahu interpreted its contents as a signal that he and the people would be sorely punished for the idolatry that was rampant in Judah. Filled with remorse and repentance, the king ordered that the guidance of the prophets be sought.

Accompanied by the elders and the people, the king ascended to the Temple where he read the scroll to the assemblage and pledged to comply with its contents. He had all idolatrous vessels removed from the Temple. He dispatched officials throughout the length and breadth of the Land to seek out and destroy all vestiges of idol worship, and to desecrate the graves of the idolaters.

A repentance like Yoshiyahu's was unprecedented and unparalleled. Nevertheless, such roots had Menashe's iniquities struck that God was unwilling to annul His decree against Judah. Yoshiyahu was killed in battle against Pharaoh Necho in Megiddo and was succeeded by his son Yehoachaz.

Yoshiyahu's death at the hands of the Egyptian pharaoh (ibid. v. 29) is a tragic burden which Israel carries on its road through history. Had he lived, the destruction might have been averted (*Lamentations* 4:20). As it was, his life was extinguished before his task was completed.[1] The people were not yet ready to answer his call to greatness. Outwardly they followed his lead, but their souls remained sick and their allegiance belonged to the familiar idols in whom Menashe and Ammon had taught them to seek comfort.

The agony was to draw out for twenty-two years more. Yoshiyahu's son, Yehoachaz (3316), reigned for only three months and all the while he returned to the evil ways of his grandfather and great-grandfather. He was deposed and imprisoned by Pharaoh Necho. The Egyptian king appointed Elyakim, son of Yoshiyahu, as the new king of Israel and changed his name to Yehoyakim. He reigned from 3316 to 3327.

> Then HASHEM, the God of their fathers, addressed them through His messengers, each and every day, always trying, because He took pity upon His people and on His habitation. But they mocked the messengers of God, despised His words and scoffed at His prophets, to a point where the anger of HASHEM rose against His people, without any possibility of abatement. So He brought up against them the king of the Chaldeans . . . (II Chronicles 36:15-17).

Yehoyakim, too, was wicked. During his reign Nebuchadnezzar became ascendant and Yehoyakim became his vassal for three years; then he rebelled. As part of His plan to destroy Judah, God sent bands of soldiers from surrounding nations to attack and harass **Yehoyakim** the Land. Yehoyakim eventually died an ignominious death while a captive in Babylonian hands (*Vayikra Rabbah* 19:5).

The cold-hearted indifference of the ruling class to the word of God became most pronounced during the reign of Yehoyakim. Jeremiah had

---

1. An entire lamentation is recited on Tishah B'Av to mourn Yoshiyahu's tragic death. See ArtScroll's *Complete Tishah B'Av Service*, Kinnah 11, p. 182.

begun to spread the word of God during the reign of Yoshiyahu and that pious king respected him, albeit with reservations. Yehoyakim, however, utterly despised this loyal messenger of God and treated his message with derision.

Jeremiah was probably the most unpopular prophet in history. For forty years, he fearlessly hammered away at the people of Israel and warned them of God's impending retribution. Everything he said, he said publicly, in the marketplace, for all to hear. The people despised him for his prophecies. He was not just unpopular — he was scorned, hated, threatened and persecuted. But he was never intimidated or silenced, because he spoke the word of God — and the word of God must be heard.

The one who detested Jeremiah most was King Yehoyakim. The height of King Yehoyakim's brazen defiance is described in chapter 36 of the Book of *Jeremiah*.

In the fourth year of his reign, eighteen years before the Destruction, God commanded Jeremiah to prepare a scroll upon which he was to record God's prediction of the evil that would befall the Land. Our Rabbis teach that Jeremiah, who was then in prison because of his intrepid prophecies, recorded the basic text of the Book of *Lamentations* (chapters 1,2, and 4). Because he was incarcerated, Jeremiah sent his devoted disciple Baruch ben Neriah to the king's place to read this prophetic warning to him. This took place on the eighth day of Kislev while the king was in his winter palace, which was warmed by a roaring fire. One of the king's officers began to read:

> "*Alas — she* (Jerusalem) *sits in solitude!*" (*Lamentations* 1:1).
> "Who cares," responded Yehoyakim, "as long as I remain king!"
> "*Judah has gone into exile because of suffering*" (ibid. 1:3).
> "Who cares! I am still king!"
> "*Her adversaries have become her ruling monarch*" (ibid. 1:5).
> "That I will never accept! I must remain king!" (*Moed Katan* 26a).

Enraged, Yehoyakim seized a sharp razor, cut out every Name of God from the scroll, and then threw God's Names and the holy scroll into the roaring fire — where it burnt until everything turned to ashes.

After the king committed this sacrilege, neither he nor any of his retinue felt any remorse or fear whatsoever. Ordinarily, when a sacred

Torah scroll goes up in flames and God's Name is obliterated, it is considered a calamity of the highest order, and one must tear his clothing in mourning, and fast and repent. Not so Yehoyakim and his court; they rejoiced over the conflagration of the Torah.

For this, Yehoyakim was doomed to die a terrible death, with his remains treated like an animal's carcass, unburied and left to rot in the street. And his subjects, who tolerated his wickedness, were doomed to destruction by sword and fire.

God told Jeremiah to take up the prophet's pen once again to rewrite the Book of *Lamentations* to which was now added chapter three, the longest and most tragic chapter of all. It begins: *I am the man who has seen affliction by the rod of His anger* (*Lamentations* 3:1).

This was Jeremiah's sorrowful destiny. He saw the destruction looming closer and closer, yet he could do nothing to prevent it, because the people and their leaders refused to listen. He tried with all his might to get the people to cry, because he knew that nothing would extinguish the flame of God's fury like sincere tears of penitence; but their hearts were hardened and not a tear would they shed.

After Yehoyakim's ignominious death, his son Yehoyachin succeeded to the throne, but reigned for only three months (*II Kings* 24:8). He was taken to Babylon with the first great wave of exiles. These exiles comprised the elite of Jerusalem's people (ibid. vs. 14-16), in particular הֶחָרָשׁ וְהַמַּסְגֵּר, *carpenters and locksmiths* (i.e.

The Final Years

the awesome Torah scholars in whose presence all mouths were "locked" in silent respect of their overwhelming scholastic superiority), who included such men as Mordechai, Daniel and Yechezkel who were to be the repository of Israel's future.[1]

Only the *lowly people of the Land* (*II Kings* 24:14) remained. Over them, Yehoyachin's uncle, Tzidkiyahu (3327-3338), would reign for the final eleven years of Israel's travail. Jeremiah was the prophet in Jerusalem, exhorting the people until the very end to turn once more to God. His message fell upon deaf ears. Tzidkiyahu failed the Almighty, and it was God's will to destroy Jerusalem. In the ninth year of Tzidkiyahu's reign, Nebuchadnezzar laid siege to Jerusalem. In the eleventh year of Tzidkiyahu's kingdom the fortifications were breached and finally everything, including the Temple, was destroyed.

---

1. See p. 72.

The following is a historic outline of the final period of the Temple and the role played by the two major participants, the prophet, Jeremiah, and the king, Tzidkiyahu.

THE LAST YEARS OF THE JEWISH MONARCHY / A TIME LINE		
KINGS OF ISRAEL	YRS.	
Menashe ben Chizkiyahu	55	
Ammon ben Menashe	2	
Yoshiyahu ben Ammon	31	
Yehoachaz ben Yoshiyahu	3 mo.	
Yehoyakim ben Yoshiyahu	11	
Yehoyachin ben Yehoyakim	3 mo.	
Tzidkiyahu ben Yoshiyahu	11	

3225 3230 3235 3240 3245 3250 3255 3260 3265 3270 3275 3280 3285 3290 3295 3300 3305 3310 3315 3320 3325 3330 3335 3340

II. The Final Period

In the year 3327, Nebuchadnezzar exiled Yehoyachin the son of Yehoyakim, but even in this moment of wrath God's mercy was aroused for His people and a flicker of compassion towards the Jews was ignited in Nebuchadnezzar's heart.

King Tzidkiyahu He proclaimed, "If there is still a descendant of King Yoshiyahu in your midst, I will appoint him as your monarch!" Masanya, son of Yoshiyahu, presented himself to the Babylonian conqueror. When Nebuchadnezzar asked him his name, Masanya said to himself, "Henceforth, I will call myself Tzidkiyahu, in the hope that righteous men (tzaddikim) shall descend from me." Unbeknownst to Tzidkiyahu, this change of name was very appropriate for him and it was God Himself who put the idea in his mind for a different reason; because in Tzidkiyahu's lifetime, God would mete out strict justice (tzedek) and retribution to the sinful nation of Israel.

Nebuchadnezzar demanded that Tzidkiyahu swear an oath of allegiance to him, which Tzidkiyahu promptly did, saying, "I swear allegiance to you by my own soul." Nebuchadnezzar was not satisfied, "I demand that you swear to me upon the holy Torah given at Sinai." Nebuchadnezzar took out a Torah scroll and Tzidkiyahu took an oath of loyalty over it (Yalkut Shimoni, Yirmiyahu 326).

Thus, at the age of 21, Tzidkiyahu became the last king of Judea (*II Kings* 24:18). Personally, Tzidkiyahu was a righteous man, so much so that he earned another name, Shalom, for he was perfect (*shaleim*) in his conduct. Upon ascending the throne, the king's first act was to release Jeremiah from the dungeon in which he had been imprisoned by Yehoyakim. Now, the prophet of God could exhort the masses to repentance so that the impending doom might still be averted.

Tzidkiyahu's personal piety, however, was not enough to save him from the bad influence of his peers — the noblemen and advisers who surrounded him. As king, he possessed the power and authority to deter his subjects from their corrupt ways, but since he failed to wield his power properly, Tzidkiyahu was held responsible for the sins of his subordinates (*Sanhedrin* 103).

The prophet Jeremiah enjoined the king to humble himself before God and before God's agent, Nebuchadnezzar, and to recognize the foreign yoke as a well-deserved punishment for Judea's sins. The arrogant princes, however, incited Tzidkiyahu to rebellion. As soon as Nebuchadnezzar departed from Jerusalem, Tzidkiyahu ignored his oath and started his plans to rebel against his Babylonian overlord.

I n the sixth year of Yehoyachin's exile (which was the sixth year of Tzidkiyahu's reign), the ugly sins of the Jews reached the point where God's Divine Presence, the *Shechinah*, could no longer dwell in their midst. Nevertheless, our compassionate God was still reluctant to
The Sixth Year forsake His children; therefore, His *Shechinah* departed gradually, in ten stages. All the while, God was hoping that His departure would awaken the Jews to the danger which threatened them and perhaps they would still repent.

The prophet Ezekiel (9:3) tells of how he observed God's *Shechinah* as it began its departure from the top of the Holy Ark (the *kappores*) to the first cherub on the Holy Ark and then to the second cherub. From there, the *Shechinah* retreated to the threshold of the Temple doorway

and then to the *Azarah*, Courtyard. Later, the *Shechinah* moved to the *Mizbeach*, Altar; the rooftop of the Temple; the wall surrounding the Courtyard and from there to inside the city of Jerusalem. From the city, the *Shechinah* fled to the Mount of Olives and finally to the wilderness outside Jerusalem. For a period of three and one half years, the *Shechinah* lingered and hovered over this barren wilderness waiting for Israel to repent but when they failed to do so, the *Shechinah* divorced itself from this lowly world and ascended to its celestial origin, as the prophet said (*Hosea* 5:15), *I shall depart, and return to My abode until they acknowledge their offense* (*Rosh Hashanah* 31a).

T he thirty-fourth chapter in the Book of *Jeremiah* describes how in the seventh year of his reign, King Tzidkiyahu gathered his entire nation into Jerusalem and exhorted them to enter into a covenant with him to proclaim freedom for all Hebrew slaves. At first, everyone, both the noble princes and the common masses, willingly agreed to follow the Torah law to liberate the Hebew slaves and maidservants after six years of bondage (*Exodus* 21:2). Soon, however, the populace had a change of heart and they forced their former servants to return to bondage.

The Seventh Year

This betrayal of the solemn covenant which, in essence, was a declaration of loyalty to God's Torah, aroused God's fury and He sent Jeremiah to issue a terrible warning to the people: "You failed to listen to Me to free your slaves. Therefore, I will make your flesh free for all to slaughter by the sword and free and open to pestilence and famine. You are henceforth free of My authority. I am no longer your Master and I shall not save you from the enemy's sword."

Thus, Israel was dragged one step closer to its ultimate doom.

I n the eighth year of his reign, King Tzidkiyahu finally put his plans for rebellion against Nebuchadnezzar into action by sending agents to Egypt to gather soldiers and horses to join in the battle against Babylonia (*Seder Olam Rabbah*, ch. 26). In doing so, he defied the expressed will of God who had sent Jeremiah to tell Tzidkiyahu: "*Bring your necks under the yoke of the Babylonian king and serve him and his people and live. Why should you die, you and your people, by the sword, in famine and*

The Eighth Year

in plague, as God had threatened for such nations as would not serve the Babylonian king?" (Jeremiah 27:12-13).

Humility and surrender and penitence was what God demanded of the Jews and of Tzidkiyahu their king. Instead, they arrogantly ignored God's will and rebelled. God rebuked them through His prophet Ezekiel. *"Shall he prosper? Shall he escape who does such things? Shall he break a covenant and yet escape?"* (Ezekiel 17:15).

Treacherously, King Tzidkiyahu pressured the high court, the Sanhedrin, to absolve him of his oath of allegiance to Nebuchadnezzar. His infidelity was an open desecration of the name of the God of Israel since the gentiles would now accuse all Jews of treachery and would claim that the word of a Jew was not to be trusted (*Nedarim* 65a and *Ramban* ibid.).

The *Midrash* (*Shochar Tov* 79:2) relates: For a period of eighteen years prior to the Temple's destruction, a Heavenly voice was issued repeatedly and it filled the halls of Nebuchadnezzar's palace saying: "Worthless servant! Arise and destroy the home of your Master" (i.e. the Holy Temple). Yet Nebuchadnezzar was afraid to do this, for he could not believe that God would destroy Jerusalem. Finally, he resorted to divination in order to determine if he should destroy God's city. He shot an arrow towards Antioch, but it crumbled to pieces and fell. The same thing happened when he shot an arrow towards Tyre and then towards Lydda. But when he shot an arrow towards Jerusalem it flew far and true in that direction. Thus, he was finally convinced that it was his destiny to destroy the holy city (see *Pesikta Eichah* 23).

Yet, Nebuchadnezzar still hesitated. Perhaps Tzidkiyahu had some merit which ultimately would overpower the might of Babylonia?

When Nebuchadnezzar was informed of Tzidkiyahu's treacherous rebellion, he knew beyond all doubt that Judea would fall.

> *Nebuchadnezzar announced, "If you, Tzidkiyahu, had only rebelled against me and not against your own God, I would have feared that your God would support you. Had you rebelled against your God and not against me, I would have continued to support you as an ally. But now that you have betrayed both God and me — you are doomed!"*
>
> (Midrash Esther Rabbah 3:1)

Nebuchadnezzar now marched against Jerusalem for the third time. The first two times were only for conquest, but now he was bent on destruction:

> The first time Nebuchadnezzar took the city and exiled
> Yehoyakim. The second time, he took the city and exiled
> Yehoyachin and tied him to his carriage as a sign of
> humiliation. The third time, he exiled Tzidkiyahu (and
> destroyed the city).
>
> (Midrash Bamidbar Rabbah 23:14)

> And it came to pass in the ninth year of his [Tzidkiyahu's]
> reign, in the tenth month, on the tenth day of the month [The
> Tenth of Teves] that Nebuchadnezzar, king of Babylonia,
> and all of his legions arrived at Jerusalem and encamped
> against it, and all around it they built a siege wall. And the
> city remained under siege until the eleventh year of King
> Tzidkiyahu."
>
> (II Kings 25:1,2)

I n truth, according to all rules of military procedure, Nebuchadnezzar's vastly superior forces should have immediately swept over the
city, but the God of Israel had different plans. In His limitless
compassion, He still sought to give Israel one last chance to repent.

The Siege Begins
Yalkut Shimoni (Eichah 1009) relates: When the evil
Nebuchadnezzar arrived with his hordes, he thought he
would take the city in no time at all. But God
invigorated the defenders of Jerusalem with renewed strength for
over three years in order to give them ample opportunity to repent.
There were extraordinary warriors in Jerusalem who battled the enemy
and killed vast numbers of them. Amongst the defenders was one
amazing hero named Avika ben Gavtari. When the Babylonians
catapulted massive stones against Jerusalem's walls in order to breach
them, this warrior would actually catch them with his bare hands and
hurl the stones back at the attackers, killing many of them. He became
so proficient at his art that he could even catch the stones with his bare
feet and hurl them at the attackers! Ultimately, it was not the enemy
who subdued this warrior; rather, he succumbed to pride and
self-confidence. Avika saw no reason to repent — and his fellow Jews
felt protected by their strong champion. One day, a mere puff of wind
came and blew Avika off Jerusalem's walls and he fell to his death. At
that moment, the walls of the city were breached and the enemy poured
in.

At the height of the siege, King Tzidkiyahu sent emissaries to Jeremiah, pleading with him, *"Please pray on our behalf to* HASHEM, *our God"* (Jeremiah 37:3). But the prophet knew that this request was really insincere, for word had reached Jerusalem that their

Jeremiah's Final Attempt new allies, their former archenemies, the Egyptians, were on their way to help lift the siege. Jeremiah knew that the people had more confidence in the Egyptian army than they had in God.

God commanded Jeremiah to tell Tzidkiyahu's emissaries: *"Behold, the army of Pharaoh which was coming to your assistance has returned to its land, Egypt. And the Babylonians will return to besiege this city and they will capture it and send it up in flames"* (Jeremiah 37:7,8).

Rashi (ibid.) explains that as the Egyptians embarked on their ships to sail to Israel, God summoned the forces of the sea and they caused inflated leather pouches which resembled the bloated bodies of drowned men to float on the water's surface. The bewildered soldiers asked one another, "What are these corpses?" And the reply was, "These are the remains of our Egyptian ancestors who were drowned because of the ancestors of the Jews to whose aid we are now running!" Thereupon, the incensed soldiers turned back from their rescue mission.

Thus Jeremiah's prophecy was fulfilled:

> *Thus says* HASHEM: *Cursed be the person who places his trust in man and makes (men of) flesh his (strong) arm. He will be like a desolate bush in the wilderness and he will never see when good comes...Blessed is the person who places his trust in* HASHEM *and then* HASHEM *will be his security* (Jeremiah 17:5-7).

As Jeremiah continued to convey God's warnings of Israel's imminent doom, he aroused the animosity and anger of the delinquent nobles and priests who preferred to ignore the painful truth that their sins were leading the nation to ruin. Not only did they hurl

His Warnings Ignored the most vicious insults at Jeremiah, but they also accused him of treachery. They claimed that the prophet of God was actually an agent of the Babylonians who sought to destroy the morale of the Jewish fighters with his dire predictions. They whipped Jeremiah mercilessly and then imprisoned him for an extended period of time. At one point,

they cast Jeremiah into a pit oozing with mud and slimy water, allowing his head to remain barely above the surface (*Yalkut Shimoni; Yirmiyahu* 308).

Finally, King Tzidkiyahu rescued the prophet from his tormentors and brought him to his palace. Tzidkiyahu begged the prophet to reveal God's true plans for the Jews.

> Then said Jeremiah to Tzidkiyahu: "Thus says HASHEM, the God of Legions, the God of Israel: 'If you will indeed go out [and surrender] to the officers of the king of Babylonia, then your soul shall live and this city will not be consumed by fire, and you and your dynasty will live on. But, if you [arrogantly] refuse to go out [to surrender] to the officers of the king of Babylonia, then this city will be given over into the hands of the Chaldeans [the Babylonians] and they shall torch it with fire and you will not escape from their hand' "
> (Jeremiah 38:17-18).

Tzidkiyahu, who was unfit for leadership, ignored the prophet's words. The king was weak hearted and feared that his subjects would turn against him and imprison and torture him if he told them the truth (ibid. v. 19). He went so far as to warn Jeremiah not to reveal his Divine prophecies to the soldiers and commanders, for they despised the truth. Moreover, he had Jeremiah incarcerated in the courtyard of the sentries in order to keep him away from the people; Jeremiah languished there until the very day Jerusalem was captured (ibid. v. 28).

S lowly but surely, the siege progressed and the hunger intensified: *All her people are sighing, searching for bread. They traded their treasures for food to keep alive* (Lamentations 1:11).

Finally, the starved populace was driven to desperation:

Starvation Amid the Siege *The tongue of the suckling infant cleaves to its palate for thirst; young children beg for bread, no one extends it to them. Those who once feasted extravagantly lie destitute in the streets; those who were brought up in scarlet clothing wallow in garbage.... Their appearance has become blacker than soot, they are not recognized in the streets; their skin has shriveled on their bones, it became dry as wood...Hands of compassionate women have boiled their own children; they became their*

food when the daughter of my people was shattered (ibid. 4:4,5,8,10).

The Midrash describes how formerly affluent daughters of Zion now walked in the streets of Jerusalem staring at each other languishing from hunger and moaning: "The ravages of hunger are hard to accept; I cannot bear them." Supporting one another, they would search through the city for food. Finding nothing to eat, they would clutch at the house pillars and fall dead. Now their infants who still nursed came crawling after them on their hands and knees. Each child, recognizing his own mother, came and put his mouth to her expecting to draw milk. But there was no milk to be drawn, and so, driven into a frenzy, their souls ebbed away in their mothers' bosoms (*Lamentations* 2:12).

Yet the city did not fall. The siege lasted for three and one half years while God's Presence remained at hand in the nearby wilderness hoping that Israel might somehow be humbled by its agony. A Heavenly voice cried out repeatedly, שׁוּבוּ בָּנִים שׁוֹבָבִים, "*Return, wayward children!*" (*Jeremiah* 3:14), and שׁוּבוּ אֵלַי וְאָשׁוּבָה אֲלֵיכֶם, "*Return unto Me, and I will return to you*" (*Malachi* 3:7). When it became painfully clear that Israel refused to repent, the *Shechinah* abandoned Israel saying (*Hosea* 5:15), אֵלֵךְ אָשׁוּבָה אֶל מְקוֹמִי, "*I shall depart and return to My* (Heavenly) *abode.*" (*Pesikta Eichah* 25).

III. Destruction

The kings of the earth did not believe, nor did any of the world's inhabitants, that the adversary or enemy could enter the gates of Jerusalem (Lamentations 4:12).

Nebuchadnezzar had witnessed God's awesome might when Sancherib, king of Assyria, laid siege to Jerusalem, and his entire army of hundreds of thousands of men was destroyed by the plague of God in one night (*II Kings* ch. 19, *II Chronicles* ch. 32). Therefore,

The Walls Are Breached Nebuchadnezzar was still afraid of attacking Jerusalem himself, so he sent his general Nevuzaradan to conquer the holy city. Nebuchadnezzar supplied his commander-in-chief with battering rams of extraordinary size and weight, but try as he might, he failed to breach the gates, and these massive "hammers" shattered to pieces. After three and one half years of

utter failure and frustration, Nevuzaradan was about to break camp and give up the futile siege. At that moment, a Heavenly voice called out to him, "Marauder, son of a marauder! The moment has arrived for the Temple to be destroyed. Attack now with whatever weapons you have!" Nevuzaradan had only one small battering ram left in his arsenal. He now attempted one final assault on the city's gates and behold — they fell asunder. The city lay open for the Babylonians to pillage and destroy at will.

Once the city was in their hands, the Babylonians ran wild and slaughtered every Jew in their path without pity. They butchered fathers and sons together, mothers and their nursing babies. The streets of the city ran red with rivers of blood. The corpses were piled up in huge heaps.

> All your enemies jeered at you; they hiss and gnash their teeth. They say: "We have devoured her! Indeed, this is the day we longed for; we have actually seen it!" (Lamentations 2:16)

The enemy committed unspeakable atrocities. They swung around little infants and smashed their heads against rocks. The sage, Ulla, related: "Nine large measures of babies' brains were found on just one boulder alone!" (Gittin 58a). Rabbi Yehoshua ben Levi reported that three hundred children were found hanging together, suspended from one branch (Midrash Eichah 5:14).

The sheer numbers were staggering: Rabbi Yehoshua ben Korcha related: "An old citizen of Jerusalem once told me that in one valley alone Nevuzaradan, the butcher, slaughtered two million, one hundred thousand people. In Jerusalem, on just one boulder, he butchered nine hundred and forty thousand" (Gittin 57a).

With Jerusalem's walls breached and with the enemy legions laying waste to the city, Tzidkiyahu realized, too late, that the fate of Judea and his own fate, as well, was sealed for doom. He attempted to escape through an eighteen-mile-long tunnel which led from the city to a cave which opened near Jericho. The **Attempt at Escape** king fled with his ten sons, but he was not destined to succeed. At this very time, a troop of Babylonian soldiers was hunting deer near Jericho. They captured their prey at the mouth of the tunnel just as Tzidkiyahu emerged.

Tzidkiyahu was taken prisoner and brought to King Nebuchadnezzar's headquarters in Rivla for judgment. The king condemned Tzidkiyahu because he had flagrantly violated his sacred oath not to rebel against Babylon. To intensify Tzidkiyahu's suffering, Nebuchadnezzar slaughtered all ten of his sons before his very eyes (II Kings 25:7). Then Nebuchadnezzar executed the entire Sanhedrin in Tzidkiyahu's presence. Nebuchadnezzar's cruelty did not stop there — he gouged out Tzidkiyahu's eyes and threw them into a fiery oven. Nebuchadnezzar then had Tzidkiyahu carried off to Babylonia in shackles where he remained a prisoner until he died (ibid.).

In his final misery, Tzidkiyahu lived up to the prophecy implicit in his name. He acknowledged the *tzedek*, justice, of God and God's prophets, saying: "Behold, Jeremiah warned, 'You will go to Babylonia; you will die in Babylonia; but your eyes will never see Babylonia!' I failed to heed his warnings and now I am indeed in Babylonia while my blind eyes do not see her!" (*Yalkut Shimoni, II Kings* chapt. 25).

T he city of Jerusalem lay in utter ruin, death and desolation everywhere. Now the enemy turned its fury on the Temple itself, the Jews' final stronghold. On the seventh day of the month of Av, the Temple's defenses fell and the Babylonian hordes poured into the Temple Courtyard.

Final Assault
God dispatched an angel to place his feet on the walls of the Temple Courtyard in order to topple them. The angel cried out, "Let the enemies press on and enter the House which has been abandoned by its Lord. Let them loot and plunder at will!" The enemies came and erected a platform in the Courtyard on the very spot where Solomon and his ministers once sat (and planned the construction of the Temple). There they now sat and conferred on how to destroy the Temple (*Yalkut Shimoni; Yirmiyahu* 20).

For the next two days — the seventh and eighth of Av — the Sanctuary in which Israel had served God for four hundred and ten years was defiled (*Taanis* 29a). The gentiles went about their business gleefully. They were now poised for the final desecration — the destruction of the Temple.

W hen the First Temple was destroyed on the Ninth of Av it was
        on the day after the Sabbath in the year following the Sabbatical
(*Shemittah*) year. The family of *Kohanim* officiating that day was that
of Yehoyariv (lit: *God will do battle*). The Levites were chanting their

**The Ninth
of Av**

psalms on the Temple platform, but instead of the
customary Psalm for the first day of the week, God
aroused them to select *Psalm 94*, whose theme referred
to the terrible calamity at hand. As they uttered the words, *He turned
upon them their own violence, and with their own evil He will cut them
off* (v. 23), the Babylonians stormed into the inner Courtyard and
silenced them, thus preventing them from concluding with the Psalm's
final words, HASHEM *our God will cut them off.*

As the sun was setting on the Ninth of Av, the enemy set the Temple
on fire and the flames continued to rage and consume the edifice
throughout the Tenth of Av (*Taanis* 29a).

Many centuries before, this day of Tishah B'Av had been designated
for calamity and woe. Eight hundred and eighty-nine years earlier, the
children of Israel had accepted the evil report of the Spies regarding the
Holy Land and wept over it. God then promised that the time would
come when Israel would have real cause to cry on Tishah B'Av. Now,
that ominous promise had been fulfilled.

The magnificent Temple which King Solomon built now lay in ruins.
The year was 3338 from Creation. God had cried out, שַׁלַּח מֵעַל פָּנַי,
"Send them away from My Presence!" (*Jeremiah* 15:1); the numerical
value of שַׁלַּח is 338, foretelling that Israel would be exiled in that fateful
year.

It only appeared as if the gentiles destroyed the Temple; in truth, it
was the Divine decree which sealed its doom and executed it. God
dispatched four angels from Heaven; in their hands were four flaming
torches which they placed at the four corners of the Temple, setting it
afire.

When the *Kohen Gadol* (High Priest) saw that the Temple was on
fire, he took the keys and cast them Heavenward, saying: "Here are the
keys of Your House; I have been an unworthy custodian of it." He
started to go, but the enemy killed him at the Altar, on the very spot
where he would offer the daily sacrifice. His daughter ran out crying,
"Woe is me! My father — delight of my eyes!" They slaughtered her,
too, and her blood mingled with her father's.

When the priests and Levites saw that the Temple was burning, they
took their harps and trumpets and let themselves fall into the flames,

and were consumed. The maidens who wove the curtains for the Sanctuary also let themselves fall into the flames so that the enemies should not violate them (*Pesikta Rabbasi* 27).

> *HASHEM vented His fury, He poured out His fierce anger; He kindled a fire in Zion which consumed its foundations (Lamentations 4:11).*
>
> *And he (Nevuzaradan) burnt down the House of HASHEM and the palace of the king and all the houses in Jerusalem and every great house he burned with fire. And all the walls of Jerusalem all around, they broke down... (Jeremiah 52:13,14).*
>
> *Alas — she sits in solitude! The city that was great with people has become like a widow (Lamentations 1:1).*

Of the vast multitudes that once filled the city, the prophet reported that only eight hundred and thirty-two survivors remained (*Jeremiah* 52:29).

Viewing his mighty accomplishments, a spirit of great pride welled up in Nevuzaradan's heart. A Heavenly voice called out to him: "A slain nation did you slay; a burnt Temple did you burn; ground-up flour did you grind." Thus did Jerusalem say to the daughter of Babylon,

The Blood of Zechariah "Had they not fought against me from on High, would you have been able to fight me?" (*Midrash Eichah* 1:13).

In the *Ezras Kohanim*, the Courtyard of the Priests, Nevuzaradan came upon a pool of seething blood. This was the blood of the *Kohen* and prophet Zechariah ben Yehoyada, who was slain by a wild mob on Yom Kippur when he attempted to admonish them for their evil ways (*II Chronicles* 24:21). This horrible murder had occurred 238 years earlier, yet the blood had not stopped boiling in anger and vengeance, for the crime was still fresh in the eyes of God.

Haughtily, Nevuzaradan declared, "I will appease this blood!" He slaughtered the members of the Sanhedrin and their blood poured over that of Zechariah — but his blood continued to seethe. Nevuzaradan then butchered young boys and girls over the blood, to no avail. He slew innocent young priests, he massacred mothers and nursing babies; he slaughtered a total of 940,000 victims, and the blood of the prophet went on seething.

Nevuzaradan exclaimed: *"Zechariah, Zechariah! I have destroyed the flower of them. Do you wish me to massacre them all?"* Then the blood rested (*Koheles Rabbah* 3:20).

Thoughts of repentance came to Nevuzaradan's mind: If the Jews, who killed one person only, have been so severely punished, what will be my fate? He left, and ultimately converted to Judaism (*Sanhedrin* 96b).[1]

J ust before the destruction of Jerusalem, God commanded his beloved, faithful prophet Jeremiah to leave the doomed city in order to carry out a special mission in the village of Anasos. The command to leave Jerusalem came at this particular time so that Jeremiah's merit would not

Aftermath: A Trail of Tears

hinder the execution of the terrible decree that the city and its Temple be destroyed. Jeremiah did not return until the Temple had already gone up in flames and the city lay in ruins. The prophet was overwhelmed with grief over the Temple's destruction but he was equally concerned over the fate of his exiled brethren. He resolved to follow the multitude of Jews who were led into captivity.

When he found a blood-drenched trail, he knew he was headed in the right direction. All too soon, he came across dead bodies, severed limbs and the pitiful corpses of tiny sucklings and babes. When Jeremiah finally caught up with the captives, he hugged and kissed them, clung to them in warm embrace and accompanied them all the way to the shores of the Euphrates River, in Babylonia, where he bid them farewell saying, "I must return to comfort the remnants of Israel who remain on holy soil."

When the captives realized that the prophet was leaving them, they burst into tears, "Our dear father Jeremiah, how can you leave us?" they wept. With deep compassion, Jeremiah responded, "I hereby bring heaven and earth to testify that I tell you the absolute truth; if only you had cried sincerely but once while you were still in Zion, you never would have been exiled." With that, Jeremiah turned toward the Holy Land, shedding bitter tears (*Pesikta Rabbasi* 26).[2]

---

1. See *Radal* to *Koheles Rabbah* 3:20. On Tishah B'Av we bemoan this terrible slaughter which describes the tragedy in detail (see ArtScroll *The Complete Tishah B'Av Service, Kinnah* 34, p. 320).

2. In the lamentations recited on Tishah B'Av, we reaccount Jeremiah's prayers and tears on behalf of his brethren both before and after the Destruction (see ArtScroll *The Complete Tishah B'Av Service, Kinnah* 26 and 27, pp. 280-287).

For the next twenty five-hundred years, Jeremiah's brethren and their descendants would be making up for those missing tears. Exiled and persecuted time and time again, the trail of the Jew's pitiful wanderings encircles the entire globe, and the trail is marked with tears. On Tishah B'Av the weeping intensifies and the flow of tears wells up into a torrent. But God has issued a special blessing for the mourners of Zion, that is, as their mourning intensifies, so does their hope. Tishah B'Av does not increase despair; rather, it intensifies our faith that the day will come, hopefully soon, when the Messiah will arrive and wipe away our tears forever.

THE DESTRUCTION
OF THE SECOND TEMPLE

I. Twilight

> HASHEM *will bring against you a nation from afar, from the*
> *end of the earth, as the eagle swoops down, a nation whose*
> *tongue you will not understand; a nation of fierce counte-*
> *nance that will not respect the old, nor show favor to the*
> *young ... And he shall besiege you in all your gates, until*
> *your high and fortified walls come down, those in which you*
> *put your trust, throughout all your land ... (Deuteronomy*
> *28:49-52).*

These verses prophesy of the destruction of Israel by the Romans. The Torah warns us that a time will come when the Jews will be estranged from God and from themselves and at that time, measure for measure, they will be punished by a hostile nation which is totally alien

Eternal Adversaries
to Israel, a nation sharing absolutely nothing in common with the Jews; not geographically, linguistically, intellectually, or emotionally. Total strangers.

Our Sages often refer to Rome as Edom, and they teach that the Romans are the descendants of Esau who was called Edom. Indeed, the aggressive warriors of Rome fulfilled Yitzchak's blessing to Esau: *By your sword shall you live (Genesis 27:40).*

The twin brothers, Esau and Jacob, were locked in a desperate struggle with one another even while in their mother's womb, and their prenatal rivalry was a portent of the perpetual historic struggle which would ultimately exist between them.

וַיִּתְרֹצֲצוּ הַבָּנִים בְּקִרְבָּהּ וַתֹּאמֶר אִם כֵּן לָמָּה זֶּה אָנֹכִי וַתֵּלֶךְ לִדְרֹשׁ אֶת
ה'. וַיֹּאמֶר ה' לָהּ שְׁנֵי גֹויִם בְּבִטְנֵךְ וּשְׁנֵי לְאֻמִּים מִמֵּעַיִךְ יִפָּרֵדוּ וּלְאֹם
מִלְאֹם יֶאֱמָץ וְרַב יַעֲבֹד צָעִיר.

And the children struggled within her [Rebecca] and she
said, "If so, why am I thus?" And she went to inquire of
HASHEM. *And* HASHEM *said to her: Two nations are in your*
womb; two regimes from your insides shall be separated;
and the might shall pass from one regime to the other, and
the elder [Esau] shall serve the younger [Jacob] (Genesis
25:22-23).

When brotherhood and love united the sons of Jacob and they were all bound by Torah teachings, they were in ascendancy over Esau, but when the sons of Jacob abandoned Torah and were rent asunder in fraternal strife — then, Esau would dominate them with brute force. This historic axiom would be demonstrated clearly in the era of the Second Temple.

When the Second Temple was built over a four-year period (3408-3412 from Creation), the Jews were not free. First they were under the rule of the Persians for thirty-four years, and then they suffered under the cruel tyranny of the Greeks for 180 years (*Avodah*

Hyrkanus and Aristobulus

Zarah 9a). The Jews were finally liberated from foreign oppression only by a display of brotherhood. The five Hasmonean (*Chashmonaim*) brothers, sons of the High Priest Mattisyahu, were tightly bound with zealous love for Torah which infused them with the power to drive out the foreigners who ravaged the Holy Land.

However, the tragic irony is that from this very same Hasmonean family came forth another set of brothers whose jealousy and selfish hatred brought ruination to the land. Alexander Yannai was a grandson of Shimon, one of the original five heroic Hasmonean brothers. Yannai ruled for twenty-seven years, but, as he was an enemy of the Torah Sages, he brought much misery and murder to the Land. Upon his death, his two sons, Hyrkanus and Aristobulus, quarreled over the throne and their power struggle plunged the country into a cruel and prolonged civil war, which centered around the Temple Mount walls.

> *The Rabbis taught: When the Hasmonean family fought one another, Hyrkanus was outside the walls and Aristobulus inside. Every day a basket with dinars was lowered and in turn, lifted the animals for the daily sacrifices. There was an old man, learned in Greek wisdom, who told the besiegers: "As long as they continue the Temple service, they will not be delivered into your hands." The next day, when the defenders lowered the basket with dinars, the besiegers sent up a pig. When it reached half the height of the wall, the pig*

stuck its hooves into the wall, and the Land of Israel shook
over an area of 400 parsaos by 400 parsaos (Sotah 49b,
Menachos 64b; but Bava Kamma 82b states that Hyrkanus
was inside and Aristobulus outside).

The pig that stuck its feet to the wall of the Temple Mount was a
shocking indication of evil days to come. Soon after this event, imperial
Rome appeared on the scene. Scripture likens Rome to the pig-like boar:
יְכַרְסְמֶנָּה חֲזִיר מִיָּעַר, *The boar of the forest ravages it (Psalms* 80:14). The
Roman boar would plunge its claws into the walls of Jerusalem and the
Holy Temple itself.

At the time when the two hostile camps were facing each other from
inside and outside the Temple Mount walls, the Roman general,
Pompey, was marching his legions throughout the lands of Asia Minor,
subduing them one after the other. In 63 BCE (3698), the two brothers
turned to Pompey's proconsul in Damascus and asked him for Rome's
intervention in their dispute. Rome's representatives were notorious for
their greed, and when the messengers of Aristobulus offered the larger
bribe, the Roman decided in his favor and commanded Hyrkanus to lift
the siege and leave Jerusalem.

The bitter end to the civil war came when Pompey returned to
Damascus after completing his victorious military campaigns. The two
brothers appeared personally before the great Roman general to lay
their cases before him. The final outcome was that the brothers
submitted the fate of their country to the will of this Roman. When, in
the end, the defenders of Jerusalem refused to accept Pompey, he
dispatched his mighty legions against the city and subdued it.

Pompey put an end to Jewish political independence and imposed a
tributary tax upon the land. The coastal cities — Gaza, Jaffa, Ashdod
and Yavneh — as well as those of Transjordan, were torn away from
Jewish rule. All that remained of the Jewish state was Judea, part of
Edom, Galilee and a small part of Transjordan. But even in this limited
territory Jewish rule was not sovereign, for it came under the
jurisdiction of the Roman proconsul in Damascus.

Although this Roman intervention violated the national self-respect
of the people and caused economic hardships, it did not lead to open
defiance. As long as the Roman proconsuls did not overstep the harsh
decrees of Pompey, the Jews accepted their lot quietly. But with the
appointment of Gabinius as Roman proconsul for Syria and Judea, the
political situation deteriorated considerably. He rebuilt the Greek cities
throughout the land and settled many non-Jews in them. The Jews

feared that the time would come when the foreigners would outnumber them and would claim ownership of the entire country.

In deciding which of the two warring Hasmonean brothers to favor, Pompey chose to install the weak, pliant Hyrkanus in power as his governor. The more dangerous Aristobulus, with his two sons, Pompey took to Rome in captivity. In fact, Hyrkanus' cunning Edomite adviser, Antipater, held the real power.

Herod Meanwhile, in Rome, in the year 49 BCE (3712) a civil war broke out. The famed Roman general, Julius Caesar, and Pompey vied for rule of the empire. Hyrkanus and Antipater cast their lot with Julius Caesar who emerged victorious from the struggle. Caesar, who was a shrewd statesman, reckoned that with the help and leadership of a wily politician like Antipater, who was of non-Jewish origin, Rome could better control the inhabitants of Judea. Caesar bestowed almost unlimited authority on this Edomite and now a foreigner of the seed of Esau truly ruled over the Jews.

Antipater treated the Land of Israel as if it were his private property. He appointed his older son governor of the Jerusalem area and he made his younger son, Herod, governor of Galilee in the north.

There is no way to describe Herod other than that he was a brutal murderer who was prepared to employ any treacherous means to satisfy his lust for power and wealth. When his father Antipater was fatally poisoned by his enemies, Herod bribed, bullied and fought his way to supreme power over Judea.

Herod assumed supreme and total power over the Land of the Jews about 103 years before the Destruction of the Second Temple (*Avodah Zarah* 9a). His rule lasted thirty-two years, from 36-4 BCE (3725-3757), a long period of time during which the Jews endured much from this tyrant. They did not even dare to cry out and protest, for fear of swift and ruthless retaliation. Only after his death, Jewish delegates came before the Roman Senate and described the anguish Herod had inflicted on them. Suffice it to quote only part of the emotional plea of the Jewish delegation, in order to understand how evil this period was in the painful history of our people: "Even if a raging beast had reigned over us, the calamity would not have been as enormous as the disasters that were inflicted upon us during the period of Herod's rule. In ancient times too, Israel saw many dark days and terrible disasters; and we were

exiled from our homeland. But what happened to the Judeans in the days of Herod has no likeness and no counterpart. Nor does the history of other peoples know of anything like it" (Josephus Flavius, *Antiquities*).

Herod wore the kingly crown by the grace of Rome, because through him Rome could better control the affairs of the Land of Israel. But he went beyond the intentions of his overlord. Rome was only concerned that the Jews should not exercise political independence as a nation. Herod however undermined their cultural and spiritual independence as well. He introduced into the Land customs and practices from other peoples of the Roman Empire, that were alien and forbidden to the Jewish people. His long rule planted the seeds that ultimately led to the Destruction of the Holy Temple and the long and bitter exile.

In order to destroy all opposition to his rule, Herod decided to wipe out all surviving members of the Hasmonean dynasty and he succeeded in tracking down and murdering every member of this royal family.[1]

According to the Talmud (*Bava Basra* 3b), there was still one surviving Hasmonean, a young girl whom Herod now wanted to take as his queen. Knowing what sort of man he was and what he did to the rest of her family, she jumped from a rooftop to her death. From then on, the Sages ruled that anyone who claimed to be a Hasmonean should be considered a descendant of non-Jewish slaves, since the Edomite Herod, who tried to pass himself off as a Hasmonean, had been a servant of the Hasmonean family.

Herod built many palaces and fortresses both in Jerusalem and throughout the land in order to protect his power and to publicize his own glory.

On the coast, Herod build a large city, with a port second to none among the many Mediterranean harbors. It took twelve years to complete. To its dedication festivities he invited Augustus Caesar [Octavian], in whose honor the city was named Caesarea. It was a magnificent city that boasted many splendid buildings, theaters and pagan temples. Most of its inhabitants were non-Jews.

Herod wanted to make Caesarea the capital city of the land and

---

1. *Ramban* (*Genesis* 49:10) writes that though the Hasmoneans were very pious, and were it not for them Torah and the observance of the commandments would have been forgotten from Israel, they sinned by assuming the monarchy of Israel which rightfully belonged to the tribe of Judah (see ibid.). Additionally, as *Kohanim* who should be wholly devoted to the service of God, there was an extra stricture against their reign (see *Numbers* 18:7). Therefore, they were punished and fell by their enemies' sword.

thus symbolize that the new Jewish state stood for the values of Herod and Caesarea, not David and Jerusalem. Had he succeeded in making the Jewish people accept Caesarea as their capital, Herod would have gone a long way toward convincing Jews that Esau / Edom — as represented by the Roman government and the Edomite king, both of whom were based in Caesarea — were superior to Israel. The Talmud expresses the contrast between Jerusalem and Caesarea with a telling statement:

> *Caesarea and Jerusalem — if someone will tell you, "Both are destroyed," do not believe it. If someone will tell you, "Both are settled," do not believe it. But [if someone will tell you], "Caesarea is destroyed and Jerusalem is settled," or "Jerusalem is destroyed and Caesarea is settled" — you may believe it (Megillah 6a).*

The historic struggle between Jacob and Esau was crystallized in the tension between Jerusalem and Caesarea. The conflict between the two rival centers of power fulfilled the prophecy revealed to Rebecca, *Two nations are in your womb ... the might shall pass from one regime to the other (Genesis 25:23)* — but they will never be equal.

N early all of Herod's grandiose building projects were intended to impress foreigners in and around *Eretz Yisrael*. He did very little for the benefit of the Jews. Only once did he feel a genuine desire to find

Herod Rebuilds the Temple

favor with the Jewish population — when he rebuilt the Holy Temple.

The Temple had been built about 320 years earlier by the returnees from the Babylonian exile, but it had not been as imposing a building as Solomon's Temple even when it was new. During its long life, it had been looted and damaged many times by foreigners and Hellenists, with the result that it had fallen into disrepair. Why would Herod, a non-Jew who hated what the Temple stood for, have wanted to rebuild it in magnificent splendor? The Talmud (*Bava Basra* 3b-4a) tells how this happened:

Herod had learned that the Torah requires that a Jewish king may only be a person *from among your brethren (Deuteronomy 17:15)*, which implies that a non-Jewish slave — like Herod — could not

become king of Israel. Not surprisingly, Herod became furious at this interpretation that disqualified him from the monarchy. "Who taught this?" he demanded. When he heard that it was the Sages, he ordered that they be killed. Hardly a sage was left by the time his rage had stilled. For his own benefit, he permitted his adviser, Bava ben Buta, to survive, but even Bava was not spared Herod's cruelty, for Herod had him blinded.

Once Herod tried to test Bava ben Buta. The king came to the blind sage without revealing who he was and spoke as if he were a fellow Jew who hated Herod. He said that Herod was an "evil serpent" and urged Bava ben Buta to curse him. Bava refused to utter a curse no matter how much his visitor provoked him.

Finally, Herod revealed his true identity and exclaimed to Bava: "It is I! Had I known that the Sages are so zealous, I would not have killed them. Now — how can I make amends?"

Bava answered that by murdering the Sages, Herod had made the world blind, because the Torah Sages show people the proper way. Now, Herod should do something for the Holy Temple, which is also called the "eyes of the world," for the prophet Ezekiel referred to the Temple as *the desire of your eyes* (Ezekiel 24:21).

Josephus reports that many Jews who heard of Herod's plan were shocked; they feared that he would destroy the old building and not build a new one. However, Herod was true to his word. He prepared all the necessary building materials in advance and only then was work begun. Some 10,000 laborers were employed in the restoration of the Temple. The work progressed rapidly, and within three years, the building stood ready in all its glory, more beautiful now than when it was first built by the exiles returning from Babylon.

Indeed, our Sages stated: "He who did not see Herod's edifice has never in his life seen a truly magnificent structure" (*Bava Basra* 4a).

But when the building of the Temple was completed, Herod offended the people in a brazen manner. Over the gate of the Temple he mounted a golden eagle, the symbol of Rome's might. This was intended to demonstrate Herod's admiration of Rome and to remind the Jews that even their House of God was subject to the grace and control of the Romans.

II. The End Draws Near

> During the last forty years before the Destruction of the
> Temple, the lot [for the Yom Kippur sacrifice] did not come
> up in the right hand [of the High Priest], the ribbon did not
> turn white [on Yom Kippur as a sign of forgiveness], the
> western candle [on the Menorah] did not burn [all day], and
> the doors of the Sanctuary opened by themselves [indicating
> that the enemy would enter easily]. Then Rabban Yochanan
> ben Zakkai rebuked them and said: "Temple, O Temple,
> why are you so frightened? I know that you will finally be
> destroyed, because Zechariah ben Ido has prophesied about
> you (Zechariah 11:1): 'Open your doors, O Lebanon, that the
> fire may devour your cedars' " (Yoma 39b).

The last forty years before the Holy Temple was destroyed were hard times for our people in the Land of Israel. Two things occurred early in that period that should have made the people realize that catastrophe was impending and that only repentance and good deeds could avert the evil decree:

The Last Forty Years

First, Rabbi Tzadok began to fast and pray that the Temple should not be destroyed. This continued until shortly before the Destruction, when Rabban Yochanan ben Zakkai removed him from the besieged city and asked the Roman emperor Vespasian for a doctor to help him regain his health. Second, the Great Sanhedrin left the Chamber of Hewn Stone and exiled itself to a place on the Temple Mount called Chanuyos, outside the Temple area. The move meant that lower courts of twenty-three judges no longer had the authority to impose the death penalty. Only when the Sanhedrin sat in the Temple area did other courts have the right to try capital cases.

The Sanhedrin took this drastic step in response to a general drift to lawlessness. Forty years before the Destruction of the Temple, the rich, the aggressive and even some High Priests began to engage gangs of robbers and murderers to tyrannize the people and enrich themselves with the loot of the weak and poor. These evildoers had acquired Roman citizenship and enjoyed the support of the procurators.

Consequently, the Jewish courts were powerless to prosecute them. Faced with a situation in which they could not enforce the law, the Sanhedrin said: "It is better not to try them at all, rather than to sentence them according to the law, without being able to carry out the law."

The Reign of Agrippa I

The last ray of hope for the Jewish people was seen in the reign of King Agrippa I, the grandson of Herod and his Jewish queen. Agrippa had been orphaned at the age of three when his father, Aristobulus, was killed by King Herod. In one of his insane suspicions, Herod — who had his own queen executed — accused his own son Aristobulus and his brother of planning to avenge their mother's death by poisoning him, Herod. Aristobulus was executed for this imaginary crime. When he was six, Agrippa was sent to Rome to be educated with the sons of the Roman aristocracy. There he grew up and became friendly with two future emperors, Caligula and Claudius. These two friendships were to advance the fortunes of both Agrippa himself and the Jewish people to whom he remained loyal despite his Roman upbringing.

It should be noted that Agrippa's mother was a niece of Herod, whose family had the halachic status of slaves.[1] Nevertheless, Agrippa's rule was a lone ray of light in the period before the Destruction, because he honored the Torah sages and did everything in his power to adhere to the Halachah. His reign lasted but three years, from 41-44 CE (3810-3804).

When he became king of all Judea, Agrippa wanted to conduct himself in the way of a Jewish king. For advice in matters of Jewish law and conduct he would turn to Rabban Gamliel the Elder, the head of the Sanhedrin, and Agrippa's piety is praised a number of times in the Mishnah for his careful observance of *mitzvos*.

Upon his arrival in Jerusalem he offered a thanksgiving sacrifice. On Shavuos, he brought the gift of First Fruits to the Temple together with the Jewish pilgrims. Upon arriving at the Temple Mount, he took the

---

1. According to *Tosafos* to *Yevamos* 45b. When acquiring an *eved Canaani*, gentile slave, a Jew must have him circumcised and immersed in a *mikveh*. With this, the slave becomes obligated in all commandments which Jewish women are obligated to do. Upon being freed by his master, the slave becomes a bona fide Jew.

basket of produce from his servants and lifted it onto his own shoulder to carry to the Temple Courtyard. During the festival of Succos in 41 CE (3802), immediately following the *Shemittah* [Sabbatical] Year, he was handed a scroll of the Torah from which to read the Book of Deuteronomy to the gathered people, as the Torah requires of a Jewish king (*Deuteronomy* 31:11). Although a king is allowed to sit while he reads, Agrippa put his own honor aside in favor of the Torah's honor: he read while standing. When he came to the verse concerning the king: *You must not put a foreigner over you, who is not your brother* (*Deuteronomy* 17:15), he wept. Seeing this, the people called to him: "Do not fear, Agrippa; you are our brother, you are our brother!" (Mishnah *Sotah* 7:8).

The Sages, however, did not approve of this reaction of the people, because his mother was from the family of Herod. Thus he was not qualified to be king of Israel and their flattery was not proper.

In response to the people's consoling exclamation, the Sages went so far as to say:

> It was taught in the name of Rabbi Nassan: At that moment the Jewish people became liable to destruction because they improperly flattered Agrippa (Sotah 41b).

Though dependent on Rome, Agrippa's rule was characterized by honor for Israel. During his reign, the land was at peace and foreign rulers were not seen. He befriended the Sages and assigned them important administrative offices. He also advanced the country economically and built many buildings throughout the land.

The Greek inhabitants of the Holy Land took a very hostile view of the revival of the Jewish community with the dedicated leadership of Agrippa and they decided to assassinate him. When he visited Caesarea, they poisoned his cup. After five days of terrible agony, Agrippa died.

Emperor Claudius of Rome eventually appointed the dead king's son, Agrippa II, to succeed his slain father. However, the real power was now in the hands of the Roman commissioners and procurators. In general, this last, weak ruler of Judea remained aloof and did nothing to help his brethren.

During the period of the last procurators, there were three Jewish factions in Jerusalem. They were not organized parties in the modern sense; rather, they represented three general viewpoints about

Rival Factions

how to deal with the Romans. The three were: those who were ready for open warfare to overthrow Roman domination (Zealots); moderates who supported the goals of the Zealots but hoped to avoid violent confrontation if at all possible; and those loyal to Rome (Friends of Rome).

The groups had vastly different goals and the cleavage between the extremes continued to widen until it resulted in civil war. The actions of various factions were responsible for harming Jewish interests and hastening the Destruction.

The Friends of Rome became numerous and strong after the death of Agrippa I, when Claudius removed control of the Temple and its treasury from loyal Jews and gave it first to Herod, Agrippa's brother, and then to Agrippa II, who was a sympathizer of the Sadducees. His appointees used their position in the Temple to gain control over the people and dislodge the Sages whom Agrippa I had placed in most positions of power. The Friends of Rome attracted Sadducees — particularly those who were so assimilated that they were barely recognizable as Jews, and corrupt High Priests, whose lust for money and power blinded them to any other consideration.

Unsurprisingly, most Jews tended to be moderates, hoping to remain loyal to the Torah without provoking war with the powerful and murderous Roman army. The Zealots, however, grew in numbers and influence as the years went by and more Jews came to the conclusion that there was no choice but to fight. They came to this decision reluctantly, because of the increasing oppression of the greedy Roman procurators and their Sadducean allies. As usually happens in the case of aggressive groups like the Zealots, hotheads and criminals joined their ranks. The violent members of the Zealots were called *Biryonim* and the criminals were called *Sicarii*.

M urder became commonplace in the streets of Judea and Jerusalem.

The killing opened the way for other lawless people to take the law

Land of Lawlessness
into their own hands, killing and plundering innocent people at will. The *Biryonim* and *Sicarii* hoodlums would excuse their crimes by inventing political reasons and making it seem as though they were resisting Rome, but their true motive was greed.

Lawlessness and violence stalked the streets of Jerusalem. In the so-called Greek cities along the coast, the non-Jewish residents looked down at the hapless Jews. In Caesarea, the Greeks even tried to strip the Jews of the city's citizenship and claimed that they were aliens. This conflict went on for a few years and ultimately the case was brought before Emperor Nero.

The decision of Nero, who was a great admirer of the Greeks and their culture, was predictable enough. He declared that the Syrian-Greek inhabitants of Caesarea were its rulers and the Jews living there had the status of aliens. Nero's verdict was one of the last causes that kindled the flames of revolt against Roman oppression.

Nero's decision regarding Caesarea was rendered during the tenure of Gessius Florus, the last procurator, who was appointed by Nero in 64 CE (3824). About Florus, Josephus Flavius, the contemporary Jewish historian of the period,[1] says:

> Though Albinus (the previous high commissioner) was a corrupt man, his successor Florus made him seem a model of righteousness by comparison. For Albinus attempted to hide his misdeeds as much as possible, while Florus boasted publicly about his abominations, acting like a hangman. He did not recoil from any robbery or murder, any evil or corruption. No one could match him as a liar and manipulator. It was beneath his dignity to rob individual persons; he plundered cities and destroyed entire communities. It was as if he had officially declared that robbery was legal, provided he was given a goodly share of the loot. To satisfy his greed,

---

1. He lived from approximately 3800-3860 (40-100 CE). When the war against Rome broke out, Josephus was appointed commander in the Galilee. After he was captured by the Romans, Josephus managed to gain the favor of the Roman general Vespasian, at whose instruction he would go before the walls of Jerusalem, exhorting the inhabitants to surrender. When Vespasian was proclaimed emperor, he freed Josephus. In gratitude, Josephus assumed Vespasian's family name Flavius.

he devastated entire districts; there were many who left their homeland and fled to other countries.

Florus outdid all his predecessors in criminal greed and cruelty. When he went to extremes, he thought of ways to cover up the traces of his crimes. In this he found no more effective method than to force the Jews into desperate acts of open defiance and revolt. He knew that whenever the Jews resisted — no matter how great the provocation — they would always be judged by the Romans as the guilty party. Under the pretext of "suppressing the uprisings," Florus felt free to do whatever he pleased, even when there was no disturbance.

To the great disappointment of the Jews, their own king, Agrippa II, sided with Florus and the Romans and not with them. Ultimately the people were so incensed by the endless injustices perpetrated against them, that they drove the hated Florus and his puppet king Agrippa from Jerusalem. Additionally, they now desired to remove the Sadducees and other assimilationists from their positions of influence in public life and particularly from the Temple service.

War in Jerusalem

But the Sadducees were still active. Though only a minority party, they would not give up their attempts to regain power even though at this time such attempts carried the seeds of civil war and national disaster.

Agrippa was not interested in the welfare of his subjects; his sole concern was to protect his power base and personal interests. He prevailed upon Cestius Gallus, the Roman governor in Antioch, to assemble his legions to march upon Jerusalem and subdue the rebels.[1]

Gallus and his army entered Jerusalem, but they did not succeed in dislodging the Jewish defenders from their fortified positions within the city. Realizing that his army was not powerful enough to conquer such an extensive and fortified area, Gallus withdrew. While he was retreating through the valley of Beis Choron, Jewish soldiers attacked from the two hills overlooking the valley and killed close to 6,000 of his men.

---

1. One should note that the incident of Kamtza and Bar Kamtza (*Gittin* 55b-56a) occurred while Nero reigned and resulted in the emperor himself sending legions to destroy the Temple. The Talmudic account of that incident is found on p. 163.

Gallus waited till sundown. Then, under cover of night, he fled with his remaining soldiers to the coastal plain, leaving behind great quantities of arms and equipment. The Jews of Jerusalem excitedly brought the spoils of war into the city and distributed them among the defenders. They well knew that the Romans would return with a much bigger army to avenge the embarrassing defeat and to reestablish their rule over Judea and all of the Land.

On the eighth day of Cheshvan, 66 CE (3827), the victors, laden with their spoils, returned triumphantly to Jerusalem. Now nothing stood in the way of establishing a Jewish government. With the removal of Florus and the defeat of Cestius Gallus, Roman authority over Judea had been removed and a Jewish government took its place. The *Nasi* of the Sanhedrin, Rabban Shimon ben Gamliel, was one of its leaders.

So great was the joy over the restoration of political independence after such long and bitter years of foreign oppression that new coins were minted which bore the inscription: "Freedom of Jerusalem."

These days of independence were not destined to last. The Divine decree of Jerusalem's Destruction still stood. The city had become filled with groundless hatred of Jew against Jew. Because of that hatred, the Destruction had been decreed, and the guilty people had not repented their sin. A very few years later the fearful end came — the Temple was burned to the ground; the Land was ruined; and its population was decimated and sent into the exile that has not yet ended.

We have seen how the spirit of unity prevailed in Jerusalem after its defenders defeated Cestius Gallus. Later, however, differences of opinion as to how to meet the impending danger sharpened, leading to conflict and outright hatred. This evil gnawed at the very soul of the

Uncontrolled Factionalism

people, destroying all that was good and promising among them.

In the camp of the Zealots, the extremists gained the upper hand. In the camp of the moderates, the Sadducees and the Friends of Rome gained fresh influence. Seeing how powerful the Romans now were, they insisted on making peace with them and reestablishing the old order.

Thus it was that in beleaguered Jerusalem, instead of combining all forces and resources to fight the common enemy, the various parties spent their strength in cruel civil wars.

When Yochanan of Gush Chalav arrived in Jerusalem, he described the heroic stand of the Galileans and proclaimed that the Romans would never conquer the strongly fortified city of Jerusalem, "even if they made themselves eagles' wings." He thus stirred the Jerusalemites with new hope in their ultimate victory.

There were other elements whose political views were mixed with criminal tendencies, including the *Sicarii* who, under the pretext of fighting the influence of the rich Friends of Rome, robbed them of their property. Rabban Shimon ben Gamliel and other friends of the defenders of Jerusalem pleaded with the Zealots to curb the extremists and stop the robberies of the *Sicarii* in order to avoid a civil war between the moderate and the extreme nationalists. But things had already gone too far; Rabban Shimon and his colleagues pleaded in vain.

The weakening of the revolutionary government gave the Friends of Rome their chance. Led by Chanan ben Chanan, they drove the Zealots from the inner city, though not from the fortified walls of the Temple Mount. Seeing that the Friends of Rome were in control of the city, Yochanan of Gush Chalav joined and became leader of the Zealots in the Temple area. Rabban Shimon ben Gamliel, realizing that the civil war had gotten completely out of control, thus precluding victory in the battle against the Romans, withdrew altogether from the political scene.

The forces of Chanan ben Chanan and the moderates who controlled the city laid siege to the Temple Mount where the Zealots were isolated. The beleaguered Zealots now did an incredible thing: they invited the Edomites to come to their aid. The Edomites lived in the south of the land and were known to be marauders who lived by the sword. They gladly accepted the invitation to come into the big city with their weapons, anticipating rich plunder. But Chanan ben Chanan closed the city gates and they could not enter. The Edomites therefore encamped their thousands outside the city and awaited their opportunity.

An Invitation to Foreigners

One stormy night, the Zealots surprised the unsuspecting guards and overcame them. They broke open the heavy bars that secured the gates and admitted their Edomite allies into the city. The soldiers of the moderate party were now trapped from both sides: from the direction of the Temple Mount they were confronted by the Zealots, and from the rear the Edomites attacked them.

The outcome was inevitable. The moderates lost and many of them were killed in the fighting. The Zealots and Edomites killed the moderate leaders and cruelly murdered peaceful citizens whom they merely suspected of loyalty to the Romans. Jerusalem was filled with fear and horror at the terrible things perpetuated that day by the fanatic elements of the Zealots and their Edomite cohorts.

Finally, sated with plunder and murder, the Edomites left the city, and Jerusalem came under the control of the Zealots and their leaders, Yochanan of Gush Chalav and Elazar ben Shimon.

The Friends of Rome did not reconcile themselves to the rule of the Zealots. Looking for an ally to help them defeat the Zealots, they turned to Shimon bar Giora, who was known for his personal hatred of Yochanan of Gush Chalav, to come to their aid.

This invitation turned out to be the last act in the drama that led to the destruction of Jerusalem. Shimon bar Giora was leader of a band of violent people who had been uprooted from their normal way of life by the years of war and lawlessness. For a time, he and his men were headquartered in Masada where they often cooperated with the Zealots led by Elazar ben Yair. Later, Shimon left Masada and made his camp elsewhere. From his new headquarters his men fought the Edomites, and attacked helpless towns and villages in order to plunder whatever they wanted. Their devotion was only to their leader, who held sway over them through the power of his tongue and the promise of loot.

The arrival of Shimon bar Giora and his men was the signal for the outbreak of civil strife that in intensity and cruelty surpassed all that had gone on before in the bleeding city. Ruthless battles were fought in the streets of Jerusalem between the forces of Yochanan of Gush Chalav, who had taken up positions on the Temple Mount, and the forces of Shimon bar Giora, who were entrenched in the Lower City.

The residents of Jerusalem, led by three wealthy citizens — Ben Tzitzis HaKsas, Nakdimon ben Gurion, and Ben Kalba Savua — who were disciples of Rabban Yochanan ben Zakkai, had for months stored provisions in anticipation of the Roman siege. The three men had filled vast warehouses with enough flour, oil and wood to help their fellow Jews survive an extended siege.[1] Now these storehouses were set on fire by Shimon bar Giora's men, in order to force the people into an immediate armed confrontation with the Romans.

1. See p. 168.

V espasian, after conquering the entire country around Jerusalem, had interrupted his campaign to capture the city upon learning that Nero had died. He awaited news of the struggle for succession to Nero's throne, but he could afford to be patient because he knew of the internal strife in Jerusalem, by which the Jews were weakening themselves.

Lost Opportunity

Unlike the situation in earlier times, the Roman Senate no longer had the power to enforce its choice of new emperor. Instead, the throne was seized by whichever aspirant had the most raw power. During the period of Vespasian's siege, the various Roman legions held the decisive influence. If an army was large enough and sufficiently loyal to its general, it simply proclaimed him emperor — and anyone choosing to contest the choice had to be ready for war.

During the pause in Vespasian's siege, three emperors were chosen in quick succession: Galba ruled from June 9, 68 to January 15, 69, when Otho had him murdered and proclaimed himself emperor. However, Vitellius' armies had declared for him and civil war broke out. Otho's forces were defeated and he committed suicide on April 15, 69. In July 69, Vespasian's troops in Judea declared for him, and they were joined by all the legions in the East. Vespasian expected that with the help of his powerful army, he would prevail in the end. To further this ambition, he planned to take his troops to fight Vitellius' legions and Vitellius was killed on December 22, 69 CE (3829).

This was an opportune moment for the Jews to come to an understanding with Vespasian under relatively easy terms, but it was not done. Due to the bloody warfare in Jerusalem, there were no men of stature and authority who were willing to listen to the advice of the Sages and make peace with the Romans. The evil of senseless hatred had blinded the people to wise counsel.

T he two leading Torah personalities at the end of the Second Temple period were Rabban Yochanan ben Zakkai, dean of the Sanhedrin, and Rabban Shimon ben Gamliel, of the family of Hillel, the *Nasi* (President). Of the two, the undisputed leader was Rabban Yochanan

Rabban Yochanan ben Zakkai — The Leading Sage

ben Zakkai. He counteracted every attempt of the Sadducees to tamper with the Halachah. The importance of his success in this defense of the Torah is highlighted by the fact that the Sages proclaimed as minor holidays the occasions when

Rabban Yochanan defeated his Sadducean opponents. The Sages forbade fasting on those days.

Rabban Shimon ben Gamliel, in his capacity as *Nasi*, participated in the central government. The Sages, led by Rabban Yochanan and Rabban Shimon, generally supported the political line of the more moderate Zealots in their resistance to Rome. However, they realized that now, because of the internal conflicts and wars, there was no chance of withstanding the Romans.

The situation in strife-torn Jerusalem was becoming more intolerable day by day. The extremists and bar Giora's violent camp imposed their will upon the population. As already mentioned, they had set fire to the storehouses which the wealthy followers of Rabban Yochanan ben Zakkai had prepared to feed the people. Rabban Yochanan now decided to do something daring and drastic at the risk of his life. He would leave Jerusalem and proceed to Vespasian's headquarters in Gofna, north of Jerusalem. The Talmud (*Gittin* 56a,b) relates this fateful event in detail:

Abba Sikra, a leader of the bandits who attached themselves to the Zealots, was a nephew of Rabban Yochanan ben Zakkai. Rabban Yochanan requested that Abba Sikra visit him in secret. When Abba Sikra came, Rabban Yochanan demanded of him, "How much longer will you starve the people to death?" Abba Sikra answered, "What can I do? As soon as I will complain, my cohorts will kill me." Said Rabban Yochanan, "Help me get out of the city; perhaps some small salvation will result from it." Abba Sikra advised his uncle to act as if he were deathly ill, and a few days later it would be made known that he had died. (Only for the burial of the dead did the extremists open the city gates; thus, by feigning death Rabban Yochanan could be carried out of the city.) Rabban Yochanan ben Zakkai accepted his nephew's advice. After he "died," two of his disciples, Rabbi Eliezer and Rabbi Yehoshua, carried the casket with their teacher in it to the outskirts of the city.

When Rabban Yochanan ben Zakkai appeared before Vespasian he greeted him, saying, "Peace upon you, O Emperor!" Vespasian replied, "You have forfeited your life for two reasons; one, because you called me Emperor, which I am not; and two, if I am Emperor, why did you not come before?" Rabban Yochanan ben Zakkai answered him, "As for what you said, that you are not an emperor — you will be one in the future, because if you were not a monarch, Jerusalem could not fall into your hands, as it is written: *And the Lebanon will fall through a mighty one* (Isaiah 10:34); *a mighty one* refers to a king, and *Lebanon* refers to the Holy Temple. As to your second question, I could not come sooner

because the *Biryonim* [i.e. the violent element] would not permit me to leave Jerusalem."

As they spoke, a messenger arrived and announced to Vespasian that he had been proclaimed Emperor.

Upon hearing the news, Vespasian decided to depart at once, and appointed another general to complete the conquest of Jerusalem.

First, however, Vespasian showed his respect for, and gratitude to, Rabban Yochanan by asking him to request whatever he wished. He made three requests:

(a) תֵּן לִי יַבְנֶה וַחֲכָמֶיהָ, *"Give me Yavneh and its Sages."* The study of the Torah must be maintained; without it, the future of Jewish life and of the Jews themselves would be doomed.

(b) He asked that the family and dynasty of Rabban Shimon ben Gamliel should not come to harm. This would insure the continued proper leadership of the nation.

(c) He asked Vespasian to provide a physician for the *tzaddik* of the generation, Rabbi Tzadok, who for the past forty years had been fasting and praying that Jerusalem and the Temple should be spared from destruction.

Vespasian kept his promise, leaving the necessary instructions. He then turned the command of his army over to his son, Titus, in order to assume the role of Emperor over the mightiest empire on earth in its new capital city, Rome — while Rabban Yochanan ben Zakkai bore the crown of leadership of the authentic spiritual empire on earth, in its new capital city, Yavneh. There, he and his disciples prayed and studied, and waited in trepidation for news from Jerusalem.

Rabban Yochanan ben Zakkai's three requests must have seemed foolish in the eyes of the gentile general who probably expected to be asked for wealth and power. But in truth, their value was of vital importance for the future of the Jewish people whose Land would be taken from them and whose Sanctuary would soon be destroyed. Rabban Yochanan knew that Israel's physical power was doomed; he looked ahead to the spiritual well-being of the people because he knew that only through Torah are we a nation — and through Torah the nation would survive.

There were some among the Sages who felt that Rabban Yochanan should have asked that Jerusalem be spared completely. Rabban Yochanan felt, however, that if he had requested so much, Vespasian would have given him nothing.

III. Destruction

As mentioned, before going to Rome to accept his new crown, Vespasian had named his son, Titus, to succeed him as commander of the siege against Jerusalem. Titus' words and actions represent the unique arrogance and ruthlessness of the entire Roman nation, the seed

Titus' March of the proud and bloodthirsty Esau. The Talmud (*Gittin* 56b) relates that Titus began his assault on Jerusalem with an insolent declaration of war — not merely against the Jews — but against the Almighty, God of Israel, Himself. Titus shouted out the verse from Scripture: אֵי אֱלֹקֵימוֹ צוּר חָסָיוּ בוֹ, *Where is their God, the Rock in Whom they have trusted?* (*Deuteronomy* 32:37; see ArtScroll's *The Complete Tishah B'Av Service*, Kinnah 16, p. 228).

Before Passover of the year 70 CE (3830), Titus marched on Jerusalem with an army of some 80,000 soldiers. Even now, with the Roman army in full view, the defenders of the city did not bury their differences and make a common front against the outside enemy.

The division of the warring camps was as follows: The Sadducees, aided by Shimon bar Giora and his band, held the Lower City, while the Zealots were entrenched on the Temple Mount. However, there was no peace even within the Zealot camp, for a moderate faction, led by Elazar ben Shimon, opposed the stand of the extreme patriots, who were led by Yochanan of Gush Chalav. There were open clashes between the two factions, with the result that the moderates concentrated their forces within the Temple itself, and the extremists surrounded them outside, on the Temple Mount. Yochanan, who led the extreme Zealots, thus found himself and his men in the middle, between Elazar within the Temple grounds and the Sadducees in the city.

In honor of Passover, many Jews ignored the danger and made their pilgrimage to Jerusalem, some of them arriving just ahead of the marching Roman army. In an act of great generosity and dedication to the Temple service, the men of Elazar ben Shimon opened the gates of the Temple so that the visitors could offer their Passover sacrifice. The men of Yochanan of Gush Chalav also entered, seemingly for the same sacred purpose, but as soon as they were inside they drew their swords which they had hidden inside their garments and threatened their opponents.

Elazar and his men wanted to avoid panic and bloodshed among the masses of Jews assembled in the Temple courts and offered no resistance. As a result of their shameful exploitation of the Passover commandment and Elazar's benevolence, Yochanan and his followers now had control over the entire Temple area, but the two groups remained in fierce opposition to one another.

The Romans did not open their attack during the festival, for they feared that despite their overwhelming numbers, they would not conquer the city. Their hope was that the peace party of the Sadducees would gain the upper hand over the Zealots and hand over the city.

The bombardment of the walls of Jerusalem began one day after the festival. Now that they stood face to face with the real enemy and the sound of war was heard throughout Jerusalem, the parties at last drew together in a common defense of their beloved city. Yochanan and his men defended the city's eastern part and Shimon bar Giora's party was in charge of its northern, southern and western parts.

This belated unity joined some 20,000 men — moderates and extremists, residents and pilgrims — into one army of brothers, whose battle for Jerusalem and the Holy Temple constitutes one of the most heroic and tragic chapters in the long history of our people.

T he Romans now launched a massive assault on the northern wall. Their battering rams pounded against it incessantly, and the impact of the rocks hurled by their catapults shook the city.

The defenders fought heroically and furiously. From atop the city's

The Battle for the City

walls, they sprayed the Romans with a rain of stones and burning torches. From time to time they made surprise attacks beyond the city walls and fought the enemy face to face, setting his war machines on fire. This phase of the war lasted fifteen days. On the seventh day of Iyar the enemy breached the third outer wall and after fierce fighting succeeded in breaching the second wall as well. The new, outer section of Jerusalem was now in the hands of the Romans. All the houses were burned to the ground and preparations were made for the attack on the Old City, the heart of Jerusalem.

Following the fall of the outer section, Yochanan of Gush Chalav withdrew and entrenched himself and his army in the Temple area, while Shimon bar Giora took over the defense of the Upper City. When Titus saw that it would not be easy to overcome the resistance of Jews

who were well fortified in their positions and who fought like lions, he tried to achieve his aim by peaceful, but treacherous, means.

At his request, Josephus approached the wall with a group of soldiers and called on the Jews to surrender, since they had no chance of winning. The reply was a shower of stones and shouts of contempt. Josephus was forced to make a humiliating dash for his life.

Now the battle for the Old City began in earnest. The Roman army had three objectives: the Temple Mount in the east, the Upper City in the west and the Lower City in the south. The Old City was protected on its north by two powerful fortifications, the Antonia Fortress that flanked the Temple Mount, and Herod's palace with its three towers that flanked the Upper City in the northwest. The Temple Mount was separated from the Upper City by a deep valley.

Titus' strategy was to first conquer the Antonia Fortress in order to occupy the Temple area, and from there to conquer the Upper City. At the end of the month of Iyar, after piling up a huge ramp of earth close to the wall and placing his war machines on it, he gave the signal for attack. But Yochanan of Gush Chalav and his men had anticipated Titus' battle plan. Under the ramp whose upper slope supported the tall wooden tower with its battering ram, Yochanan's men dug a tunnel and filled it with wood and tar which they ignited. The flames broke through to the surface causing the ramp to collapse. The catapults and battering rams fell into the flames and were totally destroyed.

W hen Titus saw that he could not subdue the defenders by force, he decided to conquer them through starvation. He commanded his soldiers to erect a stone fence and seal all the city's exits. Guards watched the fence day and night. Now it became impossible for anyone to leave the city secretly to bring in food. Jews who tried to smuggle their way out were caught and nailed to the cross in full view of those on the inside.

Victory Through Famine

A terrible hunger spread throughout the beleaguered city. All the dire prophecies of the Torah became fulfilled among the people of Jerusalem. Josephus writes:

> The roofs were filled with women and small children expiring from hunger, and the corpses of old men were piled in the streets. Youths swollen with hunger wandered like shadows in the market place until they collapsed. No one

mourned the dead, because hunger had deadened all feeling. Those who fell to the ground turned their eyes for the last time to the Temple and beheld the defenders still fighting and holding out (*The Jewish Wars*, 5:10).

Titus saw that even famine could not break the spirit of the defenders. He decided therefore to take the Antonia Fortress by direct assault. In order to build the framework for four earthen ramps he cut down all the trees around Jerusalem, and the mountain slopes became bare and desolate. The ramps were built in the month of Sivan; by then, hunger had so weakened the defenders that they no longer had the strength to attack the enemy and his machines as they had done in the past.

At the end of Sivan, the Romans began to batter the walls of Antonia and in the beginning of the month of Tammuz they breached them and conquered the fortress. On the seventeenth of Tammuz, the walls of Jerusalem were breached.

The Walls Are Breached During the many weeks of fighting and siege, the *Kohanim* in the Temple had persevered in their service. Even the stones and arrows that were hurled into the very courts of the Sanctuary did not deter them from carrying out their appointed task. But on the seventeenth of Tammuz, there was not a single lamb left for the daily sacrifice. The Altar of God was idle.

Titus ordered that the Antonia Fortress, which adjoined the Temple Mount on the northern edge of the Old City, be razed to the ground. With the fortress out of the way, Titus' army now had a wide-open approach for an assault on the Temple Mount. It did not take long before the Mount's walls were broken through.

During those days, famine took a terrible toll in Jerusalem. People died in droves. Those who were alive fought each other tooth and nail for anything, even leather and straw, that for a moment could still the unbearable pangs of hunger. *The tongue of the suckling cleaves to its palate for thirst; young children beg for bread, no one extends it to them* (*Lamentations* 4:4).

The prediction which Moses had prophesied in the name of God was now a reality: *The man who is tender among you and very delicate, his*

eye will be evil against his brother and the wife of his heart and against his children who are still left to him (Deuteronomy 28:54). The Talmud tells of a mother who ate the flesh of her dead son, as it is foretold in the Torah: *And you will eat the flesh of your sons, and the flesh of your daughters you will consume (Leviticus 26:29).*

Titus, who knew the situation in the beleaguered city, considered the time ripe for another attempt at persuasion. Once again he sent his spokesman, Josephus, hoping that his eloquence would influence his fellow Jews. Josephus presented his case as if his main concern was to save the Temple from certain destruction and pleaded with them to end their resistance. The reaction of the defenders was the same as before: they were resolved not to surrender the Holy Temple into the hands of aliens, still believing that God would come to their aid.

F or more than two weeks, fierce battles were waged in the Temple area. Trying to prevent the penetration of the enemy into the Temple Courtyard at all costs, the defenders took a desperate step — they set fire to the halls that had connected the Antonia Fortress and the

The Temple Destroyed

Temple. Many Roman soldiers were trapped and killed as they were advancing through the halls to attack the Temple.

On the eighth day of Av, the Romans approached the very walls and gates of the Temple Courtyard and attempted to break through. They had finished building their ramps and towers, their battering ram was now in position, and with it they hammered day and night against the wall, but not a single stone moved from its place. They then tried to undermine one of the Temple gates by digging and removing its foundation stones — but the gate stood firm as before. They next put up ladders against the wall and climbed to the top. But the moment they reached the highest rung the defenders pushed the ladders back, and the invaders fell to their death.

It seemed as if the Temple itself was fighting the Romans. Even the stones and arrows which they now catapulted over the wall did not make its defenders surrender. The enemy therefore set fire to the chambers adjoining the Temple. When the defenders saw to their horror that flames were licking the walls of the Temple, "their strength and their heart failed them and they stood in panic and no one tried to extinguish the flames" (Josephus). The Romans tried to exploit the

momentary dread of the Jews and rushed to the Temple. But the defenders rallied and fought them off.

The last battle took place on the ninth day of the month of Av in the morning hours. The adjoining halls had been burned, but the Sanctuary itself and its courtyards were still intact. The defenders were starved and exhausted from weeks of heavy fighting and severely outnumbered. But their love for the Temple poured new strength into their weary bodies and tired hearts, and again and again they lifted their weapons and beat the Romans back, performing deeds of incredible heroism until the last moment.

But even the most heroic resistance could not prevail after God had withdrawn His Presence from the Temple. One Roman soldier rushed to the northern chambers of the Temple. Hoisted on the shoulders of another, he reached a window and threw a firebrand into the Temple. The fire spread rapidly in all directions and before long the Temple was engulfed in flames. A piercing cry of woe came from the lips of the Jews. They tried desperately to extinguish the flames, even running into them. But it was as if the fire had come down from Heaven; nothing could put it out.

The rest of that day and into the next, the tenth day of Av, the flames rose to the very heavens, accompanied by the cries of the people of Jerusalem who saw in the loss of the Temple the loss of the spiritual content of their lives. Many could not endure the sight and cast themselves into the fire, preferring to die together with the House of God than to live without it.

When the Romans saw the Temple aflame, they rushed into it like madmen, plundering whatever they could get their hands on. The Jews whom they met they slew mercilessly, sparing neither young nor old. The number of those slain was enormous, until the very earth of the Temple Mount was covered with their bodies. The shrieks and groans of the wounded and dying, the roar of the hungry flames, the thunder of the lofty walls and turrets as they crashed to the ground reached the ears of the starved survivors in the Upper City as they watched the spectacle in horror.

Before the fire consumed the interior of the Temple, Titus and his men entered the Holy of Holies. The Talmud (*Gittin* 56b) relates that when Titus entered the Holy Temple he cursed and blasphemed the God of Israel. He unrolled a holy Torah scroll and committed unspeakable acts upon it. He then unsheathed his sword (already bloodied with the blood of countless Jewish victims) and slashed the פָּרוֹכֶת, *Curtain* (that separated the Sanctuary from the Holy of Holies),

to shreds. A miracle occurred and blood began to flow from the curtain. This blood was a Divine sign that God was suffering, as it were, over His people's tragic plight. The wicked Titus, however, interpreted it as a sign that he had slain God Himself.[1]

After they robbed the holy golden vessels, the Romans saw to it that the fire would consume whatever was still standing. Only one wall remained — the Western Wall of the Temple Mount, the *Kosel Ma'aravi* — and from there the Presence of God has never departed.[2]

The Rest of the City Destroyed

After the Destruction of the Temple, the Upper City under the command of Shimon bar Giora was still holding its own. Yochanan of Gush Chalav, the defeated commander of the Lower City and the Temple area, succeeded in escaping from the hands of the Roman soldiers through one of the tunnels of the Temple Mount and joined the defense forces of the Upper City. With the Temple lost, there was not much reason to continue the fight with the Romans. The defenders announced their readiness to surrender, provided they would be allowed to leave the city with their weapons. But Titus would not agree. Standing on the Temple Mount near the bridge that led to the Upper City, he addressed them as follows:

> You have come today to speak to me. What do you have left to save, after your Temple is lost to you? In whom do you still trust? Your people — slain by the sword. Your Temple — ruin and desolation. Your city — trodden under my feet. Even your very lives and souls are in my hands. If you will

---

1. As Titus sailed home for a triumphant celebration in Rome, a storm arose and great waves threatened to sink his ship. He declared, "It seems to me that the power of this God of the Jews extends only over the sea. He drowned Pharaoh at sea, He drowned Sisra at sea — and now He seeks to drown me at sea! If He truly is mighty, let Him do battle with me on dry land!"

A Heavenly Voice declared, "Wicked man, descendant of the wicked Esau! There exists in My world a tiny insect known as a *yitosh*. It shall do battle with you on dry land."

After Titus reached land, the insect entered his nostrils. For seven years it buzzed inside his brain, causing him great anguish. As he lay near death, Titus issued final instructions, "After I die, cremate my body and scatter my ashes upon the seven seas so that the God of the Jews will not be able to bring me to judgment."

It was to Titus that David alluded when he declared, *How long, O God, will the tormentor revile? Shall the foe blaspheme Your Name forever?* (Psalms 74:10). Even at the brink of death, this despicable soul did not desist from his blasphemy (see *Maharsha* to *Gittin* 56b; see also ArtScroll's *The Complete Tishah B'Av Service*, *Kinnah* 16, pg. 228).

2. See p. 81.

lay down your arms and surrender to me, I will let you stay alive (*The Jewish Wars* 6:6).

The defenders chose not to fall into the merciless hands of Titus and his army and rejected his offer. Instead, they continued their preparations for defense, despite their sufferings from hunger. Yochanan and Shimon and their followers took up positions in Herod's palace, and the other defenders in other parts of the Upper City.

Before their impending assault on the Upper City, the Roman soldiers went through the streets of the Lower City on a rampage of sword, fire and destruction. No house was spared. They burned the Acra Fortress and the part of the city called the Ophel on the southeastern slopes of the Temple Mount. The houses filled with dead victims of starvation were set afire.

The Upper City was well-fortified and Titus was again forced to build ramps, bulwarks and towers to bring his war machines into effective range. On the seventh day of Elul, the battering rams and catapults began to pound at the walls. A few days later, the walls were breached; the Romans stormed the city, and another bloodbath began. Many Zealots tried to avoid capture by hiding in subterranean caves and tunnels. But their fate was no better. Some of them died of hunger, others committed suicide and a few who emerged to the surface were captured by the Romans. When Yochanan of Gush Chalav left his hideout, sick and broken by famine, he was taken alive. Shimon bar Giora tried to escape through one of Jerusalem's underground passages leading to the outside. But he, too, was taken alive. Both commanders were put in chains and brought to Rome, there to be displayed before the jeering masses at the triumphal procession in honor of Titus. Shimon died soon after, and Yochanan was imprisoned for life.

T he war was over. Jerusalem was almost totally destroyed. Hundreds of thousands of corpses, victims of the sword and of hunger, filled the desolate city which Scripture calls the "Crown of Beauty" and the "Joy of the Earth." But even worse was the fate of the tens of thousands

Ruthless Victors of its surviving sons and daughters. They moved like gaunt shadows in the squalor of the alleys and the gloom of the underground tunnels until they collapsed or were captured by the Romans.

At Titus' orders, all surviving fighters and those suspected of belonging to the Zealots were killed. The old and sick were next to be murdered. Young boys and girls were gathered on the Temple Mount and subjected to another selection. Those suspected of having in some way participated in the revolt against Rome were put to the sword. Those remaining were divided according to their physical appearance and strength: those over seventeen were sent as slave laborers to the copper mines of Egypt; younger ones were sold as slaves; the largest group was sent to the Greek cities on the coast, there to provide entertainment as the victims of gladiators and beasts in the bloodthirsty sports of the circus; and the last contingent, some 700 of the tallest, handsomest of Jerusalem's youths, was taken to Rome to be marched in Titus' victory parade.

During the days of the selection of the survivors, some 11,000 more perished of hunger.

According to Josephus, 1,100,000 Jews perished during the entire period of the siege and destruction, and 97,000 were taken captive.

Thousands of captives from all over the land were taken by boat to Rome and other cities of the empire to be sold on the slave markets. Knowing that what awaited them as slaves was a life of forced immorality and other sins, many chose to die instead.

The Talmud relates the story of one such group:

> Four hundred boys and girls were taken captive for a life of shame. When they realized what was in store for them, they asked: "If we drown in the sea, do we have a share in the Resurrection of the Dead?" The oldest among them answered: "It is written, 'Hashem said: I will bring back from Bashan, I will bring back from the depths of the sea' (Psalms 68:23) — this speaks of those who drown in the sea to save themselves from sin." As soon as the girls heard this they leaped into the sea. The boys reasoned that they should surely do so ... and they too leaped into the sea. Concerning such as these, Scripture says (Psalms 44:23): "For Your sake we are killed all day, we are accounted as sheep for the slaughter" (Gittin 57b).

The he Romans celebrated the victory over Judea with great pomp and ceremony. After attending some bestial festivities in Middle Eastern cities, during which thousands of Jewish captives were tortured and murdered savagely, Titus made his triumphal entry into Rome in the

The Triumphal March in Rome

year 71 CE (3831). The Senate had decided to hold a special victory parade in his honor. Hundreds of the most beautiful young prisoners of war were made to march in the streets of Rome, while bearing on their shoulders the holy vessels of gold that had been robbed from the Temple in Jerusalem. The vessels were kept in the Temple of Jupiter in Rome, until the year 455 CE (4215), when the mighty capital was invaded and sacked by the Vandals. They plundered the city of all its treasures, including the Temple vessels, which they took with them to their capital, probably Carthage, in North Africa. Since then the whereabouts of the Temple vessels remains unknown.

A reminder of the victory parade may still be seen on the Arch of Titus, which was built in Rome in honor of the great victory. It depicts in stone relief the scene of Jewish captives carrying the holy Menorah on their backs. Also displayed in the victory parade were the two heroes of the resistance, Shimon ben Giora and Yochanan of Gush Chalav. The climax of the celebration was held at the temple of Rome's idols, but by the time the celebrants arrived there, Shimon was dead. Yochanan spent the rest of his life in prison.

The importance that the Romans attached to their victory over the Jews may still be seen today in another way. They minted a special coin, one side of which shows the likeness of Emperor Vespasian's head, while the other side shows a woman whose hands are bound and who sits weeping under a palm tree. Behind her stands an armed Roman soldier. The inscription reads: "Iudea Capta" (Judea Is Captured).

❦　❦　❦

True, Judea was defeated by Rome, but the Jewish people were not. Just as the words of the prophecy, *And I will scatter you among the nations* (*Leviticus* 26:33), came true, so did the words of consolation: *And I will remember My covenant with Jacob, and also My covenant with Isaac, and also My covenant with Abraham will I remember; and I will remember the land* (ibid. v. 42). The Roman Empire was destroyed by wild and primitive tribes and disappeared from the stage of human affairs. Only history books and ancient ruins remind us of her former existence and power. But the Jewish people live on.

"Give me Yavneh and its Sages!" Nearly 2,000 years have passed since Rabban Yochanan ben Zakkai stood before the Roman emperor and asked of him, not the preservation of the state, because it was no longer a state of the Torah, and not the preservation of the Holy Temple, because Herod's name was associated with it — but the preservation of the Oral Law of the Torah, which depended on Yavneh and its Sages. He knew that if there was the Oral Law of the Torah, there would be a people of the Torah; and if there was a people of the Torah, there would be a land of the Torah; and in the future — a state of the Torah. With "Yavneh and its Sages" he saved everything.

Now this emperor, his people, his empire — Rome, the world power: where are they now? But the people of the Torah, the people of Yavneh and its Sages are alive and vigorous, each day awaiting the coming of the righteous Messiah ... The towering personality of Rabban Yochanan ben Zakkai is likewise kept vigorously alive in the hearts of the people of the Torah, and every new generation learns to love and revere him, just as they do "Moses and Aaron among His Kohanim, and Samuel among those who invoke His Name ..." (Psalms 99:6).

"Give me Yavneh and its Sages!" There is no people on earth that has a phrase expressing this kind of pride — "And who is like Your people, Israel, one nation on earth?" (from lyunim, "Studies," by R' Eliyahu Dessler).

Yavneh became the spiritual center of the people, and the secret of its survival. Rabban Yochanan ben Zakkai re-organized the Sanhedrin, which fixed the date of each new month and the time of each leap year. From Yavneh he sent instructions to the scattered Jewish communities in matters of law and observance, and Jews from all over the Diaspora turned to Yavneh for answers and advice. Without any formal declaration, Yavneh became the new center of the Jewish people.

From Jerusalem to Yavneh

God had caused the sun of Yavneh to rise before the sun of Jerusalem had set — it became a new national center and a new heart for all the scattered remnants of the Jewish people. Yavneh was the seat of the

great *yeshivah* for the study and teaching of Torah, and for prayer, which now took the place of the sacrifices in the Temple, as the prophet wrote: *Instead of oxen, we will offer the prayer of our lips* (Hosea 14:3).

Thus Yavneh embodied the means by which God preserves His people even during the darkest and most dangerous times of our long exile, until the time comes when He, in His mercy, will redeem His people and restore us to our Land, and our Holy Temple to Jerusalem — speedily, and in our days.

IV. The Destruction of Betar

> *Five tragic events occurred on the Ninth of Av . . . [the fourth calamity was] when the great city of Betar was conquered. In that city were tens of thousands of Jews led by a great king whom all of Israel and its Sages thought was the Messiah. The city fell to the Romans and all its inhabitants were killed; it was a catastrophe akin to the Temple's destruction (Rambam, Hilchos Taaniyos 5:3).*

The destruction of Betar took place some sixty-three years after the fall of the Second Temple (which occurred in 68 CE). The chain of events leading to the fall of Betar began in the year 117 CE when the governor of Syria, Hadrian, was declared Emperor of the Roman Empire.

Hadrian's Betrayal When he ascended the throne, it seemed as if Hadrian would be a friend of the Jews because he promised them religious freedom and tolerance. He even went so far as to promise to allow them to rebuild Jerusalem and to restore the Holy Temple and its service. Needless to say, these assurances sent the spirit of the Jew soaring. Many older people still remembered the Temple when it stood — and now, the crowning glory of the Jewish people was about to be restored.

Then, suddenly, Hadrian's policies and promises changed dramatically. What had begun as a benevolent reign became one of the most repressive and brutal regimes the Jews ever had to endure. Hadrian issued new orders: A city would indeed be built — but it would *not* be Jewish. A temple would indeed be erected — but for the worship of the

idol Jupiter. The hopes of the Jewish people were dashed to pieces and a wave of bitter disappointment and deep resentment swept through the nation.

The Roman historian Dio Cassius, who lived some one hundred years after the Bar Kochba revolt, states: "At Jerusalem, Hadrian founded a city in place of the one which had been razed to the ground, naming it Aelia Capitolina [Aelia in honor of his own name, Publius Aelius Hadrianus, and Capitolina in honor of Jupiter, whose temple in Rome was on the Capitolene hill]. At the site of the Temple, he erected a new temple to Jupiter. This brought on a war of no slight importance nor brief duration, for the Jews considered it intolerable that foreign peoples should be settled in their city and foreign temples built there" (*History of Rome*, ch. 69).

At this time, the Torah leadership in the Land of Israel was in the hands of the Sanhedrin which convened in Usha where it was re-established after the Romans forced the Sages to leave the city of Yavneh. At the head of this revived center of Torah leadership in Usha was Rabbi Akiva. The elder Sage was Rabbi Yehoshua ben Chananyah who was universally respected for his great piety and sagacity.

Hadrian's betrayal aroused in many Jews a desire for rebellion. Only Rabbi Yehoshua's quiet and clever words calmed them down. The Midrash relates:

> In the days of Rabbi Yehoshua ben Chananyah the wicked [Roman] government decreed that the Temple should be rebuilt. The Cuthites went and warned [the emperor]: "The king should know that after the rebellious city [Jerusalem] has been rebuilt and its fortifications repaired, [the Jews] will stop paying land-tax, head-tax, and tribute." He replied, "What can I do? I have already issued the decree." They told him, "Send them instructions either to change the site [of the Temple] or to make it five cubits larger or five cubits smaller. If you do this, they will of their own accord abandon the project."
>
> At that time the Jews were gathered in the Valley of Beis Rimon. When the orders arrived [from the emperor], the people started to weep and some wanted to revolt against the emperor. Said some of [the sages among] them, "Let a wise man come forward and pacify the people." Said [others], "Let Rabbi Yehoshua ben Chananyah stand up, for he is a master of Scripture."

[Rabbi Yehoshua] came and told [the following parable]: "Once a lion was devouring an animal and a bone stuck in its throat. The lion announced, 'To anyone who can remove [the bone from my throat] I will give a reward.' A long-billed Egyptian heron came and stuck its beak [into the lion's throat] and removed the bone. [The heron then said to the lion,] 'Give me my reward.' [The lion] replied, "Go and boast that you entered the lion's mouth in one piece and came out in one piece.'

"And so it is with us. Let us be satisfied that we entered into [dealings with] these people in peace and came out in peace."

The powerful influence of the great sage held back the people from open revolt — but only temporarily — because Hadrian now provoked the Jewish people in such a way that an uprising was inescapable. Hadrian issued a decree prohibiting the Jews from observing the fundamentals of their faith.

The commandments that the Roman chose to outlaw were precisely those that ensure the uniqueness of the Jewish people and protect them from assimilation. As his targets, Hadrian chose the commandments of Sabbath, circumcision, and family purity. The observance of these commandments is part of Judaism's very foundation. To protect them, the Jews were ready to revolt against Rome.

And so it came about that some fifty-five years after the Destruction (in about 123 C.E., 3883), the nation faced a situation in which resistance, no matter what the cost, was the only choice.

The Bar Kochba revolt — which lasted over nine years, and passed through four main phases — was the result.

T he first phase of the revolt began as a spontaneous movement, without previous planning and certainly without any political aims. Jews who did not wish to desecrate the Sabbath hid in caves and other secret places. The same alternative was chosen by those to whom a son

Bar Kochba had been born and who wished to circumcise him. The Roman officials often employed spies to inform them of such hiding places. When such a location was raided by the Romans soldiers, the occupants, who faced death, resisted with great courage and often with considerable success. Gradually, links were formed between the people who lived in these hiding places, so that if one

group was attacked, others could come to their assistance. Before long, the attacked also became attackers, striking out at the Roman troops.

During this phase, there emerged a leader of great personal strength and military genius. His name was Shimon bar Kosiba, but Rabbi Akiva changed his name to Bar Kochba ("son of a star"), an allusion to the verse, *A star shall go forth from Jacob* (*Numbers* 24:17). The "star" of that verse would be the Messiah, and Rabbi Akiva felt that Shimon bar Kosiba was great enough to be the promised redeemer. It is important to note that Rabbi Akiva *did not say* that Bar Kochba *already was* the Messiah — he said that Bar Kochba seemed to have the potential *to become* the Messiah if he would conduct himself properly and surrender himself to God's will. Tragically, Bar Kochba disappointed Rabbi Akiva and failed to live up to the Sages' lofty expectations.

Bar Kochba succeeded in organizing the many nests of resistance into regular companies, each led by a commander. With these forces, he gradually pushed the Roman troops out of one position after another. Approximately three years after the beginning of the revolt (126 C.E., 3886), Bar Kochba led his troops toward Jerusalem. The Holy City lay relatively open to attack, since its mighty fortifications had been demolished in the Destruction. The Romans withdrew to Caesarea.

There now began a period of independent Jewish sovereignty in *Eretz Yisrael*. The Talmud refers to it as, "The kingdom of Bar Kosiba, [which lasted for] two and a half years" (*Sanhedrin* 97b).

The Romans, who seem at first to have been unaware of the

The Kingdom of Bar Kosiba

seriousness of the situation, now awoke to the danger threatening them. As Dio Cassius writes, "At first, the Romans took no account of them. Soon, however, all Judea had been stirred up, and the Jews everywhere in the world were showing signs of disturbance, were gathering together, and were giving evidence of great hostility to the Romans ... Many outside nations, too, were joining them ... Then, indeed, Hadrian sent against them his best generals" (Dio Cassius, *History of Rome*, loc. cit.).

Just how seriously the Romans regarded the threat from Bar Kochba may be judged from the size of the forces that they now marshaled for a counterattack. Julius Severus was summoned from Britian to take command of the Roman army, and was joined at its head by the emperor himself. Some sixty years earlier, the emperor Vespasian had required

three legions for the conquest of Jerusalem. Now, in addition to the two legions already in the country (the Sixth and the Tenth), Hadrian brought in no less than six more legions, besides further detachments of cavalry and infantry.

T he Romans now began their counterattack. In spite of the enormous size of their army, they were unwilling to face Bar Kochba's troops in full battle. Instead, they proceeded slowly, attacking isolated localities and interfering with food supplies. The justification for this cautious

Jerusalem strategy was revealed on the one occasion when the Romans did not hold to it. Apparently, the Twenty-**Reoccupied** second Legion advanced too deeply and too quickly into Jewish territory. As a result, this legion was totally destroyed. It was never reconstituted, and forever after was omitted from the list of units in the Roman army.

Moving slowly and carefully, the Romans occupied most of the countryside surrounding the city and were now in a position to besiege Jerusalem (circa 128-129 C.E., 3888-3889). After a siege of approximately twelve months, they recaptured Jerusalem.

T he fall of Jerusalem did not end the revolt. Bar Kochba and most of his troops withdrew to Betar, where the fighting was to continue for some three and a half years. At first, the battle went well for Bar Kochba and his men, who performed amazing feats of bravery. Unfortunately,

Betar Bar Kochba himself became arrogant, attributing his victories to his own abilities. Eventually, he accepted a slanderous accusation of treachery against his uncle, the sage Rabbi Elazar HaModa'i, and killed him in a fit of rage. When Bar Kochba killed Rabbi Elazar, a voice from Heaven proclaimed, "You have killed Rabbi Elazar HaModa'i, the strong arm and right eye of Israel. Therefore, your own arm shall wither and your right eye shall grow dim." Thereupon, Betar fell to the Romans, and Bar Kochba was slain (*Talmud Yerushalmi, Taanis* 4:5).

It is noteworthy that the defeat of the revolt and its cause were similar. As we have seen, the people revolted because their religious observances were threatened or prohibited. Bar Kochba was successful until he turned

The Tishah B'Av Tragedies — The Destruction of the Second Temple [152]

against the Torah and the Sages for whom he had fought. Once that happened, his kingdom was doomed.

On the ninth of Av, 133 C.E. (3893), after a heroic struggle, Betar was overrun and conquered by the Romans. The feats of valor of the Jewish defenders exceeded even those of the defenders of Jerusalem during the Destruction. The number of the slain was enormous. "For seven years, the non-Jews fertilized their vineyards with no other fertilizer than the blood of the Jews [slain at Betar]" (*Gittin* 57a). "[The Romans] went on killing until their horses were submerged in blood to their nostrils. The [torrents of] blood [flowed so strongly that they] overturned [huge] boulders and streamed [twenty miles to the coast and] two miles out to sea" (*Talmud Yerushalmi, Taanis* 4:5).

Roman sources likewise report the enormous Jewish losses at Betar. Dio Cassius reports that close to one half million were killed, approximately one thousand settlements laid waste, and the entire country of Judea made desolate. The Romans viewed the fall of Betar as the completion of what they had begun with the Destruction of the Temple. In their first conquest of Jerusalem they had intended to break the spirit of the Jewish nation and in the conquest of Betar they thought they had finally destroyed the nation physically.

The cost to the Romans, too, was a heavy one. Dio Cassius ends his account of the Bar Kochba revolt with these words: "Many Romans perished in this war. In writing to the Senate, therefore, Hadrian did not employ the opening phrase commonly used by the emperors: "If you and your children are in good health, it is well. I and the legions are in good health" (*Dio Cassius, History of Rome*).

V. After Betar

The fall of Betar was not the end of Jewish suffering of that period. Actually, the worst suffering was only beginning. In their thirst for revenge, the Romans now murdered and destroyed on a countrywide scale. Every inhabited place that was suspected of

"The Generation of Shmad" having taken part in the revolt — and this meant, in practice, all of Judea — was razed to the ground. Within a short time, all organized communal life in Judea came to a halt.

Even this was not the end; for the Romans' plans to destroy Israel went

much further. The Romans realized that as long as the Jews continued to study and practice the Torah, they would remain indestructible. Hence, Rome began a systematic campaign to eliminate the observance of all the *mitzvos*. Above all, the teaching of Torah was forbidden because the Romans knew that in this lay the hidden strength of the nation. The term used in the Talmudic sources to describe this period is "the generation of *shmad* (annihilation)."

The extremity of this attempt to stamp out Torah life was matched by the punishments legislated against Jews who refused to knuckle under. A Midrash gives us a glimpse of the Romans' means of enforcement:

> ...for those who love Me and who observe My commandments (Exodus 20:6): Rabbi Nassan said, "This refers to those who live in the Land of Israel and give up their lives for the sake of the commandments."
>
> "Why are you being led out to be decapitated?"
> "Because I circumcised my son to be a Jew."
> "And you — why are you being led to the stake?"
> "Because I studied the Torah."
> "And why are you being taken to be crucified?"
> "Because I ate matzah."
> "Why are you being flogged with a whip?"
> "Because I took the lulav."

The viciousness and barbaric modes of torture and punishment employed by the Romans are illustrated in the words of the Talmudic Sage Rabbi Chiya bar Abba who declared: "If a person were to order me to give up my life for the Sanctification of His Name, I would be ready to do so provided they would kill me immediately. However, [the tortures administered] in the generation of *shmad* I could not endure. And what did they do in the generation of *shmad*? They would bring iron balls, heat them white hot in fire, and put them under [the victims'] armpits and [thus] take their lives. [Also] they would bring reed slivers, stick them under their fingernails and [thus] take their lives" (*Midrash Shir HaShirim* 2:8).

Hadrian outlawed the public teaching of the Torah; anyone who disobeyed this decree would receive the death penalty. One of the few who dared continue his teaching was Rabbi Akiva. Although he was warned by his friend, Papus ben Yehudah, Rabbi Akiva replied that the Jewish people without Torah was like a fish out of water. Even though we are in danger if we study Torah, we must take the risk because we cannot survive without it (*Berachos* 61b).

The Tishah B'Av Tragedies — The Destruction of the Second Temple [154]

So it was that the great Rabbi Akiva was arrested and put in prison. The day of his arrest is known: the fifth of Tishrei (see *Shulchan Aruch, Orach Chaim* 580:2). Rabbi Akiva was executed on Yom Kippur.

One after another, wherever the Romans could find them, they executed the Sages and their students. At the head of the list of the great scholars who lost their lives in this way were the "Ten Victims of the Government" (עֲשָׂרָה הֲרוּגֵי מַלְכוּת), the ten great martyrs whom we mention every Yom Kippur in a special prayer: *These I remember and I pour out my soul* (אֵלֶּה אֶזְכְּרָה וְנַפְשִׁי אֶשְׁפְּכָה), and again during the lamentations recited on Tishah B'Av, in a eulogy that begins, *Cedars of Lebanon, Giants of Torah* (אַרְזֵי הַלְבָנוֹן אַדִּירֵי הַתּוֹרָה); see *ArtScroll's Complete Tishah B'av Service,* for a detailed discussion of this tragedy).

עַל כֵּן לֹא יֹאכְלוּ בְנֵי יִשְׂרָאֵל אֶת גִּיד הַנָּשֶׁה אֲשֶׁר עַל כַּף הַיָּרֵךְ עַד הַיּוֹם הַזֶּה כִּי נָגַע בְּכַף יֶרֶךְ יַעֲקֹב בְּגִיד הַנָּשֶׁה

Therefore the Children of Israel are not to eat the displaced sinew on the hip-socket to this day because he [Esau's angel] struck Jacob's hip-socket on the displaced sinew (Genesis 32:33).

Yalkut Reuveni cites the holy *Zohar* which teaches that the word אֶת which appears before גִּיד הַנָּשֶׁה is superfluous and only serves as an allusion to a deeper concept. The word אֶת is composed of the initial letters of אָב תִּשְׁעָה, the ninth of Av, and this teaches us that whoever

Jacob's Struggle disregards the Torah prohibition and eats the displaced sinew is as if he eats on the fast day of Tishah B'av.

Rabbi Mordechai Gifter explains this with the words of the *Midrash* (*Bereishis Rabbah* 77:4, cited in *Ramban's* commentary) which understands the angel's act of wounding Jacob as an attempt to harm his descendants, the issue of his loins. Specifically, this threat was carried out in the most violent fashion in the generation of *shmad, the generation of religious persecution during the reign of Hadrian.*

The prohibition against eating the גִּיד הַנָּשֶׁה, *displaced sinew*, reminds the Jew that Esau's power over Israel was divinely ordained long ago, in the time of the Patriarchs, and we can only terminate this exile and suffering if we repent and return to God's ways. This is also the central theme conveyed by the fast day of Tishah B'Av. Thus, one who eats the

גִּיד הַנָּשֶׁה has sinned in a fashion tantamount to eating on Tishah B'Av.

Moreover, just as the day of Tishah B'Av ends on a note of consolation, so does the *mitzvah* of the *displaced sinew* provide Israel with hope and confidence for a brighter future. For, *Sefer HaChinuch* explains, just as Jacob was only slightly wounded by Esau's angel, but otherwise emerged victorious from the struggle, so will Jacob's descendants emerge from exile triumphant, with only superficial scars. Our bodies have been beaten but our spirit endures and grows stronger, bolstered by our unswerving faith in God, our Redeemer.

W hile the Romans were furiously bent on their ruthless campaign to obliterate the soul of the Jewish nation, they also decided to eradicate the enduring symbol of the Jewish soul — the Holy Temple. True, the Temple was burnt decades earlier, but here and there traces of

The Temple Mount Is Plowed Over

its glory still remained; massive stones, foundations, masonry. The Romans decided to lower and level the entire Mount and to plow it over into an ordinary field so that no hint of the Mount's former grandeur would remain. And it was not by chance that the day on which this final destruction occurred was Tishah B'Av.

> *And on the day that was designated for punishment, the wicked Turnus Rufus plowed up the area of the Temple and its surroundings in fulfillment of the verse (Jeremiah 26:18) "Zion will be plowed like a field"* (Rambam, Hilchos Taaniyos 5:3).

Rambam's Mishneh Torah is a concise, carefully worded book of law. Beautiful stylist though he was, *Rambam* did not indulge in rhetoric in *Mishneh Torah*. Yet, after cataloging the first four tragedies of the day that seemingly exists for the tragic, *Rambam* seems to allow a groan to escape from a heart overflowing with historic Jewish woe: "And on that day that was designated for punishment," he says. It is as if he is telling us that this final indignity, the plowing of the site where the Holy of Holies had once stood, where the pillar of the Divine Presence had rested, where Abraham was ready to offer Isaac if that were God's will, where all Israel ascended yearly, seasonally, daily to become saturated with holiness — that indignity could not have occurred on any other day but Tishah B'Av.

VI. Tishah B'Av in History

The plowing up of the Temple site was not the end. On Tishah B'Av, 1492, one of history's most infamous deadlines arrived. It was on that day that the Jews of Spain had to convert or leave the country — or face torture and the *auto-da-fe*. One Jew was spared from the decree

The Spanish Inquisition — Don Yitzchok Abarbanel, the famous Torah commentator and statesman who, as finance minister of Spain, had saved profligate Ferdinand and Isabella from bankruptcy. He was too valuable to be confronted with a choice that would have forced him to leave the country. But Abarbanel spurned the "generosity" of his monarchs. He tried to induce them to withdraw the decree. Failing, he led as many as 75,000 of his fellow Jews in a march that reached the Spanish border and crossed it on Tishah B'Av. The rabbis of the time permitted Jewish citizens to play music during the trek despite the laws forbidding such merriment during the three weeks leading up to Tishah B'Av. They ruled that it was a *mitzvah* to raise the spirits and celebrate the bravery of Jews who were ready to give up everything and to face a hostile world in hunger, disease, and poverty to sanctify God's Name.

Ferdinand and Isabella with their adviser and mentor, the fiendish Torquemada, thought they had broken Jewish spirits by forcing them out of the country that had given them "golden eras" of Torah, wealth, and influence. They thought that they had proved to the wandering Jews that the Guardian of Israel was asleep and slumbering. They were wrong. Abarbanel and his followers knew the lesson of the calendar. It was Tishah B'Av, *the day that was designated for punishment*. God was not asleep. In His wrath, He remembered His wayward children, for only God could sweep away centuries of Spanish Jewry on that tragedy-laden day.

World War I began on Tishah B'Av. To contemporary people, the tragedy of our century is the Holocaust of World War II — and, indeed, the words have still not been invented to describe the extent of its loss and suffering. But we Jews have a different measuring rod. The

Two World Wars and the Holocaust

Holy Temple was burned to the ground on the *tenth* of *Av*, but we commemorate the Ninth because it was then that the fires *were* set. It is impossible to minimize the events of World War II, but, viewing this tortured century in its historic sweep, we must conclude that the fires began to rage during World War I and that it was a pivotal event in shaping the trends of Jewish experience that are still unfolding.

The German sweep into Eastern Europe beginning in 1914 uprooted Jewish communities and demolished a laboriously built tradition that took centuries to shape. Enlightenment, Bolshevism, Socalism, Nationalism, and all the other Torah demands and authority surged through the breach in the wall of tradition.

Small wonder that the devastation of the war was no less spiritual than material. The diminished stature of the rabbinate, the extreme poverty afflicting communities and *yeshivos*, the Bolshevik Revolution and the clamping of an Iron Curtain around the three million Jews of Russia, the decay of German political and economic life and the emergence of an evil genius named Hitler — all these and more were legacies of World War I.

In a deeper sense, just as World War II was a legacy of World War I, World War I was a legacy of earlier times — because World War I broke out on Tishah B'Av, *the day that was designated for punishment*. The heartbreak and tribulation of this century, too, are manifestations of the historic Tishah B'Av.

We must never forget that just as Tishah B'Av is *the day designated for punishment* it is also the day which is destined to be transformed into one of celebration when the Temple will be rebuilt. When gazing upon utter ruin it is very difficult indeed to perceive any

A Final Word of Consolation

glimmer of revival and redemption. It takes the well-trained eye and heart of the Master Sage to detect a ray of hope in the ashes. But Rabbi Akiva taught his colleagues and disciples how to do this and his words have brought healing and comfort to countless

generations of Jews down through the ages. The Talmud (*Makkos 24a*) relates:

Rabban Gamliel, Rabbi Elazar ben Azariah, Rabbi Yehoshua, and Rabbi Akiva were traveling to Jerusalem, and as they approached Mount Scopus, they saw a fox emerge from [the ruins of] the Holy of Holies. They all wept at the sight, but Rabbi Akiva smiled.

'Why are you smiling?' they asked him.

'Why do you weep?' he responded.

'Shouldn't we weep,' they answered, 'when from such a holy place concerning which the Torah commanded (Numbers 1:51) וְהַזָּר הַקָּרֵב יוּמָת *"and the stranger that comes near shall die" a fox emerges — in fulfillment of the verse "Mount Zion which lies desolate, foxes prowled over it"? (Lamentations 5:18).*

'For that reason I am smiling!' Rabbi Akiva answered. Just as we have just seen the fulfillment of the prophecy of Uriah, "one faithful witness": "Zion shall be plowed as a field and Jerusalem shall become heaps" (Jeremiah 26:18), in the future we can look forward to the fulfillment of the prophecy of another "faithful witness," Zechariah: "Old men and old women will yet sit in the streets of Jerusalem, and each will have his staff in his hand due to his old age. And the streets of the city will be filled with boys and girls playing in the streets" (Zechariah 8:4). Just as Uriah's prophecy was fulfilled, so will Zechariah's.

They answered him: 'Akiva, you have comforted us! Akiva you have comforted us!'

Talmud Selection

Gittin 55b-56a

One of the Torah portions that are permitted for study on Tishah B'Av is Tractate Gittin 55b-58a, which is comprised of narratives and Aggadic teachings about the destruction of the Second Temple. Following is an interpretative elucidation with notes, of part of this section (55b-56a).

This is taken from

THE SCHOTTENSTEIN EDITION

TALMUD BAVLI

עין משפט
נר מצוה

שלא יאמרו דבר מן התורה נקום נעשה דמן הערוה אין כורת
להטיב קרבן אחד . וח״ל וכו׳ וכן מה כח ביד חכמים
וכו׳ ומה טעם אמרו נודעה אינה מכפרת שלא
יאמרו מזבח אוכל גזילות

ומה טעם אמרו נודעה אינה מכפרת שלא
יאמרו מזבח אוכל גזילות דעולא אמר
היינו דקתני חטאת אלא לרב יהודה מאי
איריא חטאת אפי׳ עולה נמי לא מיבעיא
קאמר לא מיבעיא עולה דהכלל היא אלא
אפי׳ חטאת נמי דהלב ודם הוא דסליק
לגבי מזבח ואידך כהנים אכלי לה אפי׳
הכי קאמר שלא יאמרו מזבח אוכל גזילות

בגיורתיה

ביהודה

אשר

תוספות רי״ד

תוספות רי״ד

אַקַמְצָא וּבַר קַמְצָא חָרוּב יְרוּשְׁלַיִם – **As a result of** the incident involving **Kamtza and Bar Kamtza,**[1] **Jerusalem was destroyed:** דְּרַחְמֵיה דְּהַהוּא גַבְרָא – **A certain man,** קַמְצָא וּבַעַל דִּבְבֵיה בַּר קַמְצָא – **who had a friend** named **Kamtza and an enemy** named **Bar Kamtza,** עֲבַד סְעוּדָתָא – **made a banquet.** אָמַר לֵיה לְשַׁמָּעֵיה – **He told his attendant:** זִיל אַייתִי לִי קַמְצָא – **"Go** and **bring Kamtza** to join me at the banquet." אָזַל אַייתֵי לֵיה בַּר קַמְצָא – **[The attendant] went and** mistakenly **brought him Bar Kamtza.**

אָתָא אַשְׁכְּחֵיה דְּהַוָה יָתִיב – **When [the host] arrived** at the banquet and **found [Bar Kamtza] sitting** there, אָמַר לֵיה – **he said to [Bar Kamtza]:** מִכְּדִי – הַהוּא גַבְרָא בַּעַל דְּבָבָא דְּהַהוּא גַבְרָא הוּא – **"Look here, that man** [you] **is the enemy of that man** [me]. מַאי בָּעֵית הָכָא – **What do you want here?** קוּם פּוּק – **Get up** and **get out!"** אָמַר לֵיה – **[Bar Kamtza] said to him:** הוֹאִיל וְאָתַאי שַׁבְקָן – **"Since I am here** already **let me** stay, וִיהֵיבְנָא לָךְ דְּמֵי מַה דְּאָכִילְנָא וּשָׁתֵינָא – **and I will pay you for whatever I eat and drink."**

NOTES

1. The names of two Jews (*Rashi*).

The point of the following narrative is that the Destruction of the Temple was a result of שִׂנְאַת חִנָּם, *gratuitous hatred* [between one person and another]. As the Gemara, *Yoma* 9b, states: "In [the era of] the Second Temple, the people studied Torah and performed *mitzvos*, [so] why was the Second Temple destroyed? Because there was gratuitous hatred among the people" (*Maharsha*).

אָמַר לֵיה – [The host] said to [Bar Kamtza]: לֹא – "No, I will not let you stay!" אָמַר לֵיה – [Bar Kamtza] said to him: יְהִיבְנָא לָךְ דְּמֵי פַּלְגָא דִּסְעוּדָתֵיךְ – "I will pay you for half your banquet." אָמַר לֵיה – Again [the host] said to him: לֹא – "No!" אָמַר לֵיה – [Bar Kamtza] said to [the host]: יְהִיבְנָא לָךְ דְּמֵי כּוּלָה סְעוּדָתֵיךְ – "I will pay you for your entire banquet." אָמַר לֵיה – [The host] said to [Bar Kamtza]: לֹא – "No!" נַקְטֵיה בִּידֵיה וְאוֹקְמֵיה וְאַפְקֵיה – He took [Bar Kamtza] by his hand, stood him up and ejected him from the banquet. אָמַר – [Bar Kamtza] said to himself: הוֹאִיל וַהֲווּ יָתְבֵי רַבָּנָן וְלֹא מָחוּ בֵּיה – Since the Rabbis were seated at the banquet and did not rebuke him for the way in which he treated me, שְׁמַע מִינָּה קָא נִיחָא לְהוּ – it is evident that [what he did] was acceptable to them.[1] אֵיזִיל – I will go and אֵיכוּל בְּהוּ קוּרְצָא בֵּי מַלְכָּא – spread slander[2] against [the Rabbis] in the royal palace. אָזַל אָמַר לֵיה

לְקֵיסָר – He went and told Caesar: מָרְדוּ בָּךְ יְהוּדָאֵי – "The Jews have rebelled against you!" אָמַר לֵיה – [Caesar] said to him: מִי יֵימַר – "Who says so?" אָמַר לֵיה – [Bar Kamtza] said to [Caesar]: שְׁדַר לְהוּ קוּרְבָּנָא – "Send them an animal as a sacrifice חֲזִית אִי מְקָרְבִין לֵיה – and see whether they offer it in their Temple!"[3] אָזַל שָׁדַר בְּיָדֵיה עֶגְלָא תִּלְתָּא – [Caesar] went and sent a fine[4] calf with [Bar Kamtza]. בַּהֲדֵי דְּקָאָתֵי שְׁדָא – As he was going to Jerusalem, בֵּיה מוּמָא בְּנִיב שְׂפָתַיִם – [Bar Kamtza] caused a blemish in [the calf's] upper lip, וְאָמְרִי לָה בְּדוּקִין שֶׁבָּעַיִן – or, as some say, he caused a cataract in the eye.[5] דּוּכְתָּא דִּלְדִידַן הֲוָה מוּמָא – Either way, he ensured that the blemish was in a place where it is considered a blemish for us, i.e. for offering in the Temple, וְלְדִידְהוּ לָאו מוּמָא הוּא – but is not considered a blemish for them, i.e. for offering outside the Temple.[6] Although the animal was unfit to

---

NOTES

1. The Rabbis did not protest because they felt that doing so would be to no avail (see *Maharsha*).

2. אֲכִילַת קוּרְצִין, *eating kurtzin*, is an idiomatic expression for spreading slander. When a slanderer went to someone's house to tell him some gossip they would eat a snack — known as אֲכִילַת קוּרְצִין, *eating kurtzin* — to symbolically confirm the tale bearer's words. קוּרְצִין, *kurtzin*, is from the root קָרַץ, *to wink* — tale bearers wink as a means of imparting their message to its intended recipient without letting anyone else understand it (*Rashi* to Lev. 19:16).

3. A gentile may voluntarily bring offerings to be sacrificed on the Altar in the Temple, just as a Jew can (*Rashi*).

4. *Tosafos*.

5. *Rashi*. A cataract is a disqualifying

blemish (see *Rashi* to *Leviticus* 21:20, *Mishnah Bechoros* 38a).

A correspondent inquired of *Rashba* (*Teshuvos* 1:326, cited by *Maharatz Chayos* and *Yad David*): How is it possible to introduce a cataract in an animal's eye? *Rashba* answers that Bar Kamtza knew how to strike the eye in such a manner as to cause a cataract to develop. He also characterizes as acceptable the correspondent's own suggestion that Bar Kamtza substituted an animal that had a cataract for the animal sent by Caesar.

Rashi (*Bechoros* 16a ד״ה ואליבא), in an alternative interpretation of the term בְּדוּקִין שֶׁבָּעַיִן, translates it as *eyelids*, but *Rashi* here follows the view that it means a cataract.

6. Unlike a Jew who may offer sacrifices

אמר ליה לא אמר ליה דיובנא לך דם פלנא דסעודתיך אמר ליה דם ליה דיובנא לך דם כולה סעודתיך א"ל לא נקטת בידיה ואוקמיה ואפקיה אמר האיל חזו רבנן דיתבי ולא מחו ביה ש"מ קא ניחא להו איזיל איכול בהו קורצא בי מלכא אזל אמר ליה לקיסר מרדו בך יהודאי א"ל מי יימר א"ל שדר להו קורבנא חזית אי מקרבין ליה אזל שדר בידיה עגלא תלתא בהדי דקאתי שדא ביה מומא *בניב שפתים ואמרי לה בדוקין שבעין דוכתא דלדידן הוה מומא ולדידהו לאו מומא הוא סבר רבנן לקרובי משום שלום מלכות אמר להו רבי זכריה בן אבקולם יאמרו בעלי מומין קריבין לגבי מזבח סבר למיקטליה דלא ליזיל ולימא אמר להו רבי זכריה יאמרו מטיל מום בקדשים יהרג אמר רבי יוחנן ענוותנותו של רבי זכריה בן אבקולם החריבה את ביתנו ושרפה את היכלנו והגליתנו מארצנו שדר עילויהו לנירון קיסר כי קאתי שרא גירא למזרח אתא נפל בירושלים למערב אתא נפל בירושלים לארבע רוחות השמים אתא נפל בירושלים א"ל לינוקא פסוק לי פסוקיך אמר ליה *ונתתי את נקמתי באדום ביד עמי ישראל וגו' אמר קודשא בריך הוא *בעי לחרובי ביתיה ובעי לכפורי ידיה בההוא גברא ערק ואזיל ואיגייר ונפק מיניה ר"מ שדריה עילויהו לאספסיינוס קיסר אתא צר עלה תלת שני הוו בה הנך תלתא עתורי נקדימון בן גוריון ובן כלבא שבוע ובן ציצית הכסת נקדימון בן גוריון שנקדה לו חמה בעבורו בן כלבא שבוע שכל הנכנס לביתו כשהוא רעב ככלב יוצא כשהוא שבע בן ציצית הכסת שהיתה מטתו נגררת על גבי *כסתות איכא דאמרי שהיתה מטתו מוטלת בין גדולי רומי חד מנהו אמר להו אנא זיינא להו בחטי ושערי וחד אמר להו בדחמרא ובמלחא ומשחא וחד אמר להו בדציבי ושבח רבנן לדציבי דרב חסדא כל אקלידי הוה מסר לשמעיה בר מדציבי דאמר רב חסדא *אכלבא דחטי בעי שתן אכלבי דציבי הוה לדו למיזן עשרים וחד שתא הוו בהו נהו בריוני אמרי להו רבנן ניפוק ונעביד שלמא בהדייהו לא שבקינהו אמרי להו ניפוק ונעביד קרבא בהדייהו אמרי להו רבנן לא מסתייעא מילתא קמו קלנהו להנהו אמברי דחיטי ושערי והוה כפנא מרתא בת בייתוס עתירתא דירושלים הויא שדרתה לשלוחה ואמרה ליה זיל אייתי לי סמידא אדאזל איזדבן אתא אמר לה סמידא ליכא חיוורתא איכא אמרה ליה זיל אייתי לי א"ל חיוורתא ליכא גושקרא איכא א"ל זיל אייתי לי אדאזיל איזדבן אתא ואמר לה גושקרא ליכא קימחא דשערי איכא אמרה ליה זיל אייתי לי אדאזל איזדבן הות שליפא מסאנא אמרה איפוק ואחזי אי משכחנא מידי למיכל איתיב לה פרתא בכרעא ומתה קרי עלה רבן יוחנן בן זכאי *הרכה בך והענוגה אשר לא נסתה כף רגלה הצג על הארץ איכא דאמרי גרוגרות דר' צדוק אכלה ואיתניסא ומתה דר' צדוק יתיב ארבעין שנין בתעניתא דלא ליחרב ירושלים כי הוה אכיל מידי הוה מתחזי מאבראי וכי הוה בריא מייתי ליה גרוגרות מייץ מייהו ושדי להו כי הוה קא ניהא נפשה אפיקתה לכל דהבה וכספא שריתיה בשוקא אמרה האי למאי מיבעי לי והיינו דכתיב *כספם בחצות ישליכו אבא סקרא ריש בריוני דירושלים בר אחתיה דרבן יוחנן בן זכאי הוה שלח ליה תא בצינעא לגבאי אתא א"ל עד אימת עבדיתו הכי וקטליתו ליה לעלמא בכפנא אמר ליה מאי אעביד דאי אמינא להו מידי קטלו לי א"ל חזי לי תקנתא לדידי דאיפוק אפשר דהוי הצלה פורתא א"ל נקום נפשך בקצירי וליתי כולי עלמא ולישיילו בך ואייתי מידי סריא ואגני גבך ולימרו דנח נפשך וליעיילו בך תלמידך ולא ליעול בך איניש אחרינא דלא לרגשן בך דקליל את דאינש חיה ואינהו ידעי דחיא קליל ממיתא עביד הכי נכנס בו רבי אליעזר מצד אחד ורבי יהושע מצד אחד כי מטו לפיתחא בעו למדקריה אמר להו יאמרו רבן דקרו בעו למדחפיה אמר להו יאמרו רבן דחף פתח ליה בבא נפק כי מטא להתם אמר שלמא עלך מלכא שלמא עלך מלכא א"ל מיחייבת תרי קטלא חדא דאנא לאו מלכא אנא וקא קרית לי מלכא ותו אי מלכא אנא עד האידנא אמאי לא אתית לגבאי א"ל דקאמרת לאו מלכא אנא אברא

be offered in the Temple, סָבוּר רַבָּנַן – the Rabbis considered offering it, לְקָרוּבֵיהּ – מִשׁוּם שְׁלוֹם מַלְכוּת – for the sake of peaceful relations with the Roman government.[7] אָמַר לְהוּ רַבִּי זְכַרְיָה בֶּן אַבְקוּלָס – R' Zechariah ben Avkulus said to them: יֹאמְרוּ בַּעֲלֵי מוּמִין קְרֵיבִין לְגַבֵּי מִזְבֵּחַ – "But then [people] will say that blemished [animals] may be offered on the Altar!" סָבוּר לְמִיקְטְלֵיהּ – [The Rabbis] considered killing [Bar Kamtza] דְּלֹא לֵיזִיל וְלֵימָא – so that he would not be able to go and tell Caesar that his offering had been refused.[8] אָמַר לְהוּ רַבִּי זְכַרְיָה – R' Zechariah said to them: יֹאמְרוּ

מֵטִיל מוּם בְּקָדָשִׁים יֵהָרֵג – "But then [people] will say that one who blemishes consecrated animals is put to death!"[9]

The Gemara comments:

אָמַר רַבִּי יוֹחָנָן – R' Yochanan said: עַנְוְתָנוּתוֹ שֶׁל רַבִּי זְכַרְיָה בֶּן אַבְקוּלָס – The tolerance displayed by R' Zechariah ben Avkulus (in refusing to have Bar Kamtza put to death)[10] הֶחֱרִיבָה אֶת בֵּיתֵנוּ – destroyed our Temple, וְשָׂרְפָה אֶת הֵיכָלֵנוּ – burned down our Heichal[11] וְהִגְלִיתָנוּ מֵאַרְצֵנוּ – and exiled us from our land.[12]

The narrative is resumed:

NOTES

only in the Temple, a gentile may do so either in the Temple or elsewhere. However, there is a difference between an offering brought by a gentile in the Temple and one brought elsewhere, in that a Temple offering is disqualified if it is merely blemished, whereas an outside offering is not disqualified unless it is missing a limb (see *Rashi* here and to *Avodah Zarah* 51a ד״ה חזיא).

7. It is permissible to violate even Biblical prohibitions for the sake of maintaining good relations with the government (*Magen Avraham* 656:8; cf. *Yad David*). [Presumably, the reason for this is that a negative attitude on the part of the government toward the Jewish people could very easily lead to bloodshed, a truth that history has sadly borne out many times. All prohibitions (with the exceptions of idolatry, murder and immoral acts such as adultery and incest) are permitted for the sake of saving a life.]

8. Anyone who is, justifiably, presumed to be inciting the government against his fellow Jews may be put to death (*Meiri*). [The Gemara, *Sanhedrin* 73a, states that if one sees someone about to commit a murder, one should kill the potential murderer to prevent him from carrying out his designs.]

9. It is Biblically prohibited to blemish an animal designated as an offering. [This prohibition carries the penalty of lashes; it is not a capital offense.] People might [mistakenly] assume that Bar Kamtza was executed for violating this prohibition (*Rashi*).

10. *Rashi*. Alternatively: R' Zechariah, because of his humility, did not feel himself qualified to make the determination that Bar Kamtza posed a mortal danger to the Jewish nation. (This explains the use here of the word עַנְוְתָנוּתוֹ, which usually means "his humility") (*Geresh Yerachim*).

11. The word הֵיכָל, *Heichal*, usually refers to the chamber in the Temple that housed the Menorah, the Shulchan and the Golden Altar. Sometimes it is used to denote the Temple in its entirety (see *Tosefos Yom Tov* to *Midos* 4:6).

12. In fact, the Destruction of the Temple had already been Divinely decreed. This incident was effective only in causing the Destruction to take place at that particular time (*Maharam Shif*).
Alternatively: Only the exile had already been decreed (as punishment for the gratu-

שָׁדַר עֲלָוַויְיהוּ לְנֵירוֹן קֵיסָר – He[13] sent Nero Caesar against [the Jews]. כִּי קָאָתֵי – As he approached Jerusalem, Nero made use of divinations to see if his campaign would be successful. שָׁדָא גִּירָא לְמִזְרָח אָתָא נָפַל בִּירוּשָׁלַיִם – He shot an arrow towards the east, and it fell in Jerusalem. לְמַעֲרָב אָתָא נָפַל בִּירוּשָׁלַיִם – He shot one towards the west, and it fell in Jerusalem. לְאַרְבַּע רוּחוֹת הַשָּׁמַיִם אָתָא נָפַל בִּירוּשָׁלַיִם – He shot an arrow towards each of the four directions of the compass and every time it fell in Jerusalem.[14] אָמַר לֵיה לִינוּקָא – Then he asked a young boy: פְּסוֹק לִי פְּסוּקֵיךְ – "Tell

me your verse," i.e. the verse you are currently studying.[15] אָמַר לֵיה – [The boy] recited to him: "וְנָתַתִּי אֶת נִקְמָתִי בָּאֱדוֹם בְּיַד עַמִּי יִשְׂרָאֵל וגו' – I will take My revenge against Edom through the agency of My people Israel etc.[16] I.e. God will ultimately punish Edom[17] (for its treatment of the Jewish nation) through the agency of His people. אָמַר – [Nero] said to himself: קוּדְשָׁא בְּרִיךְ הוּא בָּעֵי לַחֲרוּבֵי בֵּיתֵיה – The Holy One, Blessed is He, wants to destroy His House וּבָעֵי לְכַפּוּרֵי יָדֵיה בְּהַהוּא גַבְרָא – and then wipe His hands clean on that man [Nero].[18] עָרַק וְאָזַל וְאִיגַּיֵּיר – He ran

---

NOTES

itous hatred that existed among the people — see 55b note 1). As far as the Temple was concerned, Caesar would have spared it had his sacrifice been offered in it. Now that his sacrifice was refused, he reasoned that since the Temple served him no purpose, it should be destroyed (*Maharsha*).

13. It is unclear to whom this pronoun refers, for who had the authority to send Nero Caesar? *Yuchasin's* (ד״ה ר׳ מאיר) et al.) text of the Gemara reads: נֵירוֹן שַׂר צְבָאוֹ, *Nero his general.* According to this reading, it was not Nero Caesar who was sent but a general of the same name (*Tzemach David* part 2, year 3830). *Seder HaDoros* (3829) cites a view that our reading should be understood likewise, i.e. *Nero Caesar sent* [a military commander] *against them.* (But *Tzemach David* [ibid.] cites dissenting views, according to which Nero Caesar himself led the campaign against Jerusalem.)

14. Since Jerusalem was to the east, what message was conveyed by the fact that the arrow shot towards the east fell in Jerusalem?

Maharsha answers: Nero was not close enough to the city for the arrow to reach it naturally. The arrow was amazingly carried by the wind all the way to Jerusalem.

Anaf Yosef answers: Nero was afraid that although the Jews had sinned, God, out of His love for His People, might interfere with the natural course of events to save them. The fact that the arrow shot towards Jerusalem reached its target and was not diverted by some miracle signified to Nero that God was not going to intervene on the Jews' behalf. And when the arrows shot in the other directions miraculously fell in Jerusalem, Nero divined that, on the contrary, it was God's will that Jerusalem be destroyed.

15. Having ascertained that the Destruction of Jerusalem had been decreed by God, Nero now wished to know whether he would be rewarded for fulfilling God's will in this matter. To this end, he asked a child to recite the verse he was studying (*Anaf Yosef*). [The message conveyed by such a method is a minor form of prophecy (*Smag* cited by *Beis Yosef Yoreh Deah* 179; see there and *Shulchan Aruch* ibid §4).]

16. *Ezekiel* 25:14.

17. Rome is regarded as heir to the Biblical nation of Edom.

18. *Anaf Yosef* asks: Since God had decreed that Jerusalem be destroyed (see note 14), why would Nero be punished for, in effect,

away **and converted** to Judaism, וְנָפַק מִינֵּיהּ רַבִּי מֵאִיר – **and R' Meir was descended from him.**

שַׁדְרֵיהּ עִילָוַויְיהוּ לְאַסְפַּסְיָינוּס קֵיסָר – **[Caesar] sent Vespasian Caesar**[19] **against [the Jews].** אָתָא צָר עֲלָהּ תְּלָת שְׁנֵי – **[Vespasian] came** and **besieged [Jerusalem] for three years.**

הֲווֹ בָּהּ הַנְהוּ תְּלָתָא עַתִּירֵי – **There were three wealthy men in [Jerusalem]:** נַקְדִּימוֹן בֶּן גּוּרְיוֹן – **Nakdimon ben Gurion,** וּבֶן כַּלְבָּא שָׂבוּעַ – **Ben Kalba Savua** וּבֶן צִיצִית הַכֶּסֶת – **and Ben Tzitzis Hakeses.**

The Gemara explains these unusual names:

נַקְדִּימוֹן בֶּן גּוּרְיוֹן – **Nakdimon ben Gurion** was so called שֶׁנָּקְדָה לוֹ חַמָּה – **because** it once happened that **the sun** miraculously **shone** (*nakdah*) **on his behalf.**[20] בֶּן כַּלְבָּא שָׂבוּעַ – **Ben Kalba Savua** was so called שֶׁכָּל הַנִּכְנָס לְבֵיתוֹ – **because anyone who en___ed his house** כְּשֶׁהוּא רָעֵב כְּכֶלֶב – **as hungry as a dog** (*kalba*)[21] יוֹצֵא כְּשֶׁהוּא שָׂבֵעַ – **left satisfied** (*savua*). בֶּן צִיצִית הַכֶּסֶת – **Ben Tzitzis Hakeses** was so called שֶׁהָיְתָה – צִיצָתוֹ נִגְרֶרֶת עַל גַּבֵּי כְּסָתוֹת – **because** wherever he walked, **his** *tzitzis*[22]

NOTES

fulfilling God's will?

A similar question was raised by the *Rishonim* in the context of the enslavement of the Jewish people in Egypt: Considering that this slavery had been Divinely ordained — as God said to Abraham (*Genesis* 15:13), וַעֲבָדוּם וְעִנּוּ אֹתָם, *They will enslave them and abuse them* — why were Pharaoh and the Egyptians punished?

The following is a synopsis of some of the approaches to this problem:

Rambam (Hil. Teshuvah 6:5): God's decree did not apply to any particular individual. Each Egyptian could have chosen not to abuse the Jews. Thus, each one who did harm a Jew was deserving of punishment.

Ramban (Genesis 15:13), though not disputing the premise that an individual can choose to avoid carrying out a preordained decree, disagrees with the general approach of *Rambam*. For, he argues, if God issues a decree (through a *prophet*), it is surely meritorious to obey the decree, and an individual who ignores it transgresses God's will. Rather, Pharaoh and the Egyptians were punished because they oppressed the Jews to a greater extent than mandated by the decree. Alternatively, one who fulfills such a decree for ulterior motives, rather than for the sake of Heaven, is deserving of punishment. [In the present

case, since there had been no *prophetic* communication, the Destruction of the Temple could not be considered the fulfillment of a Divine directive, but an act of malicious violence.]

Raavad (Hil. Teshuvah ibid.) seems to be of the opinion that once a decree has been passed, the individual who was chosen to carry it out is unable to refrain from doing so. However, God arranges that a decree of a harmful nature is performed only by one who is anyway deserving of punishment (as an alternative, *Raavad* mentions an approach similar to that of *Ramban*).

19. [At that time, Vespasian was not the emperor. He is identified here as Vespasian Caesar because ultimately he did reach this position.]

20. The sun was made to shine in the sky after the time for it to set had passed, so that Nakdimon's repayment of a loan (he had incurred on behalf of the people) would not be overdue. The full incident is recounted in Gemara *Ta'anis* 19b-20a.

21. The dog has less food available to him than any other animal (*Shabbos* 155b).

22. *Tzitzis:* the fringes worn, by Biblical command, on the corners of a four-cornered garment (see *Orach Chaim* 21:4 with *Magen Avraham* et al.).

trailed behind him **on cushions** (*keses*); i.e. he walked only on fine fabric. אִיכָּא דְּאָמְרֵי – **Some say** that he was given this name שֶׁהָיְתָה – **because** בִּסְתּוֹ מוּטֶּלֶת בֵּין גְּדוֹלֵי רוֹמִי **his seat cushion** (*keses*) **was among the nobles of Rome** whenever he went there for an audience with the emperor.[23]

The narrative is continued: חַד אָמַר לְהוּ – **One** of these three rich men **said to [the Rabbis]:** אֲנָא זָיֵינָא לְהוּ בְּחִיטֵי וְשַׂעֲרֵי – **"I will sustain [the people] with wheat and barley."** וְחַד אָמַר לְהוּ – **And** another **one said to [the Rabbis]:** בִּדְחַמְרָא וּבִדְמִלְחָא וּמִשְׁחָא – **"I will supply them with wine, salt and oil."** וְחַד אָמַר לְהוּ – **And** another **one said to [the Rabbis]:** בִּדְצִיבֵי – **"I will supply them with wood."** וְשַׁבְּחוּ רַבָּנָן לִדְצִיבֵי – **The Rabbis gave** special **praise to the** one who promised **wood.** His pledge was the most generous inasmuch as wood is required in greater quantity than other staples; as borne out by the following: דְּרַב חִסְדָּא כָּל אַקְלִידֵי הֲוָה מָסַר לְשַׁמָּעֵיהּ **Rav Chisda entrusted all his keys to his attendant** בַּר מִדְּצִיבֵי – **except for** the key to the storehouse of **wood.** דְּאָמַר רַב חִסְדָּא – **For Rav Chisda said:** אַכְלָבָא דְּחִיטֵי בָּעֵי שִׁיתִּין אַכְלָבֵי דְּצִיבֵי

To make **a storehouse** full **of wheat** into bread **requires sixty storehouses of wood.**

הֲוָה לְהוּ לְמֵיזַן עֶשְׂרִים וְחַד שַׁתָּא – **[These three men] had** enough supplies **to sustain** the residents of Jerusalem **for twenty-one years.** הָווּ בְּהוּ הַנְהוּ בַּרְיוֹנֵי – **However, among [the people] were [a band of] ruffians.**[24] אָמְרוּ לְהוּ רַבָּנָן – **The Rabbis said to [these ruffians]:** נֵיפּוֹק וְנַעֲבִיד שְׁלָמָא בַּהֲדַיְיהוּ **"Let us go out and make peace with [the Romans]."** לֹא שַׁבְקִינְהוּ – **[The ruffians] would not let them** do so. אָמְרוּ לְהוּ – **They said to [the Rabbis]:** נֵיפּוֹק וְנַעֲבִיד קְרָבָא בַּהֲדַיְיהוּ – **"Let us go out and wage war against [the Romans]."** אָמְרוּ לְהוּ רַבָּנָן – **The Rabbis said to them:** לֹא מִסְתַּיְיעָא מִילְתָא – **"It will not be successful."**[25] קָמוּ [The **[ruffians] arose and burned down the storehouses of wheat, barley** and **wood,** וַהֲוָה כַּפְנָא – **and there was a famine** in the city.[26]

The Gemara relates one of the tragic effects of the famine:

מָרְתָא בַּת בַּייתוֹס עֲתִירְתָּא דִּירוּשְׁלֵים הֲוָיָא – **Martha the daughter of Boethus was the wealthy woman of Jerusalem.** שַׁדַּרְתָּה לִשְׁלוּחַהּ וְאָמְרָה לֵיהּ **She sent out her messenger, saying to him:** זִיל אַיְיתִי לִי סְמִידָא – **"Go and**

NOTES

23. According to this explanation, "Ben Tzitzis" was his real name. "Hakeses" was added in recognition of his prestigious position (*Rashi*).

24. בַּרְיוֹנִים, *baryonim* [from the root בור, *empty*]: empty men, with a propensity to violence (*Rashi*). Here, the reference is to the ardently nationalist group whom secular history knows as the Zealots. As the

Gemara relates presently, they advocated the overthrow of Roman rule through war, and violently resisted any attempts at reconciliation.

25. The Rabbis had a tradition to this effect from our forefather Jacob (see *Maharsha*).

26. The intent of the *baryonim* was to give the populace no choice but to wage war against the Romans.

bring me some **fine flour.**" אַדְאָזַל — **By the time he went,** [the fine flour] **had been sold.** אָתָא אָמַר לָהּ — **He went** back to Martha **and told her:** סְמִידָא לֵיכָּא חִיוַּרְתָּא אִיכָּא — "**There is no** more **fine flour, but there is white bread.**" אָמְרָה לֵיהּ — **She said to him:** זִיל אַיְיתִי לִי — "**Go and bring me** some **white bread.**" אַדְאָזַל אִיזְדַּבַּן — **By the time he went,** [the white bread] **had been sold.** אָתָא וְאָמַר לָהּ — **He went** back to Martha **and told her:** חִיוַּרְתָּא לֵיכָּא גּוּשְׁקְרָא אִיכָּא — "**There is no** more white bread, **but there is coarse bread.**" אָמְרָה לֵיהּ — **She said to** him: זִיל אַיְיתִי לִי — "**Go** and **bring me** some **coarse bread.**" אַדְאָזַל אִזְדַּבַּן — **By the time he went,** [the coarse bread] **had been sold.** אָתָא וְאָמַר לָהּ — **He went** back to Martha **and told** her: גּוּשְׁקְרָא לֵיכָּא קִימְחָא דִשְׂעָרֵי אִיכָּא — "**There is no** more coarse bread, **but there is barley flour.**" אָמְרָה לֵיהּ — **She said to him:** זִיל אַיְיתִי לִי — "**Go** and **bring me** some **barley flour.**" אַדְאָזַל אִיזְדַּבַּן — **By the time he went,** [the barley flour] **had been sold.** הֲוָה שְׁלִיפָא מְסָאנָא אָמְרָה — **Although she had taken off her shoes, she said:** "אִיפּוּק וְאַחֲזֵי אִי מַשְׁכַּחְנָא מִידִי לְמֵיכַל — **I will go out and see if I can find anything to eat.**" אִיתִיב לָהּ פַּרְתָּא — **Some animal dung** בְּכַרְעָא וּמֵתָה — **stuck to her foot,** she became nauseated **and died.** קָרֵי עֲלָהּ רַבָּן יוֹחָנָן בֶּן זַכַּאי — **In reference to her, Rabban**

Yochanan ben Zakkai cited the following verse: "הָרַכָּה בְּךְ וְהָעֲנוּגָּה אֲשֶׁר לֹא נִסְּתָה כַף רַגְלָהּ" — **The delicate and pampered** [woman] **amongst you, the sole of whose foot has not tested** the **ground.** [27]

An **alternative** version of how she died: גְּרוֹגְרוֹת — אִיכָּא דְּאָמְרֵי **Some say:** דְּרַבִּי צָדוֹק אַכְלָה — **She ate the dried figs** [discarded by] **R' Tzadok,** וְאִיתְּנִיסָא וּמֵתָה — **became nauseated and died.**

The reference to **R' Tzadok** is explained: דְּרַבִּי צָדוֹק יָתִיב אַרְבְּעִין שְׁנִין בְּתַעֲנִיתָא — **R' Tzadok fasted for forty years** דְּלָא לֶיחֱרַב יְרוּשָׁלַיִם — **to avert the Destruction of Jerusalem.** [28] He was so thin כִּי הֲוָה אָכִיל מִידִי — **that when he ate anything,** הֲוָה מִיתְחֲזֵי מֵאַבָּרַאי — **it could be seen from the outside.** וְכִי הֲוָה בָּרִיא — **When he nourished himself** at night after concluding a fast, since he was not able to consume solids, מַיְיתֵי לֵיהּ גְּרוֹגְרוֹת — **they brought him dried figs.** מָיֵיץ מַיְיהוּ וְשָׁדֵי לְהוּ — **He would suck out their moisture and** then **discard them.**

The Gemara concludes the story of Martha the daughter of Boethus: כִּי הֲוָה קָא נִיחָא נַפְשָׁהּ — **As** [Martha] **was dying,** אַפִּיקְתָּה לְכָל דַּהֲבָא וְכַסְפָּא — **she took out all** her **gold and silver** שְׁדִיתֵיהּ בְּשׁוּקָא — and **threw it into the street.** אָמְרָה — **She said:** הַאי — "**What do I need this** לְמַאי מִיבָּעֵי לִי

NOTES

27. *Deuteronomy* 28:56. The verse appears in the context of the prophecy that foretells the Destruction of Jerusalem and the Temple.

28. He responded to omens of the Destruction which were discernible forty years before it actually occurred (*Maharsha*; see *Yoma* 39b).

for?" וְהַיְינוּ דִכְתִיב – **This is** a fulfillment of **that which is written**: ,,כַּסְפָּם בַּחוּצוֹת יַשְׁלִיכוּ'' – *They will throw their silver into the streets.* [29]

The Gemara continues with an account of Rabban Yochanan ben Zakkai's dramatic escape from the ruffians, and how he successfully petitioned Vespasian to spare the Torah academy in Yavneh. Vespasian was then called to Rome to become the emperor, and was replaced by Titus as head of the military campaign against Jerusalem. Titus invaded Jerusalem and desecrated the Temple. The Gemara describes the punishments that befell Titus, as well as other enemies of Israel.

NOTES

29. *Ezekiel* 7:19. The verse refers to the impending Destruction of Jerusalem.

Thus, the cycle of events put into motion by the incident of Kamtza and Bar Kamtza culminated in the Destruction of the Temple. The Gemara (57a) concludes the account of this incident and its aftermath with the following observation:

תַּנְיָא – **It was taught in a Baraisa:** אָמַר ר׳ אֶלְעָזָר – **R' ELAZAR SAID:** בָּא **COME** – וּרְאֵה כַּמָּה גְדוֹלָה כֹּחָה שֶׁל בּוֹשָׁה **AND SEE HOW GREAT IS THE POWER OF SHAME!** שֶׁהֲרֵי סִיַּיע הקב״ה אֶת בַּר קַמְצָא – **FOR THE HOLY ONE, BLESSED IS HE, ASSISTED BAR KAMTZA** in his plot to take revenge for the shame to which he had been subjected, וְהֶחֱרִיב אֶת בֵּיתוֹ – **AND HE DESTROYED HIS TEMPLE** וְשָׂרַף אֶת הֵיכָלוֹ – **AND HE BURNED HIS** *HEICHAL*.

במאי דפסקן אנפשיה: מיקלי וכוזרי קומחא: בשבבא זרע זיוזחא:
מהו כנגד מהו שבעלמא החאיל הטם לוטת אל בנות מואב: דאמר
מר: כעוזבין (דף כא:) וליף ליה מולהב הרבה ינטם בשר המלטיב
אדכב נידון בינינם בשר וקרא בדברי סופרים כחיב זוחר מדבי מצהוז
בני הכר כדבר סופרים יותר מדבר תורה או

תורה : נביא האומות עובדי ע"ז:
בלעם שהביקט נגלה פלו ורכיעש
לבד: טור מלכא מדינה שמטה
הר המלך: נפל בני המדינה
סיהרוזא עליהב דרומאו ומחטוב
גנודא: גחד: הוה בנהו ביופהור
אידרמד: לשמוח: עד דאהמחי
לבני סיהל: בלונוה דגושפנקא: מי
שהמהים לו טרה בטחובטה היה מבליק
ריחון מיל מן העול למרחוה הנרחה:
שחלים: מין מאכל שאו כמספבה

[זקן כרכים מו:] יההא אחרהך הר
המלך: משקיריו ראמשיים שטם

[סימן כ.:] חורהח דאמר מר *כל המלעיג על דברי חכמים נידון בצואה וחתרה חא חוי מה בין פשעיני ישראל לנביאי
אומת העולם עובדי ע"ז תניא אמר רבי אלעזר בא וראה כמה כמה גדולה כחה של בושה שהרי סייע הקב"ה את
בר קמצא והחריב את ביתו ושרף את היכלו : ארגנגולא וארגנגולא חריב מר פרו ורב כתרנגולא כלומר פרו ורבו עד דהו
מפקי חתנא וכלהא מפקי קמייהו תרנגולא ותרנגולתא כלומר פרו ורבו כתרנגולי יומא חד הוה קא חליף
גנדא דרומאו שקליניהו מנייהו נפלו עלייהו מנדנהו אתו אמרו ליה לקסר מרד בך יהודאי אתא עלייהו הוה
בהו ההוא בר דרומא דהוה קפיץ מילא וקטל וקטל שקיל מלכא גלימא דמאניה וצלי אמר רבונה
דעלמא כוליה אי ניחא לך לא חמסרינהו להנהו גברא בידיה דדוד גברא אכשליה פומה
לבר דרומא ואמר °הלא אתה אלהים זנחתנו ולא חצא אלהים בצבאותינו דוד נמי אמר הכי דוד אתגמדי קא
מחמה על לביח הכסא אתא דדיקנא שמטתה לרביעיות ונח נפשיה והוה האיל ואיחרחיש ליה ניסא הא זימנא
אישבקיניה שבקיניה ואול אידמחי ואכל שטן וארלקיץ שרני עד דאתחזי בלויונא דנושפנקה ברתוק מלא
אמר מידחא קא חדו כי יהודאי הדר אתא עלייהו א"ר אם תלח מאה אלף שליפי סייפא עיילי למטר מלכא וקטלו
בת חלמא יומי יומי ותלחמא לליוותא ובכך נימא עלייהו ובכך אי חוי ינד בני נבני °בלע"ה אל חמל אחא כל
נאות יעקב כי אתא רבין אמר רבי יוחנן אלו ששים רבוא עיירות היו לו לינאי המלך בהר המלך דאמר רב
יהודה אמר רב אסר ששים רבוא עיירות היו לו לינאי המלך בהר המלך וכל אחת ואחת היו בה כיוצאי מצרים
חוץ משלוש שהיו בהן כפלים כיוצאי מצרים אלו שלושים כפר שיחולים וכפר שהוריה וכפר ביש דלא יהבי
ביתא לאושפיזא כפר שיחולים שהוחה פרנסתן מן שהלים כפר דכריא אמר רבי יוחנן שהיו נשטחוזל וילדות
זכרים תחלה וילדות ובנקבה באחרונה ופסקית אמר עולא לדידי חוי לי ההוא אתרא שהון ריבוותא

[דניאל יא וי'] כחובות
קב: תצ"ט ועי"ג ע"ק
ג.]

קני לא מחזיק אמר ליה ההוא צדוק לרבי חנינא שקרו משקרית אמר ליה °ארץ צבי כתיב בה מה צבי
זה אין עורו מחזיק את בשרו אף ארץ ישראל חלקה אף חלק רב מביה רב חנא א"ר זבי גבי חדדי אמר א"ר אכא דשמע ליה
מלחא מכפר סבניא של מצרים לימא פתח חד מנייהו ואמר מעשה באדם ארוסתו שנשבו לבן העובד
כובבים והשאם זה לזה אמרה ליה בבקשה ממך לא ישאן לי שאין לי כחובה מנך א"ד נגע לו עד יום
מותו וכשמת אמרה להן סיפרו ליה שפטם ביצרו יותר מיוסף דאילו ביוסף לא הוה לא אלא חדא שטתא
והאי כל יומא ויומא ואילו יוסף לא בחדא מטה לאו אלו אשרו אהא אשרו פתח אחד
ואמר מעשה ועמדו ארבעים מדיני בידני נחמר השטר ארת ובקין ודבק שבאו לחלוק באר נגרה
מאורסה ביום הכפרים תביאום לבית דין וסקלום והכר השער למקום פתח אחד ואמר מעשה באדם
אחד שנתן עיני באשה לגרושה והחה כתובתה מרובה כד עשה הלך חימן מה ששביעו האוכיל והשקן
שכח והשבול מ"י מטה ארת והבא לבין ביתה יהטול גורבול בינתין העמד לפן עדים ובא ארת זה זק
אחד מתלמידי שמאי הזקן והבא ד לן בוטם שמו אמר להן כך מקובלני משמאי הזקן לובן ביזה בלא האור
ושבכבת זרע דוהה מן האור בדקו ומצאו כדבריו התביאהו לב"ד חלקוהו והגבו כתובתה מצבו א"ל אבי
לרב וכתיב ומארו דהו צדיקים כלי האי דאי מן מטמא אינעשו א"ל °משום דלא האבול מי ירושלם דכתיב
°שבחאו את ירושלם ותלו בה כל אוהבים שש שאתה משש כל המוהבאהים עליה : אשקא דריספק חריב
בירתר דהו נדיני כי הוה מתינילי יוקא שהלי ארוא יוקרתא שהרי תרניתא וכי רהו מנגבכר קיצו לתו ועובד
גנגא יומא חד הוה קא חלפא ברחתה דקטר אחבר שהנכנס לכרך בדרים קצו מיה ועיילי לה אתו נפל עלייהו מנדנו
א"ד אתו אמרו ליה לקסר מרד בך יהודאי אתא עלייהו א"ד א"א אבד
א"ד יוהנן אלו יוהנן אלו שמנים [אלף] קרני מלחמה שנכנסו לכרך ביתר בשעה שלכדוה הרגו בה אנשים נשים וטף
עד שהלך דמן ונפל לים הגדול שמא תאמר קרובה היתה רחוקה היתה מיל תניא רבי אליעזר הגדול
אמר שני נחלים יש בבקעת ידים אחד מושך אילך ואחד מושך אילך ושערו חכמים שבאותה שעה חלקם
מים ואחד דם במחניתא תנא שבע שנים בצדו עובדי כובבים את כרמיהן מדמן של ישראל בלא זבל
אמר

*) כלומר אהבת נפיט נ' יפר וזה מנ'ה גופו וממונו . **) בלעם. ודיט כ'ולא דוחחת כלומר מלאחני לא רחן וממומלתו לא נסתר גם לשמלוה כאת.

אֵיכָה
eichah

The Book of Eichah/Lamentations is read on the night of Tishah
B'Av. The following pages are reproduced from the ArtScroll Series
Book of Megillos. A comprehensive commentary, by Rabbi Meir
Zlotowitz, with Overviews by Rabbi Noson Scherman is available
in the ArtScroll Tanach Series.

א

א **אֵיכָ֣ה | יָשְׁבָ֣ה בָדָ֗ד הָעִיר֙ רַבָּ֣תִי עָ֔ם הָֽיְתָ֖ה כְּאַלְמָנָ֑ה רַבָּ֣תִי בַגּוֹיִ֗ם שָׂרָ֙תִי֙ בַּמְּדִינ֔וֹת הָיְתָ֖ה לָמַֽס. ב בָּכ֨וֹ תִבְכֶּ֜ה בַּלַּ֗יְלָה וְדִמְעָתָהּ֙ עַ֣ל לֶֽחֱיָ֔הּ אֵֽין־לָ֥הּ מְנַחֵ֖ם מִכָּל־אֹֽהֲבֶ֑יהָ כָּל־רֵעֶ֙יהָ֙ בָּ֣גְדוּ בָ֔הּ הָ֥יוּ לָ֖הּ לְאֹֽיְבִֽים. ג גָּֽלְתָ֨ה יְהוּדָ֤ה מֵעֹ֙נִי֙ וּמֵרֹ֣ב עֲבֹדָ֔ה הִ֚יא יָֽשְׁבָ֣ה בַגּוֹיִ֔ם לֹ֥א מָֽצְאָ֖ה מָנ֑וֹחַ כָּל־רֹֽדְפֶ֥יהָ הִשִּׂיג֖וּהָ בֵּ֥ין הַמְּצָרִֽים. ד דַּרְכֵ֨י צִיּ֜וֹן אֲבֵל֗וֹת מִבְּלִי֙ בָּאֵ֣י מוֹעֵ֔ד כָּל־שְׁעָרֶ֙יהָ֙ שֽׁוֹמֵמִ֔ין כֹּֽהֲנֶ֖יהָ נֶֽאֱנָחִ֑ים בְּתֽוּלֹתֶ֥יהָ נּוּג֖וֹת וְהִ֥יא מַר־לָֽהּ. ה הָי֨וּ צָרֶ֤יהָ לְרֹאשׁ֙ אֹֽיְבֶ֣יהָ שָׁל֔וּ כִּֽי־יְהוָ֥ה הוֹגָ֖הּ עַ֣ל רֹב־פְּשָׁעֶ֑יהָ עֽוֹלָלֶ֛יהָ הָֽלְכ֥וּ שְׁבִ֖י לִפְנֵי־צָֽר. ו וַיֵּצֵ֥א °מִן בת־צִיּ֖וֹן כָּל־הֲדָרָ֑הּ הָי֣וּ שָׂרֶ֗יהָ כְּאַיָּלִים֙ לֹא־מָֽצְא֣וּ מִרְעֶ֔ה וַיֵּֽלְכ֥וּ בְלֹא־כֹ֖חַ לִפְנֵ֥י רוֹדֵֽף. ז זָֽכְרָ֣ה יְרֽוּשָׁלִַ֗ם יְמֵ֤י עָנְיָהּ֙ וּמְרוּדֶ֔יהָ כֹּ֚ל מַֽחֲמֻדֶ֔יהָ אֲשֶׁ֥ר הָי֖וּ מִ֣ימֵי קֶ֑דֶם בִּנְפֹ֧ל עַמָּ֣הּ בְּיַד־צָ֗ר וְאֵ֤ין עוֹזֵר֙ לָ֔הּ רָא֣וּהָ צָרִ֔ים שָֽׂחֲק֖וּ עַ֥ל מִשְׁבַּתֶּֽהָ. ח חֵ֤טְא חָֽטְאָה֙ יְר֣וּשָׁלִַ֔ם עַל־כֵּ֖ן לְנִידָ֣ה הָיָ֑תָה כָּֽל־מְכַבְּדֶ֤יהָ הִזִּיל֙וּהָ֙ כִּֽי־רָא֣וּ עֶרְוָתָ֔הּ גַּם־הִ֥יא נֶֽאֶנְחָ֖ה וַתָּ֥שָׁב אָחֽוֹר. ט טֻמְאָתָ֣הּ בְּשׁוּלֶ֗יהָ לֹ֤א זָֽכְרָה֙ אַֽחֲרִיתָ֔הּ וַתֵּ֣רֶד פְּלָאִ֔ים אֵ֥ין מְנַחֵ֖ם לָ֑הּ רְאֵ֤ה יְהוָה֙ אֶת־עָנְיִ֔י כִּ֥י הִגְדִּ֖יל אוֹיֵֽב. י יָד֙וֹ פָּ֣רַשׂ צָ֔ר עַ֖ל כָּל־מַֽחֲמַדֶּ֑יהָ כִּֽי־רָֽאֲתָ֤ה גוֹיִם֙ בָּ֣אוּ מִקְדָּשָׁ֔הּ אֲשֶׁ֣ר צִוִּ֔יתָ לֹֽא־יָבֹ֥אוּ בַקָּהָ֖ל לָֽךְ. יא כָּל־עַמָּ֤הּ נֶֽאֱנָחִים֙ מְבַקְשִׁ֣ים לֶ֔חֶם נָֽתְנ֧וּ °מחמודיהם בְּאֹ֖כֶל לְהָשִׁ֣יב נָ֑פֶשׁ רְאֵ֤ה יְהוָה֙ וְהַבִּ֔יטָה כִּ֥י הָיִ֖יתִי זֽוֹלֵלָֽה. יב ל֣וֹא אֲלֵיכֶ֗ם כָּל־עֹ֣בְרֵי דֶ֔רֶךְ הַבִּ֖יטוּ וּרְא֑וּ אִם־יֵ֤שׁ מַכְאוֹב֙**

°מִבַּת ק

°מַֽחֲמַדֵּיהֶם ק

1/1. THE DESOLATION OF JERUSALEM

The prophet Jeremiah wrote סֵפֶר קִינוֹת, the *Book of Lamentations*, which Yehoyakim burned 'on the fire that was in the brazier' [Jeremiah 36:23]. The book consisted of three chapters [1, 2, and 4] which Jeremiah rewrote. He later added chapters 3 and 5 (*Rashi*).

2. Many Tishah B'Av customs are inferred from the verses in *Eichah*. An example is *Maharam Rothenburg's* inference from the phrase, *she weeps bitterly in the night,* that *Eichah* is chanted publicly on Tishah B'Av only in the evening and not in the morning [unlike *Megillas Esther* which is read publicly on Purim both evening and morning] (*Sefer Minhagim 34*).

3. Heathen nations also go into exile, however, since they eat the bread and drink the wine of their captors, they do not experience real exile and privation. For Israel, however, which is forbidden to eat their bread or drink their wine, the exile is real (*Midrash*).

8. *Jerusalem sinned greatly.* [lit. 'Jerusalem sinned a sin.'] A sin consists of two parts: the sinful act itself and the thoughts and satisfaction surrounding it. Each part of the sin is evaluated separately and punished separately (*Kiddushin 40a*). Therefore the verse uses a twin expression of sin — חֵטְא חָטְאָה (*Hagaon Rav Moshe Feinstein* זצ"ל).

9. *On her hems.* Her sins were plainly evident for all to see (*Rashi*).

11. JERUSALEM ITSELF LAMENTS

12. Israel says to the nations: 'May there not occur to you what has occurred to me' (*Midrash*).

[1] **A**las — she sits in solitude! The city that was great with people has become like a widow. The greatest among nations, the princess among provinces, has become a tributary. [2] She weeps bitterly in the night and her tear is on her cheek. She has no comforter from all her lovers; all her friends have betrayed her, they have become her enemies. [3] Judah has gone into exile because of suffering and harsh toil. She dwelt among the nations, but found no rest; all her pursuers overtook her in narrow straits. [4] The roads of Zion are in mourning for lack of festival pilgrims. All her gates are desolate, her priests sigh; her maidens are aggrieved, and she herself is embittered. [5] Her adversaries have become her master, her enemies are at ease, for HASHEM has aggrieved her for her abundant transgressions. Her young children have gone into captivity before the enemy. [6] Gone from the daughter of Zion is all her splendor. Her leaders were like deer that found no pasture, but walked on without strength before the pursuer. [7] Jerusalem recalled the days of her affliction and sorrow — all the treasures that were hers in the days of old. With the fall of her people into the enemy's hand and none to help her, her enemies saw her and gloated at her downfall. [8] Jerusalem sinned greatly, she has therefore become a wanderer. All who once respected her disparage her, for they have seen her disgrace. She herself sighs and turns away. [9] Her impurity is on her hems, she was heedless of the consequences. She has sunk astonishingly, there is no one to comfort her. 'Look, HASHEM, at my misery, for the enemy has acted prodigiously!' [10] The enemy spread out his hand on all her treasures; indeed, she saw nations invade her sanctuary — about whom You had commanded that they should not enter Your congregation. [11] All her people are sighing, searching for bread. They traded their treasures for food to keep alive. 'Look, HASHEM, and behold what a glutton I have become!' [12] May it not befall you — all who pass by this road. Behold and see, if there is any pain

כְּמַכְאֹבִ֗י אֲשֶׁ֤ר עוֹלַל֙ לִ֔י אֲשֶׁ֥ר הוֹגָ֖ה יְהֹוָ֑ה בְּי֖וֹם

יג חֲר֥וֹן אַפּֽוֹ׃ **מִ**מָּר֛וֹם שָֽׁלַח־אֵ֥שׁ בְּעַצְמֹתַ֖י וַיִּרְדֶּ֑נָּה

פָּרַ֨שׂ רֶ֤שֶׁת לְרַגְלַי֙ הֱשִׁיבַ֣נִי אָח֔וֹר נְתָנַ֙נִי֙ שֹֽׁמֵמָ֔ה

כָּל־הַיּ֖וֹם דָּוָֽה׃ יד **נִ**שְׂקַד֩ עֹ֨ל פְּשָׁעַ֜י בְּיָד֗וֹ יִשְׂתָּ֣רְג֤וּ

עָלוּ֙ עַל־צַוָּארִ֔י הִכְשִׁ֖יל כֹּחִ֑י נְתָנַ֣נִי אֲדֹנָ֔י בִּידֵ֖י

לֹא־אוּכַ֥ל קֽוּם׃ טו **סִ**לָּ֨ה כָל־אַבִּירַ֤י ׀ אֲדֹנָי֙ בְּקִרְבִּ֔י

קָרָ֥א עָלַ֛י מוֹעֵ֖ד לִשְׁבֹּ֣ר בַּחוּרָ֑י גַּ֚ת דָּרַ֣ךְ אֲדֹנָ֔י

לִבְתוּלַ֖ת בַּת־יְהוּדָֽה׃ טז **עַ**ל־אֵ֣לֶּה ׀ אֲנִ֣י בוֹכִיָּ֗ה עֵינִ֤י ׀

עֵינִי֙ יֹ֣רְדָה מַּ֔יִם כִּֽי־רָחַ֥ק מִמֶּ֛נִּי מְנַחֵ֖ם מֵשִׁ֣יב נַפְשִׁ֑י

הָי֤וּ בָנַי֙ שֽׁוֹמֵמִ֔ים כִּ֥י גָבַ֖ר אוֹיֵֽב׃ יז **פֵּ**רְשָׂ֨ה צִיּ֜וֹן

בְּיָדֶ֗יהָ אֵ֤ין מְנַחֵם֙ לָ֔הּ צִוָּ֧ה יְהֹוָ֛ה לְיַעֲקֹ֖ב סְבִיבָ֣יו

צָרָ֑יו הָיְתָ֧ה יְרוּשָׁלַ֛͏ִם לְנִדָּ֖ה בֵּינֵיהֶֽם׃ יח **צַ**דִּ֥יק ה֛וּא

יהוה כִּ֥י פִ֖יהוּ מָרִ֑יתִי שִׁמְעוּ־נָ֣א כָל־°עַמִּ֗ים וּרְאוּ֙ °הָעַמִּים ק׳

מַכְאֹבִ֔י בְּתוּלֹתַ֥י וּבַחוּרַ֖י הָלְכ֥וּ בַשֶּֽׁבִי׃ יט **קָ**רָ֤אתִי

לַֽמְאַהֲבַי֙ הֵ֣מָּה רִמּ֔וּנִי כֹּהֲנַ֥י וּזְקֵנַ֖י בָּעִ֣יר גָּוָ֑עוּ כִּֽי־

בִקְשׁ֥וּ אֹ֙כֶל֙ לָ֔מוֹ וְיָשִׁ֖יבוּ אֶת־נַפְשָֽׁם׃ כ **רְ**אֵ֣ה יְהֹוָ֞ה

כִּֽי־צַר־לִ֗י מֵעַי֙ חֳמַרְמָ֔רוּ נֶהְפַּ֤ךְ לִבִּי֙ בְּקִרְבִּ֔י כִּ֥י

מָר֖וֹ מָרִ֑יתִי מִח֥וּץ שִׁכְּלָה־חֶ֖רֶב בַּבַּ֥יִת כַּמָּֽוֶת׃

כא **שָֽׁ**מְע֞וּ כִּ֧י נֶאֱנָחָ֣ה אָ֗נִי אֵ֤ין מְנַחֵם֙ לִ֔י כָּל־אֹ֨יְבַ֜י

שָֽׁמְע֤וּ רָֽעָתִי֙ שָׂ֔שׂוּ כִּ֥י אַתָּ֖ה עָשִׂ֑יתָ הֵבֵ֥אתָ יוֹם־

קָרָ֖אתָ וְיִֽהְי֣וּ כָמֹ֑נִי׃ כב **תָּ**בֹ֨א כָל־רָעָתָ֤ם לְפָנֶ֙יךָ֙

וְעוֹלֵ֣ל לָ֔מוֹ כַּאֲשֶׁ֥ר עוֹלַ֖לְתָּ לִ֑י עַ֥ל כָּל־פְּשָׁעָ֖י כִּֽי־

רַבּ֥וֹת אַנְחֹתַ֖י וְלִבִּ֥י דַוָּֽי׃

ב א **אֵיכָה֩** יָעִ֨יב בְּאַפּ֤וֹ ׀ אֲדֹנָי֙ אֶת־בַּת־צִיּ֔וֹן הִשְׁלִ֤יךְ

מִשָּׁמַ֙יִם֙ אֶ֔רֶץ תִּפְאֶ֖רֶת יִשְׂרָאֵ֑ל וְלֹא־זָכַ֥ר הֲדֹם־

רַגְלָ֖יו בְּי֥וֹם אַפּֽוֹ׃ ב **בִּ**לַּ֨ע אֲדֹנָ֜י °לֹ֣א חָמַ֗ל אֵ֤ת כָּל־ °וְלֹא ק׳ ב

14. God collected all Zion's transgressions and metaphorically 'knit' them together into a heavy garment which He thrust upon her neck in one heavy, cumulative load, effectively weighing her down, and sapping her strength until she was unable to withstand the enemy.

15. *He proclaimed a set time against me,* i.e., the Ninth of Av *(Taanis 29a).*

17. In this parenthetic verse there is a momentary shift from first person (Zion lamenting) to third person. Jeremiah becomes the speaker and acknowledges that God is the executor of the calamity.

18. [Zion itself resumes the lament, and confesses publicly and without reservation that God is righteous and justified in what He had done.]

21. Let them share my suffering, — but let them have no part in my ultimate restoration *(Midrash).*

2/1. *Daughter of Zion* is a poetic form, used to denote Jerusalem or its populace.

like my pain which befell me; which HASHEM has afflicted me on the day of His wrath. ¹³ From on high He sent a fire into my bones, and it crushed them. He spread a net for my feet hurling me backward. He made me desolate; in constant misery. ¹⁴ The burden of my transgressions was accumulated in His hand; they were knit together and thrust upon my neck — He sapped my strength. The Lord has delivered me into the hands of those I cannot withstand. ¹⁵ The Lord has trampled all my heroes in my midst; He proclaimed a set time against me to crush my young men. As in a winepress the Lord has trodden the maiden daughter of Judah. ¹⁶ Over these things I weep; my eyes run with water because a comforter to revive my spirit is far from me. My children have become forlorn, because the enemy has prevailed. ¹⁷ Zion spread out her hands; there was none to comfort her. HASHEM commanded against Jacob that his enemies should surround him; Jerusalem has become as one unclean in their midst. ¹⁸ It is HASHEM Who is righteous, for I disobeyed His utterance. Listen, all you peoples and behold my pain: My maidens and my youths have gone into captivity. ¹⁹ I called for my lovers but they deceived me. My priests and my elders perished in the city as they sought food for themselves to keep alive. ²⁰ See, HASHEM, how distressed I am; my insides churn! My heart is turned over inside me for I rebelled grievously. Outside the sword bereaved, inside was death-like. ²¹ They heard how I sighed, there was none to comfort me. All my enemies heard of my plight and rejoiced, for it was You Who did it. O bring on the day You proclaimed and let them be like me! ²² Let all their wickedness come before You, and inflict them as You inflicted me for all my transgressions. For my groans are many, and my heart is sick.

¹ **A**las — The Lord in His anger has clouded the daughter of Zion. He cast down from heaven to earth the glory of Israel. He did not remember His footstool on the day of His wrath. ² The Lord consumed without pity all the dwell-

נְאוֹת יַעֲקֹב הָרַס בְּעֶבְרָתוֹ מִבְצְרֵי בַת־יְהוּדָה

ג הִגִּיעַ לָאָרֶץ חִלֵּל מַמְלָכָה וְשָׂרֶיהָ. גָּדַע בָּחֳרִי־
אַף כֹּל קֶרֶן יִשְׂרָאֵל הֵשִׁיב אָחוֹר יְמִינוֹ מִפְּנֵי
אוֹיֵב וַיִּבְעַר בְּיַעֲקֹב כְּאֵשׁ לֶהָבָה אָכְלָה סָבִיב.

ד דָּרַךְ קַשְׁתּוֹ כְּאוֹיֵב נִצָּב יְמִינוֹ כְּצָר וַיַּהֲרֹג כֹּל
מַחֲמַדֵּי־עָיִן בְּאֹהֶל בַּת־צִיּוֹן שָׁפַךְ כָּאֵשׁ חֲמָתוֹ.

ה הָיָה אֲדֹנָי | כְּאוֹיֵב בִּלַּע יִשְׂרָאֵל בִּלַּע כָּל־
אַרְמְנוֹתֶיהָ שִׁחֵת מִבְצָרָיו וַיֶּרֶב בְּבַת־יְהוּדָה
תַּאֲנִיָּה וַאֲנִיָּה. וַיַּחְמֹס כַּגַּן שֻׂכּוֹ שִׁחֵת מֹעֲדוֹ

ו שִׁכַּח יהוה | בְּצִיּוֹן מוֹעֵד וְשַׁבָּת וַיִּנְאַץ בְּזַעַם־אַפּוֹ

ז מֶלֶךְ וְכֹהֵן. זָנַח אֲדֹנָי | מִזְבְּחוֹ נִאֵר מִקְדָּשׁוֹ
הִסְגִּיר בְּיַד־אוֹיֵב חוֹמֹת אַרְמְנוֹתֶיהָ קוֹל נָתְנוּ

ח בְּבֵית־יהוה כְּיוֹם מוֹעֵד. חָשַׁב יהוה | לְהַשְׁחִית
חוֹמַת בַּת־צִיּוֹן נָטָה קָו לֹא־הֵשִׁיב יָדוֹ מִבַּלֵּעַ

ט וַיַּאֲבֶל־חֵל וְחוֹמָה יַחְדָּו אֻמְלָלוּ. טָבְעוּ בָאָרֶץ
שְׁעָרֶיהָ אִבַּד וְשִׁבַּר בְּרִיחֶיהָ מַלְכָּהּ וְשָׂרֶיהָ
בַגּוֹיִם אֵין תּוֹרָה גַּם־נְבִיאֶיהָ לֹא־מָצְאוּ חָזוֹן

י מֵיהוה. יֵשְׁבוּ לָאָרֶץ יִדְּמוּ זִקְנֵי בַת־צִיּוֹן הֶעֱלוּ
עָפָר עַל־רֹאשָׁם חָגְרוּ שַׂקִּים הוֹרִידוּ לָאָרֶץ

יא רֹאשָׁן בְּתוּלֹת יְרוּשָׁלָ͏ִם. כָּלוּ בַדְּמָעוֹת עֵינַי
חֳמַרְמְרוּ מֵעַי נִשְׁפַּךְ לָאָרֶץ כְּבֵדִי עַל־שֶׁבֶר בַּת־

יב עַמִּי בֵּעָטֵף עוֹלֵל וְיוֹנֵק בִּרְחֹבוֹת קִרְיָה. לְאִמֹּתָם
יֹאמְרוּ אַיֵּה דָּגָן וָיָיִן בְּהִתְעַטְּפָם כֶּחָלָל בִּרְחֹבוֹת

יג עִיר בְּהִשְׁתַּפֵּךְ נַפְשָׁם אֶל־חֵיק אִמֹּתָם. מָה־
°אֲעִידֵךְ ק׳ אֲעוֹדֵךְ מָה אֲדַמֶּה־לָּךְ הַבַּת יְרוּשָׁלַ͏ִם מָה
אַשְׁוֶה־לָּךְ וַאֲנַחֲמֵךְ בְּתוּלַת בַּת־צִיּוֹן כִּי־גָדוֹל

3. *He withdrew His right hand, i.e., He refrained from doing battle for His children (Rashi).*

4. In this verse God is depicted, not only in His passive role as the One who withdrew His support, but as One who actively participated in Israel's destruction.

He consumed all her citadels. He thus vented His anger by directing His actions 'on wood and stone' [i.e., on inanimate objects rather than on human lives] so as to avoid the total slaughter of the Jews themselves *(Palgei Mayim).*

7. *As though it were a festival day.* The heathens clamored joyously at the destruction of the Temple, matching the fervor of Israel's joyous chants on its holidays *(Alshich; Rashi).*

9. *Minchas Shay* explains that the ט of טָבְעוּ, *sunk,* is written as a smaller letter in *Megillah* scrolls to allude to ט, the Ninth, of Av when the Temple was destroyed.

10. This verse is cited as a basis for the Halachic customs of sitting on the ground on Tishah B'Av. The 12th-century *Sefer HaEshkol* says: After the final meal, we go to the synagogue without shoes and sit on the ground as it is written: 'sit on the ground in silence.'

ings of Jacob; in His anger He razed the fortresses of the daughter of Judah down to the ground; He profaned the kingdom and its leaders. ³ He cut down, in fierce anger, all the dignity of Israel; He withdrew His right hand in the presence of the enemy. He burned through Jacob like a flaming fire, consuming on all sides. ⁴ He bent His bow like an enemy. His right hand poised like a foe, He slew all who were of pleasant appearance. In the tent of the daughter of Zion He poured out His wrath like fire. ⁵ The Lord became like an enemy. He consumed Israel; He consumed all her citadels, He destroyed its fortresses. He increased within the daughter of Judah moaning and mourning. ⁶ He stripped His Booth like a garden, He destroyed his place of assembly. HASHEM made Zion oblivious of festival and Sabbath, and in His fierce anger He spurned king and priest. ⁷ The Lord rejected His altar, abolished His Sanctuary; He handed over to the enemy the walls of her citadels. They raised a clamor in the House of HASHEM as though it were a festival. ⁸ HASHEM resolved to destroy the wall of the daughter of Zion. He stretched out the line and did not relent from devouring. Indeed, He made rampart and wall mourn; together they languished. ⁹ Her gates have sunk into the earth, He has utterly shattered her bars; her king and officers are among the heathen, there is no Torah; her prophets, too, find no vision from HASHEM. ¹⁰ The elders of the daughter of Zion sit on the ground in silence; they have strewn ashes on their heads, and wear sackcloth. The maidens of Jerusalem have bowed their heads to the ground. ¹¹ My eyes fail with tears, my insides churn; my liver spills on the ground at the shattering of my people, while babes and sucklings swoon in the streets of the city. ¹² They say to their mothers, 'Where is bread and wine?' as they swoon like a dying man in the streets of the town; as their soul ebbs away in their mothers' laps. ¹³ With what shall I bear witness for you? To what can I compare you, O daughter of Jerusalem? To what can I liken you to comfort you, O maiden daughter of Zion? — Your ruin is as vast as the sea; who can

יד כַּיָּם שִׁבְרֵךְ מִי יִרְפָּא־לָךְ. **נְבִיאַיִךְ** חָזוּ לָךְ שָׁוְא
וְתָפֵל וְלֹא־גִלּוּ עַל־עֲוֺנֵךְ לְהָשִׁיב °שְׁבִיתֵךְ וַיֶּחֱזוּ °שְׁבוּתֵךְ ק
לָךְ מַשְׂאוֹת שָׁוְא וּמַדּוּחִים. **סָפְקוּ** עָלַיִךְ כַּפַּיִם טו
כָּל־עֹבְרֵי דֶרֶךְ שָׁרְקוּ וַיָּנִעוּ רֹאשָׁם עַל־בַּת
יְרוּשָׁלָ͏ִם הֲזֹאת הָעִיר שֶׁיֹּאמְרוּ כְּלִילַת יֹפִי
מָשׂוֹשׂ לְכָל־הָאָרֶץ. **פָּצוּ** עָלַיִךְ פִּיהֶם כָּל־אֹיְבַיִךְ טז
שָׁרְקוּ וַיַּחַרְקוּ־שֵׁן אָמְרוּ בִּלָּעְנוּ אַךְ זֶה הַיּוֹם
שֶׁקִּוִּינֻהוּ מָצָאנוּ רָאִינוּ. **עָשָׂה** יְהֹוָה אֲשֶׁר זָמָם יז
בִּצַּע אֶמְרָתוֹ אֲשֶׁר צִוָּה מִימֵי־קֶדֶם הָרַס וְלֹא
חָמָל וַיְשַׂמַּח עָלַיִךְ אוֹיֵב הֵרִים קֶרֶן צָרָיִךְ. **צָעַק** יח
לִבָּם אֶל־אֲדֹנָי חוֹמַת בַּת־צִיּוֹן הוֹרִידִי כַנַּחַל
דִּמְעָה יוֹמָם וָלַיְלָה אַל־תִּתְּנִי פוּגַת לָךְ אַל־תִּדֹּם
בַּת־עֵינֵךְ. **קוּמִי** | רֹנִּי בליל [בַלַּיְלָה] לְרֹאשׁ אַשְׁמֻרוֹת יט
שִׁפְכִי כַמַּיִם לִבֵּךְ נֹכַח פְּנֵי אֲדֹנָי שְׂאִי אֵלָיו כַּפַּיִךְ
עַל־נֶפֶשׁ עוֹלָלַיִךְ הָעֲטוּפִים בְּרָעָב בְּרֹאשׁ כָּל־
חוּצוֹת. **רְאֵה** יְהֹוָה וְהַבִּיטָה לְמִי עוֹלַלְתָּ כֹּה אִם־ כ
תֹּאכַלְנָה נָשִׁים פִּרְיָם עֹלֲלֵי טִפֻּחִים אִם־יֵהָרֵג
בְּמִקְדַּשׁ אֲדֹנָי כֹּהֵן וְנָבִיא. **שָׁכְבוּ** לָאָרֶץ חוּצוֹת כא
נַעַר וְזָקֵן בְּתוּלֹתַי וּבַחוּרַי נָפְלוּ בֶחָרֶב הָרַגְתָּ
בְּיוֹם אַפֶּךָ טָבַחְתָּ לֹא חָמָלְתָּ. **תִּקְרָא** כְיוֹם מוֹעֵד כב
מְגוּרַי מִסָּבִיב וְלֹא הָיָה בְּיוֹם אַף־יְהֹוָה פָּלִיט
וְשָׂרִיד אֲשֶׁר־טִפַּחְתִּי וְרִבִּיתִי אֹיְבִי כִלָּם.

ג **אֲנִי** הַגֶּבֶר רָאָה עֳנִי בְּשֵׁבֶט עֶבְרָתוֹ. **אוֹתִי** נָהַג א־ב
וַיֹּלַךְ חֹשֶׁךְ וְלֹא־אוֹר. **אַךְ** בִּי יָשֻׁב יַהֲפֹךְ יָדוֹ כָּל־ ג
הַיּוֹם. **בִּלָּה** בְשָׂרִי וְעוֹרִי שִׁבַּר עַצְמוֹתָי. **בָּנָה** עָלַי ד־ה
וַיַּקַּף רֹאשׁ וּתְלָאָה. **בְּמַחֲשַׁכִּים** הוֹשִׁיבַנִי כְּמֵתֵי ו

heal you? [14] Your prophets envisioned for you vanity and foolishness, and they did not expose your iniquity to bring you back in repentance; they prophesied to you oracles of vanity and deception. [15] All who pass along the way clap hands at you; they hiss and wag their head at the daughter of Jerusalem: 'Could this be the city that was called Perfect in Beauty, Joy of All the Earth?' [16] All your enemies jeered at you; they hiss and gnash their teeth. They say: 'We have devoured her! Indeed, this is the day we longed for; we have actually seen it!' [17] HASHEM has done what He planned; He carried out His decree which He ordained long ago; He devastated without pity. He let the enemy rejoice over you; He raised the pride of your foes. [18] Their heart cried out to the Lord. O wall of the daughter of Zion: Shed tears like a river, day and night; give yourself no respite, do not let your eyes be still. [19] Arise, cry out at night in the beginning of the watches! Pour out your heart like water in the Presence of the Lord; lift up your hands to Him for the life of your young children, who swoon from hunger at every street corner. [20] Look, HASHEM, and behold, whom You have treated so. Should women eat their own offspring, the babes of their care? Should priest and prophet be slain in the Sanctuary of the Lord? [21] Out on the ground, in the streets they lie, young and old; my maidens and my young men have fallen by the sword. You slew them on the day of Your wrath; You slaughtered them and showed no mercy. [22] You invited, as though at festival time, my evil neighbors round about. So that, at the day of HASHEM'S wrath, there were none who survived or escaped. Those who I cherished and brought up, my enemy has wiped out.

15. *They hiss and wag their head ...* In mock and derision, not over your loss, Jerusalem, but for themselves, as the Sages proclaimed: Had the heathens known how much they would lose by destroying the Temple, they would not have done it. The Divine blessing that had rested upon Israel and, through it, upon the entire world, left with the Destruction (*Alshich*).

18. The greatest sin of all is that we, in our time, stopped mourning properly for Jerusalem. I am convinced that, in punishment for this, our exile has lasted so long, we have never been able to find rest, and we are always being persecuted. Historically, whenever we found some security in any of the lands of our exile, we forgot Jerusalem and did not set it at the foremost place in our minds (*Rav Yaakov Emden*).

21. Had the Destruction come on a day other than 'the day of Your wrath,' i.e., Tishah B'Av, it would have been tempered with mercy and restraint. Having come on the day You specifically set aside for display of Your anger, it was untempered and complete (*Lechem Dimah*).

3/1. JEREMIAH'S PERSONAL LAMENT.

Jeremiah laments that he saw more affliction than the other prophets who foretold the Destruction. For it was destroyed not in their days, but in his (*Rashi*). Thus this chapter begins, אֲנִי הַגֶּבֶר, *I am the man*, which has the same numerical value [271] as יִרְמְיָהוּ, *Jeremiah* [*Tzfunos Yisrael*].

[1] I am the man who has seen affliction by the rod of His anger. [2] He has driven me on and on into unrelieved darkness. [3] Only against me did He turn His hand repeatedly all day long. [4] He has worn away my flesh and skin; He broke my bones. [5] He besieged and encircled me with bitterness and travail. [6] He has placed me in darkness like the

ז-ח עוֹלָם. גָּדַר בַּעֲדִי וְלֹא אֵצֵא הִכְבִּיד נְחָשְׁתִּי. גַּם

ט כִּי אֶזְעַק וַאֲשַׁוֵּעַ שָׂתַם תְּפִלָּתִי. גָּדַר דְּרָכַי בְּגָזִית

י נְתִיבֹתַי עִוָּה. דֹּב אֹרֵב הוּא לִי °אֲרִיה °אֲרִי ק׳

יא בְּמִסְתָּרִים. דְּרָכַי סוֹרֵר וַיְפַשְּׁחֵנִי שָׂמַנִי שֹׁמֵם.

יב-יג דָּרַךְ קַשְׁתּוֹ וַיַּצִּיבֵנִי כַּמַּטָּרָא לַחֵץ. הֵבִיא בְּכִלְיֹתַי

יד בְּנֵי אַשְׁפָּתוֹ. הָיִיתִי שְּׂחֹק לְכָל־עַמִּי נְגִינָתָם כָּל־

טו-טז הַיּוֹם. הִשְׂבִּיעַנִי בַמְּרוֹרִים הִרְוַנִי לַעֲנָה. וַיַּגְרֵס

יז בֶּחָצָץ שִׁנָּי הִכְפִּישַׁנִי בָּאֵפֶר. וַתִּזְנַח מִשָּׁלוֹם

יח נַפְשִׁי נָשִׁיתִי טוֹבָה. וָאֹמַר אָבַד נִצְחִי וְתוֹחַלְתִּי

יט-כ מֵיהוָה. זְכָר־עָנְיִי וּמְרוּדִי לַעֲנָה וָרֹאשׁ. זָכוֹר

כא תִּזְכּוֹר °וְתָשִׁיחַ עָלַי נַפְשִׁי. זֹאת אָשִׁיב אֶל־לִבִּי °וְתָשׁוֹחַ ק׳

כב עַל־כֵּן אוֹחִיל. חַסְדֵי יהוה כִּי לֹא־תָמְנוּ כִּי לֹא־

כג כָלוּ רַחֲמָיו. חֲדָשִׁים לַבְּקָרִים רַבָּה אֱמוּנָתֶךָ.

כד-כה חֶלְקִי יהוה אָמְרָה נַפְשִׁי עַל־כֵּן אוֹחִיל לוֹ. טוֹב

כה יהוה לְקֹוָו לְנֶפֶשׁ תִּדְרְשֶׁנּוּ. טוֹב וְיָחִיל וְדוּמָם

כו לִתְשׁוּעַת יהוה. טוֹב לַגֶּבֶר כִּי־יִשָּׂא עֹל בִּנְעוּרָיו.

כח-כט יֵשֵׁב בָּדָד וְיִדֹּם כִּי נָטַל עָלָיו. יִתֵּן בֶּעָפָר פִּיהוּ

ל אוּלַי יֵשׁ תִּקְוָה. יִתֵּן לְמַכֵּהוּ לֶחִי יִשְׂבַּע בְּחֶרְפָּה.

לא-לב כִּי לֹא יִזְנַח לְעוֹלָם אֲדֹנָי. כִּי אִם־הוֹגָה וְרִחַם

לג כְּרֹב חֲסָדָו. כִּי לֹא עִנָּה מִלִּבּוֹ וַיַּגֶּה בְּנֵי־אִישׁ.

לד-לה לְדַכֵּא תַּחַת רַגְלָיו כֹּל אֲסִירֵי אָרֶץ. לְהַטּוֹת

לו מִשְׁפַּט־גָּבֶר נֶגֶד פְּנֵי עֶלְיוֹן. לְעַוֵּת אָדָם בְּרִיבוֹ

לז אֲדֹנָי לֹא רָאָה. מִי זֶה אָמַר וַתֶּהִי אֲדֹנָי לֹא צִוָּה.

לח-לט מִפִּי עֶלְיוֹן לֹא תֵצֵא הָרָעוֹת וְהַטּוֹב. מַה־יִּתְאוֹנֵן

מ אָדָם חָי גֶּבֶר עַל־חֲטָאָו. נַחְפְּשָׂה דְרָכֵינוּ

מא וְנַחְקֹרָה וְנָשׁוּבָה עַד־יהוה. נִשָּׂא לְבָבֵנוּ אֶל־

Or the first-person narrative refers to the suffering of the entire nation as a collective entity personified as an individual (Midrash).

14. Jeremiah is lamenting how, whenever he prophesied impending disaster, the Jews would laugh at him and taunt him. Because of their inattentiveness to his prophecies, disaster befell them (Palgei Mayim).

16. The Talmud relates that on the eve of Tishah B'Av, after Rav would complete his regular meal, he would dip a morsel of bread into ashes and say 'This is the essence of the Erev Tishah B'Av meal, in fulfillment of the verse: ... He made me cower in ashes' (Yerushalmi Taanis 4:6).

22. Rashi, whose translation we followed, gives an alternate translation: חַסְדֵי ה', it is due to HASHEM's kindness, כִּי לֹא תָמְנוּ, that we were not annihilated for our transgressions, כִּי לֹא כָלוּ רַחֲמָיו — because His mercies are not exhausted [see Numbers 17:28].

26-27. Since we are certain that God will not eternally neglect us, we accept God's afflictions in quiet resignation, and silently anticipate God's ultimate salvation. As for our suffering in the interim ... It is better to bear the yoke in one's youth — while one has the vigor to withstand the tribulations, rather than when old and lacking the stamina (Alshich).

31. In the last several verses, the prophet exhorted man to completely debase himself in resignation before God. Now, he justifies his advice by extolling the compassion of God.

37-40. Rashi groups together four verses and explains: One should never ascribe his suffering to chance, because from whom else but from God do good and evil emanate? Therefore a man should not complain — but should blame his own sins, search his ways and repent.

eternally dead. [7] He has walled me in so I cannot escape; He has weighed me down with chains. [8] Though I would cry out and plead, He shut out my prayer. [9] He has walled up my roads with hewn stones; He tangled up my paths. [10] He is a lurking bear to me, a lion in hiding. [11] He has strewn my paths with thorns and made me tread carefully; He made me desolate. [12] He bent His bow and set me up as a target for the arrow. [13] He shot into my vitals the arrows of His quiver. [14] I have become a laughing stock to all my people; object of their jibes all day long. [15] He filled me with bitterness, sated me with wormwood. [16] He ground my teeth on gravel, He made me cower in ashes. [17] My soul despaired of having peace, I have forgotten goodness. [18] And I said, 'Gone is my strength and my expectation from HASHEM.' [19] Remember my afflictions and my sorrow; the wormwood and bitterness. [20] My soul remembers well — and makes me despondent. [21] Yet, this I bear in mind; therefore I still hope: [22] HASHEM's kindness surely has not ended, nor are His mercies exhausted. [21] They are new every morning; great is Your faithfulness! [24] 'HASHEM is my portion,' says my soul, therefore I have hope in Him. [25] HASHEM as good to those who trust in Him; to the soul that seeks Him. [26] It is good to hope submissively for HASHEM's salvation. [27] It is good for a man that he bear a yoke in his youth. [28] Let one sit in solitude and be submissive, for He has laid it upon him. [29] Let him put his mouth to the dust — there may yet be hope. [30] Let one offer his cheek to his smiter, let him be filled with disgrace. [31] — For the Lord does not reject forever; [32] He first afflicts, then pities according to His abundant kindness. [33] For He does not torment capriciously, nor afflict man ... [34] Nor crush under His feet all the prisoners of the earth; [35] nor deny a man justice in the presence of the Most High. [36] To wrong a man in his conflict — the Lord does not approve. [37] Whose decree was ever fulfilled unless the Lord ordained it? [38] Is it not from the mouth of the Most High that evil and good emanate? [39] Of what shall a living man complain? A strong man for his sins! [40] Let us search and examine our ways and return to HASHEM. [41] Let us lift our hearts with our hands to

מב כַּפָּיִם אֶל־אֵל בַּשָּׁמָיִם. **נַ**חְנוּ פָשַׁעְנוּ וּמָרִינוּ אַתָּה

מג לֹא סָלָחְתָּ. **סַ**כֹּתָה בָאַף וַתִּרְדְּפֵנוּ הָרַגְתָּ לֹא

מד-מה חָמָלְתָּ. **סַ**כֹּתָה בֶעָנָן לָךְ מֵעֲבוֹר תְּפִלָּה. **סְ**חִי

וּמָאוֹס תְּשִׂימֵנוּ בְּקֶרֶב הָעַמִּים. **פָּ**צוּ עָלֵינוּ פִּיהֶם

מו כָּל־אֹיְבֵינוּ. **פַּ**חַד וָפַחַת הָיָה לָנוּ הַשֵּׁאת וְהַשָּׁבֶר.

מז **פַּ**לְגֵי־מַיִם תֵּרַד עֵינִי עַל־שֶׁבֶר בַּת־עַמִּי. **עֵ**ינִי

מח-מט נִגְּרָה וְלֹא תִדְמֶה מֵאֵין הֲפֻגוֹת. **עַ**ד־יַשְׁקִיף וְיֵרֶא

נ יְהוָה מִשָּׁמָיִם. **עֵ**ינִי עוֹלְלָה לְנַפְשִׁי מִכֹּל בְּנוֹת

נא עִירִי. **צ**וֹד צָדוּנִי כַּצִּפּוֹר אֹיְבַי חִנָּם. **צָ**מְתוּ בַבּוֹר

נב-נג חַיָּי וַיַּדּוּ־אֶבֶן בִּי. **צָ**פוּ־מַיִם עַל־רֹאשִׁי אָמַרְתִּי

נד נִגְזָרְתִּי. **קָ**רָאתִי שִׁמְךָ יְהוָה מִבּוֹר תַּחְתִּיּוֹת. **קוֹ**לִי

נה-נו שָׁמָעְתָּ אַל־תַּעְלֵם אָזְנְךָ לְרַוְחָתִי לְשַׁוְעָתִי.

נז **קָ**רַבְתָּ בְּיוֹם אֶקְרָאֶךָּ אָמַרְתָּ אַל־תִּירָא. **רַ**בְתָּ

נח-נט אֲדֹנָי רִיבֵי נַפְשִׁי גָּאַלְתָּ חַיָּי. **רָ**אִיתָה יְהוָה עַוָּתָתִי

ס שָׁפְטָה מִשְׁפָּטִי. **רָ**אִיתָה כָּל־נִקְמָתָם כָּל־

סא מַחְשְׁבֹתָם לִי. **שָׁ**מַעְתָּ חֶרְפָּתָם יְהוָה כָּל־

סב מַחְשְׁבֹתָם עָלָי. **שִׂ**פְתֵי קָמַי וְהֶגְיוֹנָם עָלַי כָּל־

סג הַיּוֹם. **שִׁ**בְתָּם וְקִימָתָם הַבִּיטָה אֲנִי מַנְגִּינָתָם.

סד-סה **תָּ**שִׁיב לָהֶם גְּמוּל יְהוָה כְּמַעֲשֵׂה יְדֵיהֶם. **תִּ**תֵּן

סו לָהֶם מְגִנַּת־לֵב תַּאֲלָתְךָ לָהֶם. **תִּ**רְדֹּף בְּאַף

וְתַשְׁמִידֵם מִתַּחַת שְׁמֵי יְהוָה.

א **אֵ**יכָה יוּעַם זָהָב יִשְׁנֶא הַכֶּתֶם הַטּוֹב תִּשְׁתַּפֵּכְנָה **ד**

ב אַבְנֵי־קֹדֶשׁ בְּרֹאשׁ כָּל־חוּצוֹת. **בְּ**נֵי צִיּוֹן הַיְקָרִים

הַמְסֻלָּאִים בַּפָּז אֵיכָה נֶחְשְׁבוּ לְנִבְלֵי־חֶרֶשׂ

מַעֲשֵׂה יְדֵי יוֹצֵר. **גַּ**ם־°תנין חָלְצוּ שַׁד הֵינִיקוּ °תַּנִּים ק׳ ג

גּוּרֵיהֶן בַּת־עַמִּי לְאַכְזָר °כי ענים בַּמִּדְבָּר. **דָּ**בַק °כַּיְעֵנִים ק׳ ד

46. Instead of completely ignoring us — as one would normally ignore 'filth and refuse' — our enemies taunted and jeered at us giving us no peace; not even allowing us to wallow, undisturbed, in our misery (Ibn Yachya).

51. This is a personal lament of Jeremiah who was of an aristocratic priestly family. He anguished that his weeping contorted his face and aggrieved his spirit more than any inhabitant of the city. His family was particularly affected, and suffered more than others because, as priests, they had been selected for holiness and the service of God (Rashi).

57. The phrase 'Do not be afraid!' appears throughout Scripture. It was said not only on isolated occasions, but to virtually every one of the fathers of our people; it is a divine promise that Israel need not fear.

64-66. In these verses God is asked to mete out retribution to Israel's enemies, in kind, for all their evil.

4/2. Midrash Lekach Tov, commenting on the precious character of the people of Jerusalem, notes that when residents of Jerusalem sat down to eat they would hang a cloth over their door as a signal to the poor that they might come to share their meal [see also Bava Basra 93b].

God in heaven: ⁴² 'We have transgressed and rebelled — You have not forgiven. ⁴³ You have enveloped Yourself in anger and pursued us; You have slain mercilessly. ⁴⁴ You wrapped Yourself in a cloud that no prayer can pierce. ⁴⁵ You made us a filth and refuse among the nations.' ⁴⁶ All our enemies jeered at us; ⁴⁷ panic and pitfall were ours, ravage and ruin. ⁴⁸ My eye shed streams of water at the shattering of my people. ⁴⁹ My eye will flow and will not cease — without relief — until HASHEM looks down and takes notice from heaven. ⁵¹ My eyes have brought me grief over all the daughters of my city. ⁵² I have been constantly ensnared like a bird by my enemies without cause. ⁵³ They cut off my life in a pit and threw stones at me. ⁵⁴ Waters flowed over my head; I thought, 'I am doomed!' ⁵⁵ I called on Your name, HASHEM, from the depths of the pit. ⁵⁶ You have heard my voice; do not shut your ear from my prayer for my relief when I cry out. ⁵⁷ You always drew near on the day I would call You; You said, 'Do not be afraid.' ⁵⁸ You always championed my cause, O Lord, you redeemed my life. ⁵⁹ You have seen, HASHEM, the injustices I suffer; judge my cause. ⁶⁰ You have seen all their vengeance, all their designs against me. ⁶¹ You have heard their insults, HASHEM; all their designs regarding me. ⁶² The speech and thoughts of my enemies are against me all day long. ⁶³ Look, in everything they do, I am the butt of their taunts. ⁶⁴ Pay them back their due, HASHEM, as they have done. ⁶⁵ Give them a broken heart; may Your curse be upon them! ⁶⁶ Pursue them in anger and destroy them from under the heavens of HASHEM.

¹ **A**las — The gold is dimmed! The finest gold is changed! Sacred stones are scattered at every street corner! ² The precious children of Zion, who are comparable to fine gold — alas, are now treated like earthen jugs, work of a potter. ³ Even 'Tanim' will offer the breast and suckle their young; the daughter of my people has become cruel, like ostriches in the desert. ⁴ The tongue of the suckling

לְשׁוֹן יוֹנֵק אֶל־חִכּוֹ בַּצָּמָא עֽוֹלָלִים שָׁאֲלוּ לֶחֶם

ה פֹּרֵשׂ אֵין לָהֶם. **הָאֹכְלִים** לְמַעֲדַנִּים נָשַׁמּוּ בַּחוּצוֹת הָאֱמֻנִים עֲלֵי תוֹלָע חִבְּקוּ אַשְׁפַּתּֽוֹת.

ו **וַיִּגְדַּל** עֲוֹן בַּת־עַמִּי מֵחַטַּאת סְדֹם הַהֲפוּכָה כְמוֹ־רָגַע וְלֹא־חָלוּ בָהּ יָדָֽיִם. **זַכּוּ** נְזִירֶיהָ מִשֶּׁלֶג צַחוּ

ז מֵחָלָב אָֽדְמוּ עֶצֶם מִפְּנִינִים סַפִּיר גִּזְרָתָֽם. **חָשַׁךְ**

ח מִשְּׁחוֹר תָּאֳרָם לֹא נִכְּרוּ בַּחוּצוֹת צָפַד עוֹרָם עַל־עַצְמָם יָבֵשׁ הָיָה כָעֵץ. **טוֹבִים** הָיוּ חַלְלֵי־חֶרֶב

ט מֵֽחַלְלֵי רָעָב שֶׁהֵם יָזֻבוּ מְדֻקָּרִים מִתְּנוּבֹת שָׂדָֽי.

י **יְדֵי** נָשִׁים רַחֲמָנִיּוֹת בִּשְּׁלוּ יַלְדֵיהֶן הָיוּ לְבָרוֹת לָמוֹ בְּשֶׁבֶר בַּת־עַמִּי. **כִּלָּה** יהוה אֶת־חֲמָתוֹ שָׁפַךְ

יא חֲרוֹן אַפּוֹ וַיַּצֶּת־אֵשׁ בְּצִיּוֹן וַתֹּאכַל יְסֹדֹתֶֽיהָ. **לֹא**

יב הֶאֱמִינוּ מַלְכֵי־אֶרֶץ °וְכֹל יֹשְׁבֵי תֵבֵל כִּי יָבֹא צַר °כֹּל ק׳

יג וְאוֹיֵב בְּשַׁעֲרֵי יְרוּשָׁלָֽםִ. **מֵחַטֹּאת** נְבִיאֶיהָ עֲוֺנֹת כֹּהֲנֶיהָ הַשֹּׁפְכִים בְּקִרְבָּהּ דַּם צַדִּיקִים. **נָעוּ** עִוְרִים

יד בַּחוּצוֹת נְגֹאֲלוּ בַּדָּם בְּלֹא יוּכְלוּ יִגְּעוּ בִּלְבֻשֵׁיהֶֽם.

טו **סוּרוּ** טָמֵא קָרְאוּ לָמוֹ סוּרוּ סוּרוּ אַל־תִּגָּעוּ כִּי נָצוּ גַם־נָעוּ אָמְרוּ בַּגּוֹיִם לֹא יוֹסִפוּ לָגֽוּר. **פְּנֵי**

טז יהוה חִלְּקָם לֹא יוֹסִיף לְהַבִּיטָם פְּנֵי כֹהֲנִים לֹא נָשָׂאוּ °זְקֵנִים לֹא חָנָֽנוּ. °עֽוֹדֵינָה תִּכְלֶינָה עֵינֵינוּ °זְקֵנִים ק׳ / °עוֹדֵינוּ ק׳

יז אֶל־עֶזְרָתֵנוּ הָבֶל בְּצִפִּיָּתֵנוּ צִפִּינוּ אֶל־גּוֹי לֹא

יח יוֹשִֽׁעַ. **צָדוּ** צְעָדֵינוּ מִלֶּכֶת בִּרְחֹבֹתֵינוּ קָרַב קִצֵּנוּ

יט מָלְאוּ יָמֵינוּ כִּי־בָא קִצֵּֽנוּ. **קַלִּים** הָיוּ רֹדְפֵינוּ מִנִּשְׁרֵי שָׁמָיִם עַל־הֶהָרִים דְּלָקֻנוּ בַּמִּדְבָּר אָרְבוּ

כ לָֽנוּ. **רוּחַ** אַפֵּינוּ מְשִׁיחַ יהוה נִלְכַּד בִּשְׁחִיתוֹתָם

כא אֲשֶׁר אָמַרְנוּ בְּצִלּוֹ נִחְיֶה בַגּוֹיִם. **שִׂישִׂי** וְשִׂמְחִי

eichah 4:5-21

5. In the verse Jeremiah further laments the fall of the people from their previous heights to the nethermost depths to which they have fallen. People who were brought up eating only the finest delicacies and dressed only in the most luxurious clothing, now lay faint from hunger in the streets, and scrounged through garbage heaps for the most meager scraps of food *(Lechem Dimah).*

10. The impending Destruction, and the ravages and famine of war, caused compassionate mothers to become so depraved that with their own hands they boiled their children and they consumed them without even leaving flesh for other members of the family *(Alshich).*

The Shelah comments that this phrase also contains moralistic criticism of overly compassionate and over-indulgent mothers who, for example, let their children sleep late rather than go to synagogue or to school. With this 'misplaced compassion' they 'roast' and destroy their children's souls.

18. *So we could not walk in our streets.* When a Jew went to market they would pounce on him screaming 'Jew! Jew!' *(Lekach Tov).*

21. The words 'rejoice and exult' are spoken sarcastically: 'Rejoice while you can because you will not escape punishment for your sins' *(Midrash Lekach Tov).*

cleaves to its palate for thirst; young children beg for bread, no one extends it to them. ⁵ Those who feasted extravagantly lie destitute in the streets; those who were brought up in scarlet clothing wallow garbage. ⁶ The iniquity of the daughter of my people is greater than the sin of Sodom, which was overturned in a moment without mortal hands being laid on her. ⁷ Her princes were purer than snow, whiter than milk; their appearance was ruddier than rubies, their outline was like sapphire. ⁸ Their appearance has become blacker than soot, they are not recognized in the streets; their skin has shriveled on their bones, it became dry as wood. ⁹ More fortunate were the victims of the sword than the victims of famine, for they pine away, stricken, lacking the fruits of the field. ¹⁰ Hands of compassionate women have boiled their own children; they became their food when the daughter of my people was shattered. ¹¹ HASHEM vented His fury, He poured out His fierce anger; He kindled a fire in Zion which consumed its foundations. ¹² The kings of the earth did not believe, nor did any of the world's inhabitants, that the adversary or enemy could enter the gates of Jerusalem. ¹³ It was for the sins of her prophets, the iniquities of her priests, who had shed in her midst the blood of the righteous. ¹⁴ The blind wandered through the streets, defiled with blood, so that none could touch their garments. ¹⁵ 'Away, unclean one!' people shouted at them; 'Away! Away! Don't touch! For they are loathsome and wander about.' The nations had said: 'They will not sojourn again.' ¹⁶ The anger of HASHEM has divided them, caring for them no longer; they showed no regard for the priests nor favor for the elders. ¹⁷ Our eyes still strained in vain for our deliverance; in our expectations we watched for a nation that could not save. ¹⁸ They dogged our steps so we could not walk in our streets; our end drew near, our days are done, for our end has come. ¹⁹ Our pursuers were swifter than eagles in the sky; they chased us in the mountains, ambushed us in the desert. ²⁰ The breath of our nostrils, HASHEM's anointed, was caught in their traps; he, under whose protection, we had thought, we would live among the nations. ²¹ Rejoice and exult, O daughter of Edom, who

בַּת־אֱד֑וֹם °יוֹשַׁבְתְּ ק׳ יוֹשֶׁבֶת בְּאֶ֣רֶץ ע֔וּץ גַּם־עָלַ֛יִךְ תַּעֲבָר־

כב כּ֗וֹס תִּשְׁכְּרִ֣י וְתִתְעָרִ֑י. תַּם־עֲוֺנֵ֞ךְ בַּת־צִיּוֹן֙ לֹ֤א

יוֹסִיף֙ לְהַגְלוֹתֵ֔ךְ פָּקַ֤ד עֲוֺנֵךְ֙ בַּת־אֱד֔וֹם גִּלָּ֖ה עַל־

חַטֹּאתָֽיִךְ.

ה

א זְכֹ֤ר יְהֹוָה֙ מֶֽה־הָ֣יָה לָ֔נוּ הַבֵּ֖ט וּרְאֵ֥ה אֶת־

חֶרְפָּתֵֽנוּ. נַחֲלָתֵ֨נוּ֙ נֶהֶפְכָ֣ה לְזָרִ֔ים בָּתֵּ֖ינוּ לְנׇכְרִֽים.

ג יְתוֹמִ֤ים הָיִ֙ינוּ֙ °וְאֵ֣ין ק׳ אֵ֣ין אָ֔ב אִמֹּתֵ֖ינוּ כְּאַלְמָנֽוֹת.

ד-ה מֵימֵ֙ינוּ֙ בְּכֶ֣סֶף שָׁתִ֔ינוּ עֵצֵ֖ינוּ בִּמְחִ֥יר יָבֹֽאוּ. עַ֤ל

ו צַוָּארֵ֙נוּ֙ נִרְדָּ֔פְנוּ יָגַ֖עְנוּ °וְלֹ֣א ק׳ לֹ֣א הֽוּנַ֥ח־לָֽנוּ. מִצְרַ֙יִם֙

ז נָתַ֣נּוּ יָ֔ד אַשּׁ֖וּר לִשְׂבֹּ֥עַ לָֽחֶם. אֲבֹתֵ֤ינוּ חָֽטְאוּ֙

ח °אֵינָ֔ם ק׳ וְאֵינָ֔ם / °וַאֲנַ֖חְנוּ ק׳ אֲנַ֙חְנוּ֙ עֲוֺנֹתֵיהֶ֣ם סָבָֽלְנוּ. עֲבָדִים֙ מָ֣שְׁלוּ

בָ֔נוּ פֹּרֵ֖ק אֵ֣ין מִיָּדָֽם. בְּנַפְשֵׁ֙נוּ֙ נָבִ֣יא לַחְמֵ֔נוּ מִפְּנֵ֖י

י חֶ֥רֶב הַמִּדְבָּֽר. עוֹרֵ֙נוּ֙ כְּתַנּ֣וּר נִכְמָ֔רוּ מִפְּנֵ֖י

יא זַלְעֲפ֥וֹת רָעָֽב. נָשִׁים֙ בְּצִיּ֣וֹן עִנּ֔וּ בְּתֻלֹ֖ת בְּעָרֵ֥י

יב יְהוּדָֽה. שָׂרִים֙ בְּיָדָ֣ם נִתְל֔וּ פְּנֵ֥י זְקֵנִ֖ים לֹ֥א נֶהְדָּֽרוּ.

יג-יד בַּחוּרִים֙ טְח֣וֹן נָשָׂ֔אוּ וּנְעָרִ֖ים בָּעֵ֥ץ כָּשָֽׁלוּ. זְקֵנִים֙

טו מִשַּׁ֣עַר שָׁבָ֔תוּ בַּחוּרִ֖ים מִנְּגִינָתָֽם. שָׁבַת֙ מְשׂ֣וֹשׂ

טז לִבֵּ֔נוּ נֶהְפַּ֥ךְ לְאֵ֖בֶל מְחֹלֵֽנוּ. נָֽפְלָה֙ עֲטֶ֣רֶת רֹאשֵׁ֔נוּ

יז אֽוֹי־נָ֥א לָ֖נוּ כִּ֥י חָטָֽאנוּ. עַל־זֶ֗ה הָיָ֤ה דָוֶה֙ לִבֵּ֔נוּ עַל־

יח אֵ֖לֶּה חָשְׁכ֥וּ עֵינֵֽינוּ. עַ֤ל הַר־צִיּוֹן֙ שֶׁשָּׁמֵ֔ם שׁוּעָלִ֖ים

יט הִלְּכוּ־בֽוֹ. אַתָּ֤ה יְהֹוָה֙ לְעוֹלָ֣ם תֵּשֵׁ֔ב כִּסְאֲךָ֖ לְד֥וֹר

כ וָדֽוֹר. לָ֤מָּה לָנֶ֙צַח֙ תִּשְׁכָּחֵ֔נוּ תַּעַזְבֵ֖נוּ לְאֹ֥רֶךְ יָמִֽים.

כא הֲשִׁיבֵ֨נוּ יְהֹוָ֤ה ׀ אֵלֶ֙יךָ֙ וְֽנָשׁ֔וּבָה חַדֵּ֥שׁ יָמֵ֖ינוּ כְּקֶֽדֶם.

כב כִּ֚י אִם־מָאֹ֣ס מְאַסְתָּ֔נוּ קָצַ֥פְתָּ עָלֵ֖ינוּ עַד־מְאֹֽד.

The following verse is recited aloud by the congregation,
then repeated by the reader:

הֲשִׁיבֵנוּ יהוה אֵלֶיךָ וְנָשׁוּבָה, חַדֵּשׁ יָמֵינוּ כְּקֶדֶם.

dwells in the land of Uz; to you, too, will the cup pass, you will be drunk and will vomit. [22] Your iniquity is expiated, O daughter of Zion, He will not exile you again; He remembers your iniquity, daughter of Edom, He will uncover your sins.

5/1. Chapter Five is composed of 22 verses like chapters 1, 2 and 4. It differs from the previous four chapters in that it is not alphabetically arranged.

[1] Remember, HASHEM, what has befallen us; look and see our disgrace. [2] Our inheritance has been turned over to strangers; our houses to foreigners. [3] We have become orphans, fatherless; our mothers are like widows. [4] We pay money to drink our own water, obtain our wood at a price. [5] Upon our necks we are pursued; we toil, but nothing is left us. [6] We stretched out a hand to Egypt, and to Assyria to be satisfied with bread.

7. Our misfortune is the result of our sins which intermingled with the sins of our ancestors. This follows the doctrine of *punishing the iniquity of the fathers upon the children ... of those that hate Me (Exodus 20:5).* God punishes children for the sins of the fathers only if the children 'hate Me,' i.e., they persist in committing those same sins *(Sanhedrin 27b).*

Rav Yisrael Salanter explained this verse morally: Fathers who do not train their children in the ways of Torah are considered sinners, even when *they are no more,* i.e., after their deaths. Because their children continue the sinful ways for which their fathers are responsible, they, the children *suffer for their father's iniquities,* suffering for which the parents bear the onus.

[7] Our fathers have sinned and are no more, and we have suffered for their iniquities. [8] Slaves ruled us, there is no rescuer from their hands. [9] In mortal danger we bring out bread, because of the sword of the wilderness. [10] Our skin was scorched like an oven, with the fever of famine. [11] They ravaged women in Zion; maidens in the towns of Judah. [12] Leaders were hanged by their hand, elders were shown no respect. [13] Young men drag the millstone, and youths stumble under the wood. [14] The elders are gone from the gate, the young men from their music. [15] Gone is the joy of our hearts, our dancing has turned into mourning. [16] The crown of our head has fallen; woe to us, for we have sinned. [17] For this our heart was faint, for these our eyes dimmed:

18. Mount Zion's desolation is so utter, that foxes, which usually dwell in ruins, prowl freely and undisturbed over it *(Ibn Ezra).*

[18] for Mount Zion which lies desolate, foxes prowled over it. [19] Yet You, HASHEM, are enthroned forever, Your throne is ageless. [20] Why do You ignore us eternally, forsake us for so long? [21] Bring us back to You, HASHEM, and we shall return, renew our days as of old. [22] For even if You had utterly rejected us, You have already raged sufficiently against us.

The following verse is recited aloud by the congregation, then repeated by the reader:

Bring us back .... It is customary to repeat verse 21 rather than end with the rebuke of verse 22 *(Rashi).*

Bring us back to You, HASHEM, and we shall return, renew our days as of old.

❧ Selected Tishah B'Av Laws and Customs

⋲§ Selected Tishah B'Av Laws and Customs

Compiled by Rabbi Hersh Goldwurm

The laws and customs of Tishah B'Av are numerous, and in some instances too complex to be summarized here. The following compilation is not meant to be exhaustive, and is meant only as a learning and familiarizing tool.

This digest cannot cover all eventualities and should be regarded merely as a guide; in case of doubt, one should consult a competent halachic authority. When a particular *halachah* is in dispute, we generally follow the ruling of the *Mishnah Berurah*. On occasion, however (usually when *Mishnah Berurah* does not give a definitive ruling or when a significant number of congregations do not follow *Mishnah Berurah's* ruling), we cite more than one opinion. As a general rule, each congregation is bound by its tradition and the ruling of its authorities.

These laws and customs have been culled, in the main, from the most widely accepted authorities: the *Shulchan Aruch Orach Chaim* [here abbreviated O.C.] and *Mishnah Berurah* [M.B.]. For halachic questions, one should consult the *Shulchan Aruch* and its commentaries and/or a halachic authority.

EREV TISHAH B'AV — TISHAH B'AV EVE

⋲§ The Afternoon

1. The afternoon before the Tishah B'Av fast takes on some of the mourning aspects of the fast day itself. One should not go on a pleasure trip or even on a pleasurable stroll. [Rather, one should devote his time to reflect on the theme of the upcoming day.] (*Rama O.C.* 553:2).

2. Similarly, from the hour of noon before the fast it is customary to learn only the Torah subjects that one may learn on Tishah B'Av itself (see §38), i.e. matters that pertain to the fast or to mourning. Therefore, even when Tishah B'Av falls on the Sabbath (so that the fast is observed on Sunday) or Sunday, it is customary to refrain from learning matters other than those permitted on Tishah B'Av on the Sabbath afternoon before the fast; the recitation of *Pirkei Avos* is deferred to

the following week (*Rama O.C.* 553:2). However, many *poskim* point out that the custom has no Talmudic basis and argue that it is better to study whatever Torah subjects one wishes, rather than to desist from learning altogether. Therefore if one wishes to be lenient in this matter we do not deter him (*M.B.* 553:8).

⋲§ Minchah

3. The *Minchah* prayer should be recited early enough to allow time to eat a small meal — the *se'udah hamafsekes* (see §5) — between the prayer and the beginning of the fast.

4. *Minchah* is recited in the usual manner; *Tachanun* is omitted. Since Tishah B'Av itself has the status of a quasi-festival on which *Tachanun* is omitted, it is also omitted at *Minchah* of the preceding afternoon (*O.C.* 552:2).

❧ The Se'udah Hamafsekes

5. The meal that immediately precedes the fast — the *se'udah hamafsekes*, literally the *meal that interposes* — should reflect the mourning theme of the impending fast day. The *Gemara* (*Taanis* 30a) relates that on the eve of Tishah B'Av, the Tanna R' Yehudah bar Ilai's meal consisted only of stale bread with salt and a jug of water, which he would consume while seated between the oven and the stove. *Rambam* writes (*Taanis* 5:9): "The following was the practice of the devout people of ancient times: On the eve of Tishah B'Av one would be served dry bread . . . and after it, drink a jug of water, in sadness, desolation and with tears, like one who has the body of a dear one in his presence. This, or [a practice] resembling this, should be the practice of Torah scholars. In all my life I have not eaten a cooked dish on the eve of Tishah B'Av — even one of lentils — except when [Tishah B'Av or its eve] falls on the Sabbath."

6. The above practices, however, were the stringent practices of the extremely devout; they are not binding upon every Jew. The *halachah* follows the Mishnah (*Taanis* 26b), which states that at the final meal before the fast, one may not eat more than one cooked dish. Meat and wine are entirely forbidden. (The ban upon meat and wine need not concern us, since it is customary to refrain from these foods from Rosh Chodesh Av.) It should be noted that in this context fish is also categorized as meat. Thus, even fish may not be eaten at the *se'udah hamafsekes* (*O.C.* 352:2).

7. The *Gemara* (30a) applies two qualifications to the food restrictions in the meals of Tishah B'Av eve: (a) They apply only to meals eaten after the hour of noon; and (b) only to the meal that immediately precedes the fast — hence, the restrictions apply only to the *se'udah hamafsekes*, provided it is eaten in the afternoon. Hence, if one eats more than one meal in the afternoon, the restrictions apply to the final full meal of the day, and if one's last meal was eaten before noon, it is not subject to these restrictions (*O.C.* 552:9).

8. One may eat even many different types of raw fruit and vegetables (*O.C.* 552:4), but not two cooked fruit or vegetable dishes; even if they are also fit to be eaten raw (e.g. apple sauce), they qualify as cooked dishes (*O.C.* 552:3). Therefore, some *poskim* prohibit hot coffee or tea at the *se'udah hamafsekes* (in addition to one cooked dish). Some permit this, arguing that the prohibition applies only to solid foods, not to drinks (*Shaarei Teshuvah* 552:1).

9. Roasted (and fried) foods are considered cooked dishes in this regard (*O.C.* 552:3), as are also pickled foods (*Shaarei Teshuvah* 552:1).

10. Even two batches of the same food could be considered two dishes in this regard: if they were cooked in two different pots and thereby differ in some way, even if the difference is only in consistency, e.g. one has a thick texture while the other is more watery. But if both batches are identical they are considered one food (*O.C.* 552:3 with *M.B.* §8).

11. Two foods that were cooked together are considered two dishes,

unless it is customary to cook these foods together year round, e.g. peas with onions (O.C. 552:3).

12. One should also curtail one's pleasure at this meal, by cutting down on the amount and type of drinks consumed. Beer and other intoxicating drinks should be avoided completely. One should not eat salads after the meal, as is the custom year round (O.C. 552:1).

13. The prevalent custom, which is also the ancient Ashkenazic custom, is to eat a regular meal in the afternoon before *Minchah*. There are no restrictions on this meal, and it is customary to eat well at this meal so that fasting will not be difficult the next day. However, if one feels that the fast will not harm him and he wishes to be stringent in this matter, he is to be commended. After *Minchah*, the *se'udah hamafsekes* is eaten, subject to the restrictions noted above (*Rama O.C. 552:9*). Moreover, one should take care not to overeat at the first meal, because if one has no appetite to eat afterwards, the meal may be considered as inconsequential, so that the first meal will be the actual *se'udah hamafsekes*.

◆§ Customs of the Se'udah Hamafsekes

14. At the *se'udah hamafsekes* it is customary to eat [bread and] a hard-boiled egg, because eggs are a mourner's food. At the conclusion of the meal one dips a piece of bread in ashes and says, "This is the Tishah B'Av meal" (O.C. 552:5, 6, with M.B.).

15. The meal is eaten sitting on the ground or a low seat, but one need not remove one's shoes. After the

meal, however, one may sit on a chair (O.C. 552:7).

16. Three males should not sit together during the meal, so that they will not have to recite *Birkas Hamazon* together with *zimun*. Even if they did eat together, they should nevertheless not say *zimun* (O.C. 552:8 with M.B.).

◆§ After the Se'udah Hamafsekes

17. After the meal has been concluded and *Birkas Hamazon* been recited, until sundown one may still eat and do other things that are prohibited on the fast itself (O.C. 553:1).

18. If, however, one explicitly (i.e. orally) expressed the resolve not to eat anymore, he is considered to have taken the fast upon himself, and is obligated to observe all the strictures of the fast (eating, drinking, washing, etc.) — except for the wearing of shoes, which is permitted until sundown (O.C. 553:1 with M.B. §4). The same is true if one did not mention "eating," but said that he accepts the fast upon himself (M.B. §1).

19. The above-mentioned acceptance of the fast is valid only if it is done before *plag haminchah*, i.e. within approximately one and one half hours before sundown (or more precisely, 5/48 of the time between sunrise and sunset). Consequently, if the resolve not to eat was expressed prior to that time, one need not observe *all* the strictures of the fast, but, in accordance with his explicit vow, one is forbidden to eat (M.B. §4).

20. According to the *Shulchan Aruch* (O.C. 553:1) only an oral

declaration has validity, so that if one resolved only mentally not to eat or to accept the fast, one may still eat thereafter. Some *poskim* dispute this ruling, however, and obligate one to fast even if he made merely a mental resolution to *fast*; but if he resolved mentally not to *eat*, the resolution is not binding. In view of the above, it is advisable to declare (either orally or mentally) at the conclusion of the meal that one does not wish to accept the fast prematurely (M.B. §2).

21. Immediately upon sundown, the fast takes effect, and all of its strictures apply. Therefore one must take care to stop eating and drinking before sundown, but there is no obligation to "add" from the daytime to the fast, as there is on the eve of the Sabbaths and festivals (O.C. 553:2 with M.B. §3).

22. Since wearing shoes is prohibited on Tishah B'Av, one must take off his shoes before sundown. Moreover if *Maariv* is recited before sundown, the shoes should be taken off before *Borchu* (i.e. the beginning of the service) is recited. Some advise that the shoes be taken off before one goes to the synagogue. However, once the sun sets one must remove them even if one has not yet gone to the synagogue (O.C. 553:2 with M.B. §5).

◆§ Tishah B'Av Eve on the Sabbath

23. When Tishah B'Av occurs on Sunday or on the Sabbath itself (so that the fast is observed on Sunday), none of the strictures regarding the *se'udah hamafsekes* apply. One may eat meat and drink wine and set the table "as King Solomon did in his time." Moreover, it is a sin to deprive oneself of these foods if one does so in observance of the mourning of Tishah B'Av (O.C. 552:10 with M.B. §23). [It goes without saying that customs such as sitting on the ground, eating a hard-boiled egg and dipping the bread in ashes are not observed.]

24. Some say that one should not eat the third meal of Sabbath — the *se'udah shlishis* — together with a group, but others argue that if one always eats this meal together with his associates (e.g. the group meets in the synagogue for a public *se'udah shlishis*), one must also do so now, for to refrain would be a public observance of mourning on the Sabbath. All agree that at home the meal should be eaten with the family sitting together, and that *Birkas Hamazon* be recited with *zimun* (O.C. 552:10 with M.B. §23).

25. As on a weekday, the fast begins at sundown (O.C. 552:10 with M.B. §24). At this time all eating, drinking, etc. must stop, and the five restrictions are observed. However, wearing of shoes is permitted until *Borchu* is recited. The members of the congregation remove their shoes after the recitation and the *chazzan* does so before it; they should first recite the formula: בָּרוּךְ הַמַּבְדִּיל בֵּין קוֹדֶשׁ לְחוֹל, *Blessed is He Who separates between holy and secular* (O.C. 553:2). [Nowadays it is customary in many congregations to recite *Maariv* some time after the Sabbath has ended, so that people will have time to remove their shoes and change into their weekday clothing at home, before they go to the synagogue. They should of course recite the above-mentioned formula first.]

26. Regarding Torah study on Tishah B'Av eve when it occurs on the Sabbath, see above §2.

27. The verses of צִדְקָתְךָ, *Tzid-kas'cha*, which are said at the conclusion of the *chazzan's* repetition of the Sabbath *Minchah*, are omitted (*O.C.* 552:12).

∼§ Tishah B'Av on the Sabbath

28. Even when Tishah B'Av falls on the Sabbath itself, none of the restrictions of the fast day apply, because to observe them would be a public manifestation of mourning on the Sabbath. Regarding marital relations see *O.C.* 554:19, *M.B.* §39-40.

29. Torah study is permitted until noon (*M.B.* 553:9). Thereafter, the restrictions are the same as those of a Tishah B'Av eve that falls on the Sabbath; see above §2.

30. The prayer *Av Harachamim* is recited after the Torah reading (*M.B.* 552:30).

THINGS PROHIBITED ON THE FAST DAY

∼§ The Five Restrictions

31. Fasting on Tishah B'Av is a broader concept than mere abstention from food and drink. It includes abstention from five activities: (1) eating and drinking; (2) washing one's body; (3) anointing oneself; (4) wearing leather shoes; and (5) marital relations. It is not within the scope of this summary to discuss in detail the ramifications of these restrictions. However, a few words about the restriction on washing, especially about washing the hands before a prayer service, are appropriate here.

32. It is absolutely forbidden to wash even a minute part of the body, whether in hot or cold water, or even to dip one's finger in water (*O.C.* 554:7). However, one may wash his hands three times upon arising in the morning [נְטִילַת יָדַיִם] except that one may wash only the minimum-required area — the fingers, but not the palm of the hand (*O.C.* 554:10).

33. If one has performed his bodily functions and is returning to his prayers (i.e. to recite the *Shemoneh Esrei*), he may also wash his fingers (as above; *O.C.* 554:9, 613:2, *M.B.* 4). If it is his custom all year round to wash three times, he may wash his fingers three times (*Matteh Ephraim* 613:5). One may also wash his hands in preparation for *Minchah* (*M.B.* 554:21).

34. However, if one has merely urinated and will not recite the *Shemoneh Esrei*, it is questionable whether he may wash his hands. In order to avoid this problem, one should touch a covered part of the body, thus incurring an unquestionable obligation to wash his hands before reciting the blessing of אֲשֶׁר יָצַר (see *O.C.* 613:3, *M.B.* 4,6).

35. One who merely entered a bathroom may not wash his hands, even if this is one's practice throughout the year. Rather, one should wipe his hands, on a clean cloth or board, in lieu of washing (*M.E.* 613:7). However, if one is upset at praying with unwashed hands, one may wash them (*Eleph LaMatteh* 613:7). [Presumably the device of touching oneself on a

covered part of the body is applicable here too.]

36. If one has touched a covered part of the body and wishes to pray or recite a blessing, one should wash all the fingers of that hand. But if one has touched dirt or mud, he may wash only the soiled area (O. C. 554:9, M.B. 613:6).

37. Although it is customary to wash one's face and rinse one's mouth every morning before praying, it is forbidden to do so on Tishah B'Av. However, if one has mucous on his eyes, he may moisten his fingers and rub them over his eyes (O.C. 554:11).

⋖§ Other Prohibitions

38. Though we cannot detail all the laws of Tishah B'Av here, the following is a brief listing: One may not study Torah, except for things pertaining to mourning of Tishah B'Av, because the study of Torah brings joy. One may study, with commentary, the Biblical books of *Job*, the "unpleasant" passages in *Jeremiah* (omitting the verses of consolation), and *Eichah*. One may also study the Midrash to *Eichah*, the third chapter of *Moed Kattan* (which discusses the laws of mourning), the passages in the Talmud (*Gittin* 55b-58a) that discuss the Destruction of the Temple, and the story of the Destruction of the Temple in the book of *Yossipon* (O.C. 554:1-2, M.B. §3).

39. One does not greet his fellows on Tishah B'Av; not even to say good morning. If one is greeted by someone who is unaware of this law, one should answer quietly and with a serious mien. It is better to tell him that on Tishah B'Av one does not extend greetings. One should also not give a present on Tishah B'Av (O.C. 554:20, M.B. 41-2).

40. Work should be avoided until noon. See O.C. 554:22-4. One should refrain from smoking on Tishah B'Av. If this is very difficult, one may smoke in private after the hour of noon (M.B. 555:8). Some say that one should not stroll on the streets on Tishah B'Av because this may cause him to engage in frivolity (O.C. 554:21).

41. On the night of Tishah B'Av and on the morning, until noon, one sits on the ground or on a low stool (O.C. 559:3, M.B. §3).

MAARIV

42. *Maariv* begins in the usual manner. After בָּרְכוּ the congregation sits on the floor or on low stools and the lights are dimmed. The *paroches* is removed from the front of the Holy Ark. On Tishah B'Av the prayers are said slowly and tearfully, in the manner of mourners (O.C. 559:1).

43. The regular *Maariv* service is recited [on Saturday night with the addition of אַתָּה חוֹנַנְתָּנוּ]. After *Shemoneh Esrei* the Full *Kaddish* is recited [including the verse תִּתְקַבֵּל] (M.B. 559:4).

44. On Saturday night, although *Havdalah* is not recited [see below], a multi-wicked candle is lit and the blessing בּוֹרֵא מְאוֹרֵי הָאֵשׁ is recited (O.C. 556:1).

45. *Eichah* (the Book of *Lamenta-*

tions) is chanted aloud by the reader. The prevalent custom is that the entire congregation reads along in an undertone (see *M.B.* 559:15. See also *Taz*, *Magen Avraham*, and *Pri Megadim* to 559:4). After *Eichah* has been concluded, the evening *Kinnos* are recited.

46. After the *Kinnos*, the congrega-

tion recites וְאַתָּה קָדוֹשׁ, omitting the verse וַאֲנִי זֹאת בְּרִיתִי; the reader recites the Full *Kaddish*, but omits the verse תִּתְקַבֵּל; and the congregation recites עָלֵינוּ, followed by the Mourner's *Kaddish*. [At the end of the Sabbath, וִיהִי נֹעַם and וְיִתֶּן לְךָ are omitted, and *Havdalah* is postponed until Sunday night.]

SHACHARIS

47. Candles are not lit at the *chazzan's* lectern for *Shacharis*, but they are lit for *Minchah* (*M.B.* 559:15).

48. Donning of the *tallis* and *tefillin* is postponed until *Minchah*. The *tallis kattan (tzitzis)* is worn, however, but the accompanying blessing is omitted. (*O.C.* 555:1)

49. The morning blessings are recited as usual. Although the blessing שֶׁעָשָׂה לִי כָּל צָרְכִּי was instituted to thank God for providing us with shoes, it is the general custom among Ashkenazim (even those who follow *Nusach Sefard*) to recite it even though shoes are not worn on Tishah B'Av (*M.B.* 554:31, see *Shaarei Teshuvah* and *Pri Megadim* to *O.C.* 46:8). However, Sephardim omit the blessing (see *Kaf HaChaim* 46:17), and the Vilna Gaon (*Maaseh Rav*) is reported to have recited the blessing only at night, after the fast.

50. The entire prayer service which precedes פְּסוּקֵי דְזִמְרָה (the *Verses of Praise*), including אֵיזֶהוּ מְקוֹמָן, may be said [Although *Eizehu Mekoman* is a chapter of Mishnah — which may not be studied on Tishah B'Av — it is part of the regular prayer order, and is therefore not omitted.] (*O.C.* 554:4, *M.B.* 7). However, *Rama* states (*O.C.*

559:4) that פִּטּוּם הַקְּטֹרֶת is omitted (because, *M.B.* explains, its recitation is not considered to be sufficiently widespread for it to be considered part of the "order of the day").

Mishnah Berurah (554:7) maintains that according to *Rama's* view, the passage of *Tamid* is the only Scriptural passage referring to offerings that may be recited. Nevertheless, in many communities the entire service is recited, without omission, as already indicated.

51. Individuals recite *Shemoneh Esrei* at *Shacharis* as usual, without any additions. The *chazzan*, however, inserts the blessing עֲנֵנוּ in his repetition. See §61 for laws pertaining to this blessing. *Birkas Kohanim* is omitted (see *Dagul Merevavah* to *O.C.* 559) as is *Tachanun*.

52. The prayer service continues with reading from the Torah, followed by the Half *Kaddish* and *Haftarah*. The Torah is returned to the Ark and *Kinnos* are recited. It is preferable that their recitation extend until close to noon (*O.C.* 559:2).

53. After the recitation of *Kinnos*, the prayer service continues with אַשְׁרֵי and וּבָא לְצִיּוֹן (with the omission of the verse וַאֲנִי זֹאת ...), the Full

Kaddish, with the omission of תִּתְקַבֵּל; followed by עָלֵינוּ and the Mourner's *Kaddish*. The Song of the Day is deferred until *Minchah*.

54. During the recitation of *Kinnos*, one should not talk about extraneous matters nor leave the syna-gogue, in order to fully concentrate on mourning for the destruction of the Temple (*O.C.* 559:5).

55. It is commendable that every individual read *Eichah* again during the daytime (*Shelah* cited by *Magen Avraham*, beginning of 559).

MINCHAH

56. Candles are lit at the *chazzan's* lectern for *Minchah* (*Pri Mega-dim* in *Eishel Avraham* 559:3). The *paroches* [Ark curtain] is put back in place (*Kaf HaChaim* 559:19).

57. The *talis* and *tefillin* are donned (*O.C.* 555:1), and the remainder of the *Shacharis* prayer is said.

58. *Minchah* on Tishah B'Av is the same as that of a regular fast day, except that נַחֵם, *Nacheim*, is inserted in the Shemoneh Esrei (see §64). The Torah reading and the *Haftarah* are identical to that of a regular fast day, with the exception of *Avinu Malkeinu* and *Tachanun*, which are omitted.

59. In *Shemoneh Esrei*, עֲנֵנוּ, *Aneinu*, [*Answer us*] is inserted, as on other fast days. In addition, נַחֵם, *Nacheim*, [*Comfort*] is inserted. See below, §64.

60. The *chazzan* repeats the *Shemo-neh Esrei* as usual and inserts the above two prayers (see below). He also recites the Priestly Blessing, as on other fast days (*Kitzur Shulchan Aruch* 124:19). The *Shemoneh Esrei* is followed by the Full *Kaddish* (with תִּתְקַבֵּל), then עָלֵינוּ, and the Mourner's *Kaddish*.

עֲנֵנוּ / Aneinu ✥

61. A special fast-day prayer — עֲנֵנוּ

— is interjected both in the silent *Shemoneh Esrei* and in the *chazzan's* repetition. This prayer may be recited only by one who is fasting; for someone not fasting to recite this prayer which refers specifically to "our public fast" would be fraudulent (see *O.C.* 565:3 in *Rama*). This inser-tion is made by the *chazzan* in his repetition of both *Shacharis* and *Min-chah*, but in the silent *Shemoneh Esrei* it is recited only during *Minchah* (*O.C.* 565:3). In the *chazzan's* prayer, *Aneinu* takes the form of a complete benediction, concluding with ... בָּרוּךְ בְּעֵת צָרָה, *Blessed* ... *in time of distress* (*O.C.* 566:1), בָּרוּךְ ... גּוֹאֵל יִשְׂרָאֵל and רְפָאֵנוּ. The individual's recitation is included in the benedic-tion שְׁמַע קוֹלֵנוּ (*O.C.* 565:1). In order for the *chazzan* to recite the blessing in his repetition of the *Shemoneh Esrei*, there must be ten congregants who are fasting. Some authorities rule that it is sufficient that there be seven fasting individuals (*O.C.* 566:3, *M.B.* §14). Individuals recite *Aneinu* in their own *Shemoneh Esrei* even if no one else is fasting.

62. If an individual forgot to insert עֲנֵנוּ in its proper place and has already said the word HASHEM in the concluding blessing of שְׁמַע קוֹלֵנוּ, he must conclude with שׁוֹמֵעַ תְּפִלָּה and continue with רְצֵה. He may

Selected Laws and Customs **[202]**

insert עֲנֵנוּ at the end of the *Shemoneh Esrei* before אֱלֹהַי נְצוֹר. If he finished *Shemoneh Esrei* before realizing his error, he should not repeat the *Shemoneh Esrei* (*M.B.* 119:16,19).

63. If the *chazzan* forgot to insert עֲנֵנוּ in its proper place, but has not yet said the word *HASHEM* of the concluding blessing of רְפָאֵנוּ, he should interrupt his recitation, and recite עֲנֵנוּ. Thereafter he should begin רְפָאֵנוּ again and continue. If he has already uttered the word *HASHEM*, he must conclude the blessing רוֹפֵא חוֹלֵי and continue his prayer as usual. In this case, the *chazzan* inserts עֲנֵנוּ in the benediction שְׁמַע קוֹלֵנוּ, as do individuals in the silent prayer, but omits the concluding formula ... בָּרוּךְ בְּעֵת צָרָה. If he realized his error after he uttered the word *HASHEM* in the concluding formula of שְׁמַע קוֹלֵנוּ, he must continue with שׁוֹמֵעַ תְּפִלָּה. In that case, he may recite עֲנֵנוּ (omitting the concluding blessing) after הַמְבָרֵךְ אֶת עַמּוֹ יִשְׂרָאֵל בַּשָּׁלוֹם (*O.C.* 119:4 *M.B.* §16,19).

נַחֵם / Nacheim

64. In addition to עֲנֵנוּ, a special prayer (נַחֵם, *Comfort*), mourning the destruction of the Holy Temple and supplicating that it be rebuilt, is inserted in the benediction וְלִירוּשָׁלַיִם, *and to Jerusalem*, (both in the silent and *Chazzan's Shemoneh Esrei*) of *Minchah*. The concluding blessing of וְלִירוּשָׁלַיִם is changed (both for individuals and for the *chazzan*) to בָּרוּךְ ... מְנַחֵם צִיּוֹן וּבוֹנֵה יְרוּשָׁלָיִם, *Blessed ... Who consoles Zion and rebuilds Jerusalem*. If one forgot to recite this prayer in its appropriate place, he inserts it in the benediction רְצֵה, before the word וְתֶחֱזֶינָה, but in that case one omits the concluding formula ... מְנַחֵם צִיּוֹן (*O.C.* 557:1, *M.B.* §2). However, if one recited נַחֵם erroneously in the benediction שְׁמַע קוֹלֵנוּ, it need not be repeated in רְצֵה (*Be'ur Halachah*). If one has already concluded the רְצֵה benediction with הַמַּחֲזִיר שְׁכִינָתוֹ לְצִיּוֹן (or even said the word *Hashem*), he continues his prayer, and need not repeat *Shemoneh Esrei* (*O.C.* 557).

AFTERNOON

65. Although some restrictions are relaxed in the afternoon, e.g. one may sit on a chair etc., this applies only to practices that are based on custom. However, all halachic stric- tures that apply to the fast, i.e. eating, drinking, wearing shoes, studying Torah, et al., are in force until nightfall, when stars become visible (*M.B.* 553:3).

MAARIV

66. The regular *Maariv* is recited. On Sunday night, *Havdalah* is recited, with the following exceptions: a) *Havdalah* commences with the blessing over wine; the preliminary verses that are reciting at the end of the Sabbath are omitted; b) The blessings over spices and the candles are omitted. Even those who do not drink the *Havdalah* wine during the nine days may do so now; they need not give the wine to a child to drink. [One should not eat before reciting *Havdalah*.] (*O.C.* 556:1, *M.B.* §3).

◄§ Kiddush Levanah

67. According to *Rama* (*O.C.* 426:2), *Kiddush Levanah* should not be recited on the night following Tishah B'Av, because it should be recited joyously, but we are still in mourning. However, many *poskim* dispute this ruling and permit the recitation of *Kiddush Levanah*. Nevertheless, one should first eat something and don his shoes (*M.B.* §11). However, if this is the only time he will be able to recite *Kiddush Levanah* with a *minyan*, some permit its recitation even if one has not yet broken his fast (*Shaar HaTziyun* §9).

◄§ The Night After the Fast

68. The strictures that were observed during the Nine Days apply also to the night following Tishah B'Av and the next day until noon. Thus, one does not eat meat, take a haircut, launder clothing, etc. until noon of the next day (*O.C.* 558:1, *M.B.* §3).

However if Tishah B'Av was on Thursday, one may wash clothing and take a haircut or shave on Friday morning in preparation for the Sabbath (*M.B.* 558:3), *Shaarei Teshuvah* §2).

69. If Tishah B'Av fell on the Sabbath so that the fast was observed on the tenth of Av, one need not observe the strictures of the Nine Days [e.g. bathing, haircut, laundering] on the night after the fast. However, one should abstain from meat and wine [except for the *Havdalah* wine] on the night itself (*O.C.* 558:1, *M.B.* §4).

This volume is part of
THE ARTSCROLL SERIES®
an ongoing project of
translations, commentaries and expositions
on Scripture, Mishnah, Talmud, Halachah,
liturgy, histroy, the classic Rabbinic writings,
biographies, and thought.

For a brochure of current publications
visit your local Hebrew bookseller
or contact the publisher:

Mesorah Publications, ltd

4401 Second Avenue
Brooklyn, New York 11232
(718) 921-9000